DATE			

The Critical Response
to Truman Capote

**Recent Titles in
Critical Responses in Arts and Letters**

The Critical Response to Mark Twain's
Huckleberry Finn
Laurie Champion, editor

The Critical Response to Nathaniel
Hawthorne's *The Scarlet Letter*
Gary Scharnhorst, editor

The Critical Response to Tom Wolfe
Doug Shomette, editor

The Critical Response to Ann Beattie
Jaye Berman Montresor, editor

The Critical Response to Eugene O'Neill
John H. Houchin, editor

The Critical Response to Bram Stoker
Carol A. Senf, editor

The Critical Response to John Cheever
Francis J. Bosha, editor

The Critical Response to Ann Radcliffe
Deborah D. Rodgers, editor

The Critical Response to Joan Didion
Sharon Felton, editor

The Critical Response to Tillie Olsen
Kay Hoyle Nelson and Nancy Huse, editors

The Critical Response to George Eliot
Karen L. Pangallo, editor

The Critical Response to Eudora Welty's
Fiction
Laurie Champion, editor

The Critical Response to Dashiell Hammett
Christopher Metress, editor

The Critical Response to H. G. Wells
William J. Scheick, editor

The Critical Response to Raymond Chandler
J. K. Van Dover, editor

The Critical Response to Herman Melville's
Moby Dick
Kevin J. Hayes, editor

The Critical Response to Kurt Vonnegut
Leonard Mustazza, editor

The Critical Response to Richard Wright
Robert J. Butler, editor

The Critical Response to Jack London
Susan N. Nuernberg, editor

The Critical Response to Saul Bellow
Gerhard Bach, editor

The Critical Response to William Styron
Daniel W. Ross, editor

The Critical Response to Katherine
Mansfield
Jan Pilditch, editor

The Critical Response to Anais Nin
Philip K. Jason, editor

The Critical Response to Tennessee
Williams
George W. Crandell, editor

The Critical Response to Andy Warhol
Alan R. Pratt, editor

The Critical Response to Thomas Carlyle's
Major Works
D. J. Trela and Rodger L. Tarr, editors

The Critical Response to John Milton's
Paradise Lost
Timothy C. Miller, editor

The Critical Response to Erskine Caldwell
Robert L. McDonald, editor

The Critical Response to Gloria Naylor
*Sharon Felton and Michelle C. Loris,
editors*

The Critical Response to Samuel Beckett
Cathleen Culotta Andonian, editor

The Critical Response to Ishmael Reed
Bruce Allen Dick, editor
With the assistance of Pavel Zemliansky

The Critical Response to Truman Capote

Edited by
Joseph J. Waldmeir
and John C. Waldmeir

Critical Responses in Arts and Letters, Number 32
Cameron Northouse, *Series Adviser*

GREENWOOD PRESS
Westport, Connecticut • London

Library of Congress Cataloging-in-Publication Data

The critical response to Truman Capote / edited by Joseph J. Waldmeir
and John C. Waldmeir.
    p. cm.—(Critical responses in arts and letters, ISSN
1057–0993 ; no.32)
  Includes bibliographical references and index.
  ISBN 0–313–30666–4 (alk. paper)
  1. Capote, Truman, 1924– —Criticism and interpretation.
I. Waldmeir, Joseph J. II. Waldmeir, John Christian, 1959– .
III. Series.
PS3505.A59Z635 1999
813′.54—dc21   98–48934

British Library Cataloguing in Publication Data is available.

Library of Congress Catalog Card Number: 98–48934
ISBN: 0–313–30666–4
ISSN: 1057–0993

First published in 1999

Greenwood Press, 88 Post Road West, Westport, CT 06881
An imprint of Greenwood Publishing Group, Inc.

Printed in the United States of America

The paper used in this book complies with the
Permanent Paper Standard issued by the National
Information Standards Organization (Z39.48–1984).

10 9 8 7 6 5 4 3 2 1

COPYRIGHT ACKNOWLEDGMENTS

FOR LOUIS MICHAEL AND HELEN CATHERINE

CONTENTS

Series Foreword by Cameron Northouse   xiii

Acknowledgments   xv

Chronology   xvii

Introduction   1

I.   OVERVIEWS AND INTERVIEWS

Plate du Jour: Soul Food: Truman Capote on Black Culture
Cecil M. Brown   31

The Metaphorical World of Truman Capote
John W. Aldridge   37

The Daydream and Nightmare of Narcissus
Ihab H. Hassan   49

Capote As Gay American Author
Peter G. Christensen   61

II.   GENRES AND INDIVIDUAL WORKS

Stage and Fiction

On Capote's Grass Harp
Eric Bentley   69

The Grass Menagerie
George Jean Nathan   73

The Stage: House of Flowers
Richard Hayes   77

Short Stories

Capote's Tale
Leslie Fiedler   79

Truman Capote: The Revelation of the Broken Image
Paul Levine   81

From Gothic to Camp
Irving Malin   95

Novels

Other Voices, Other Rooms: Oedipus Between the Covers
Marvin E. Mengeling   99

A Blizzard of Butterflies
H. P. Lazarus   107

Birth of a Heroine
Ihab H. Hassan   109

A Final Door
Terrence Rafferty   115

III. FACT INTO FICTION

Capote's Crime and Punishment
Diana Trilling   121

The Kansas Farm Murders
Kenneth Tynan   129

The "Non-Fiction" Novel
  William Wiegand   135

Real Toads in Real Gardens: Reflections on the Art of
    Non-Fiction Fiction and the Legacy of Truman Capote
  David Galloway   143

Religion and Style in *The Dogs Bark* and *Music for Chameleons*
  John C. Waldmeir   155

"Fire, Fire, Fire Flowing Like a River, River, River": History
    and Postmodernism in Truman Capote's *Handcarved Coffins*
  Jack Hicks   167

IV. CAPOTE AND OTHERS

Gothic As Vortex: The Form of Horror in
    Capote, Faulkner, and Styron
  J. Douglas Perry   179

Glimpses of "A Good Man" in Capote's *In Cold Blood*
  Jon Tuttle   193

Variations on a Dream: Katherine Anne Porter and Truman Capote
  William L. Nance   197

An American Tragedy and *In Cold Blood*:
    Turning Case History into Art
  John J. McAleer   205

V. BIBLIOGRAPHY

Major Works and Themes
  Peter G. Christensen   221

Selected Bibliography   231

VI. INDEX   239

SERIES FOREWORD

Critical Responses in Arts and Letters is designed to present a documentary history of highlights in the critical reception to the body of work of writers and artists and to individual works that are generally considered to be of major importance. The focus of each volume in this series is basically historical. The introductions to each volume are themselves brief histories of the critical response an author, artist, or individual work has received. This response is then further illustrated by reprinting a strong representation of the major critical reviews and articles that have collectively produced the author's, artist's, or work's critical reputation.

The scope of *Critical Responses in Arts and Letters* knows no chronological or geographical boundaries. Volumes under preparation include studies of individuals from around the world and in both contemporary and historical periods.

Each volume is the work of an individual editor, who surveys the entire body of criticism on a single author, artist, or work. The editor then selects the best material to depict the critical response received by an author or artist over his/her entire career. Documents produced by the author or artist may also be included when the editor finds that they are necessary to a full understanding of the materials at hand. In circumstances where previous isolated volumes of criticism on a particular individual or work exist, the editor carefully selects material that better reflects the nature and directions of the critical response over time.

In addition to the introduction and the documentary section, the editor of each volume is free to solicit new essays on areas that may not have been adequately dealt with in previous criticism. Also, for volumes on living writers and artists, new interviews may be included, again at the discretion of the volume's editor. The volumes also provide a supplementary bibliography and are fully indexed.

While each volume in *Critical Responses in Arts and Letters* is unique, it is also hoped that in combination they form a useful, documentary history of the critical response to the arts, and one that can be easily and profitably employed by students and scholars.

Cameron Northouse

ACKNOWLEDGMENTS

We could not have completed this volume without the help and friendship of several individuals. Nancy Ward of Alumni Memorial Library at Saint Mary's College and Darlyne Koch at the University of Mary Library searched for and ordered a tremendous amount of material on Capote. Dr. Tom Johnson, Vice President of Academic Affairs at the University of Mary, supported the project through its most difficult period. Carol Oberfoell sacrificed many weekends to prepare the manuscript. We thank them all.

CHRONOLOGY

1924　Truman Streckfus Persons, son of Nina Faulk Persons and Joseph Persons, born in New Orleans on 30 September. Parents would be divorced in 1931.

1927　Sent to live in rural Alabama with three elderly women and an elderly uncle, including Miss Sook Faulk, later portrayed in his fiction.

1939　Mother remarried Joseph Garcia Capote, who legally adopted Truman and changed his name. Began to attend a series of boarding schools including Trinity School and St. John's Academy in New York, finally to be enrolled in Greenwich High School in Millbrook, Connecticut, where he was encouraged by English teacher Catherine Wood. Began sending stories to literary journals.

1942　Employed by *The New Yorker*.

1943　First short story, "The Walls Are Cold," published in *Decade of Short Stories*.

1945　"Miriam" published in June *Mademoiselle* and given an O. Henry Memorial Award in 1946.

1946　"The Headless Hawk" published in November *Harper's Bazaar* and selected for inclusion in *The Best American Short Stories 1947*.

1947　"Shut a Final Door" published in August *Atlantic* and given an O. Henry Award in 1948.

1948   *Other Voices, Other Rooms* published in January.

1949   *Tree of Night and Other Stories* published in February.

1950   *Local Color* published in September.

1951   *The Grass Harp* published in September.

1952   Stage version of *The Grass Harp* opened March 27 on Broadway at Martin Beck Theater.

1953   Mother committed suicide.

1954   John Huston's film *Beat the Devil* released, for which Capote wrote the script. Musical version of short story "House of Flowers" opened December 30 on Broadway at Alvin Theater.

1956   *The Muses Are Heard: An Account*, based on his travels in the Soviet Union with the American cast of *Porgy and Bess*, published in November.

1957   "The Duke in His Domain," an interview with Marlon Brando, published in *The New Yorker* of November 9.

1958   *Breakfast at Tiffany's* published in November.

1959   Richard Avedon's book of photographs *Observations*, with text by Capote, appeared. Began research on the murder of the Clutter family for his next book after reading an account of the crime in Holcomb, Kansas, in the *New York Times* of November 16.

1963   *The Selected Writings of Truman Capote* published in February.

1966   *In Cold Blood* published in January after having been serialized in *The New Yorker* on 25 September, 2, 9, and 16 October 1965. *A Christmas Memory* published in November. Hosts "The Party of the Decade" in December at the Hotel Plaza in New York.

1967   Film version of *In Cold Blood* by Richard Brooks released.

1968   *The Thanksgiving Visitor* published in September.

1971   Had operation for cancer.

1972   *Truman Capote Behind Prison Walls*, a ninety-minute documentary presented on ABC television 7 December.

1973   *The Dogs Bark: Public People and Private Places* published in August.

1975   First excerpt from the unfinished "Answered Prayers" manuscript, "Mojave," published in June *Esquire*, to be followed in the same magazine by "La Côte Basque, 1965" in November, "Unspoiled Monsters" in May 1976, and "Kate McCloud" in December 1976.

1976   Plays role of Lionel Twain in Neil Simon's film *Murder by Death*.

1980   *Music for Chameleons* published.

1984   Died 25 August in Los Angeles.

1987   Posthumous publication of unfinished *Answered Prayers*.

INTRODUCTION

Truman Capote gained his first success as a young, precocious short short writer. He published his first story, "The Walls Are Cold," when he was nineteen years old, and by the time of the publication of "Miriam," his fifth story, in 1945 when he was twenty-one, he was hailed by Herschell Brickell, editor of the annual *O. Henry Memorial Award Prize Stories* as "the most remarkable new talent of the year." Brickell called "Miriam" "one of the best short stories" in the 1946 collection, and predicted "that Mr. Capote will take his place among the best short story writers of the rising generation."

Among the writers of that rising generation were two, Norman Mailer and Gore Vidal, who were destined to become Capote's greatest public antagonists, willy-nilly helping him develop a persona, mostly on TV, as a witty, feisty, fearsome little guy. But more importantly, from the outset their work was very different in both form and content from Capote's. Mailer's and Vidal's first major publications were novels, not short stories. Furthermore, they were historical, political, cultural, social critical war novels (Vidal's *Williwaw*, 1946, and Mailer's *The Naked and the Dead*, 1948), hence were in the mainstream of naturalistic realism in American fiction.

By way of contrast, *Other Voices, Other Rooms* (1949), Capote's first novel, focused on character rather than event. Its characters were internalized rather than externalized and represented no historical or socio/political position outside themselves as do the characters in ideological novels like *The Naked and the Dead*. For these reasons, it was also shorter, more compact; it needed no marshaling of evidence to support its argument, and it swam quite buoyantly outside the naturalist/realist stream. At least until *In Cold Blood*, much the same could be said of most of Capote's fiction, including the two other short novels, *The Grass Harp* and *Breakfast at Tiffany's*.

Many critics, accustomed to the socially committed fiction of the day, found the characters weak and unsympathetic, and their stories uninteresting. Most favorable critics, however, fascinated by Capote's style, by the poetic clarity with which he could portray even the most unattractive scene, character, or image found his work intensely interesting. They speculated that what he was doing was not only turning **away** from the prevailing social fiction of the day but turning **toward** the pre-war Southern tradition in American fiction best represented by Faulkner, Eudora Welty, Carson McCullers, and Flannery O'Connor. They felt that though he took no social/political position, he did take a cultural one. There is some justification for this thinking. After all, Capote was a Southerner, and his settings and characters are mostly Southern, indeed, many of them seem to fit the definition of "grotesque" as the word has been used to describe characters portrayed by those four Southern writers.

However, despite his obvious links to this twentieth-century Southern tradition, Capote was not a Southern writer with Southern preoccupations and concerns as Faulkner almost always was and the other three writers often were. His characters, whether in stories set in New York or New Orleans or in the rural South, whether comically grotesque or grotesquely weird, are only secondarily Southerners when they are Southerners at all. They are primarily luckless, hapless, loveless aliens within and victims of a world, a society, they never made and don't know how to cope with or even be a part of. Their reaction is often paranoid or manic depressive; their actions are frequently violently psychotic. But just as often, in their lonely insecurity, they escape to worlds of their own creation, romantically misty/spooky, even frightening worlds. They invent companions for themselves, doppelgänger alter egos which threaten and frighten as often as they soothe and comfort; or they deliver themselves into the hands of convincing con artists, whose cure for fear and weakness, though it may work, comes at too high a price; or they simply climb defiantly into a tree, and wait.

Not surprisingly, Capote himself qualified as one of his own alienated characters. His famous statement which appeared as a headline in the *Village Voice*, "I'm an alcoholic. I'm a drug addict. I'm a homosexual. I'm a genius," established his outsider credentials and contributed to the notoriety of his public persona. But it was this mini-rebellion reflected in the form and content of his art which is of lasting significance to contemporary letters. It excited and influenced a myriad young college writers—writers who were too young to have experienced the war, hence were, like Capote, out of the political/ideological loop and were desperate to escape the naturalism-realism box which ideology was trapping them into. Capote made it respectable to be an "artist" again rather than a propagandist, made it possible to write without feeling they were in competition with the social critical establishment. And because the young writers could identify with him and with his far-out characters, Capote in effect midwifed the birth of the anti-hero into the fiction of the 1950s.

And in 1966, he introduced Perry Smith and Dick Hickock, two consummate alienated anti-heroes, into a documentary novel about the vicious murders of the

Clutter family in Holcomb, Kansas. The novel is written with the poetic style and grace that marks Capote's best work, but it is a style and grace so anomalous to the deed itself as to invest the murders with a terror and horror more cathartic than any other manner of telling about them could do.

But the creation of *In Cold Blood,* Capote's masterpiece, was the result of a slow, gradual, maturation rather than the sudden blooming suggested above. From the appearance of the first successful short stories in the 1940s to the publication of his third novel, *Breakfast at Tiffany's* in 1958, Capote worked assiduously at his art, producing a dozen individual short stories—many collected in *A Tree of Night* (1949)—and the novels *Other Voices, Other Rooms* (1948) and *The Grass Harp* (1951). As he worked, he developed gradually both his understated style and his seemingly overstated characters. He also branched out into the theatrical, writing the script for the film *Beat the Devil* (1954) and the book and lyrics for the Broadway musical, *House of Flowers* (1956). In addition, capitalizing on his growing notoriety he honed a talent for the sort of personal, self-involved nonfiction which he perfected in *In Cold Blood*. During those years, he did dozens of nonfiction pieces from reviews to travelogues for magazines like *Vogue, Mademoiselle,* and *The New Yorker*; and he produced *Local Color* (1950), a collection of travel essays, and *The Muses Are Heard* (1956) about the Russian tour of *Porgy and Bess* by an American Company.

However, between the murders in Kansas in 1959 and the publication of *In Cold Blood* in 1966, he published merely 15 items. He was spending most of his time researching the book, interviewing all concerned including Smith and Hickock, getting his facts straight like any good reporter, marshaling his evidence toward the presentation of his factual fiction. And the rest of his time he spent writing the book; indeed, six of the 15 published items during those six years were concerned with *In Cold Blood* directly, including four very long excerpts from it in four consecutive weeks of *The New Yorker*.

His obsessive meticulousness paid off; the book is considered to be, as referred to above, his masterpiece. As an experiment in narrative journalism—or journalistic narrative—reporting on a particularly vicious murder partly at least from the apparently sympathetic point of view of the murderers, the book was widely and vociferously attacked on moral as well as artistic grounds—and just so loudly defended as well. And at the same time, because it represented an extension of Capote's early rebellion in form and content, *In Cold Blood* reinforced his influence over and significance to contemporary world letters.

The book became the climax of Capote's career as a writer, however (though it opened ever wider the door to his career as a public persona); from then on, everything he wrote was measured against *In Cold Blood,* and found to be anti-climactic. But Capote consciously contributed to this perception; with the exception of the story, "The Thanksgiving Visitor" (1968), almost everything he produced invited comparison to *In Cold Blood*—as nonfiction fiction, as reportage, as biography and/or autobiography. *The Dog's Bark* (1973) is concerned with *Public People and Private Places;* four excerpts from the *roman à clef, Answered Prayers* appeared in *Esquire* during 1975 and 1976; and in 1980, *Music for Chameleons* was published. In his "Preface" to that book, Capote referred to its composition as "a modified version of [the] technique" he developed while attempting to solve the problem of journalistic objectivity which he faced in writing *In Cold Blood.* Perhaps the best example of his solution is *Handcarved Coffins,* a nonfiction novella which is the largest part of *Music for Chameleons.* Like *Blood,* it too is about murder most grisly; but unlike *Blood,* it is murder unsolved, shrouded in mystery.

Truman Capote died in August 1984. *Answered Prayers,* the book he considered would be the epitome of that technique he perfected after and as a result of *In Cold Blood* was never completed, though he got a great deal of mileage out of it with publication of excerpts in *Esquire* and in *Music for Chameleons.* It was finally published in 1987 by Random House as *An Unfinished Novel,* and as such, it had no chance to supplant *In Cold Blood* as his greatest work, despite Capote's hopes and prayers.

This anthology of critical commentary on Truman Capote brings together a representative selection of approaches and attitudes, both favorable and unfavorable, toward his work. The overall organization of the essays into four sections—Overviews and Interviews, Genres and Individual Works, Fact into Fiction, and Capote and Others—allows us great latitude in covering all aspects of Capote criticism as it appears in reviews, review articles, essays published in newspapers and periodicals and as chapters in books. Throughout each section we refer briefly to those publications which, though worthy of inclusion in the collection, could not be included because of spatial limitations. Within each general section, we have tried to illustrate the shifts and changes, the growth in critical response to Capote's work as the body of that work grew and expanded from the brilliant early short stories and novels, through the genre *tour de force* that was *In Cold Blood,* into the experiments in style and content that characterize *Music for Chameleons* and about which Capote wrote, "I had found a framework into which I could assimilate everything I knew about writing." The anthology ends with a bibliographical essay and a selected bibliography of works by and about Truman Capote. All publications cited in this Introduction are included in that bibliography.

OVERVIEWS AND INTERVIEWS

Capote had a great deal to say, in his persona or role of celebrity-interviewee, about the art of fiction and its relation to journalism, about the influence on his own work of both his contemporaries and his immediate masters, about any number of social and societal issues and people. As he said to Pati Hill in a 1957 interview " . . . I'm pretty sure conversation will always come first with me. . . . Heavens, girl, can't you see I like to talk?" Many of the best interviews with Capote, including this one by Pati Hill, have been collected by M. Thomas Inge in *Truman Capote: Conversations* (1987); and there was an interesting book-length collection of one-on-one interviews which Capote granted to Lawrence Grobel (*Conversations with Capote*, 1985) and which includes a Foreword by James Michener.

Most of these interviews are by now quite familiar, so we have chosen to include one less well known, more refractory, even controversial. It was with Cecil M. Brown from *Rolling Stone* magazine, and was done in 1974 in Key West. It rambles rather much, probably because it is done at three a.m. after a long party with Tennessee Williams, but in the course of it, Capote offers some interesting off-the-cuff speculation on the "Jewish Literary Mafia" which, he argues, built up Jewish writers after World War II—Bellow, Mailer, Irwin Shaw, Roth, Podhoretz—and which now (in 1974) is in the process of tearing them down because they are no longer doctrinaire. He argues further that these prominent Jewish writers, themselves members of the J.L.M., are in the process of destroying Black writers by creating them in the J.L.M. image; they are destroying James Baldwin, whom Capote calls a Jewish writer, just as they destroyed Richard Wright. It is a convoluted argument, highly relevant in the early seventies after the civil rights advances of the sixties. Throughout, Capote offers himself as a champion of Black Culture, especially in music and film, but he seems to offer as his credentials a sort of Black Culture intellectual anti-Semitism which became unfortunately prophetic over the following eventful years.

There have been a number of biographies, even critical biographies of Truman Capote culminating in Gerald Clarke's monumental *Capote* (1988), as well as in George Plimpton's collection of oral reminiscences by Capote's "friends" (*Truman Capote,* 1997). But there have been few primarily critical book-length overviews of his work. The earliest was William L. Nance's *The Worlds of Truman Capote* (1970) followed by Helen Garson's brief *Truman Capote* (1980). Perhaps the best of the overview books was Kenneth T. Reed's *Truman Capote* (1981), and the best of the in-depth studies of any single aspect of Capote's work is Helen Garson's *Truman Capote: A Study of the Short Fiction* (1992).

We, of course, do not have the luxury of including a book-length study in the Overview portion of this anthology; indeed, we haven't space to include more than three of the many excellent individual essays which have been published. But the three we have included represent exceptionally well three diverse though related directions in Capote criticism.

The first of these essays is John W. Aldridge's "The Metaphorical World of Truman Capote" (1951). Significantly, it was the first essay devoted exclusively to Capote (specifically, to *Other Voices, Other Rooms* and *A Tree of Night*) and it became the one essay which all succeeding scholars had to consider when they dealt with the early work. Aldridge argues that Capote's precocious early work promised to lead the American novel away from the journalistic realism of World War II literature and the immediately post-war novel. But his preciosity proved to be mere preciosity; his work is **only** about itself. His world "seems to be a concoction rather than a synthesis." Aldridge points out that Capote's symbols, which should explain what is outside the text or be explained by it, are actually narcissistic metaphors, inbred, incestuous, attaching only to people and events within the text, clarifying no reality except the text. *Other Voices* has nothing to say about the world outside itself; it is "simply the metaphorically reinforced story of Joel Knox." Nor do the short stories carry symbolic significance outside themselves; they become little more than the images of grotesquerie and horror upon which they depend.

The second Overview essay is Ihab Hassan's "Daydream and Nightmare of Narcissus" (1960). It deals with the "daylight" and "nocturnal" styles of Capote's fiction seeing both as developments of "a self-regarding impulse which Narcissus has traditionally embodied," bringing together supernatural dread which is nocturnal, and reality and humor which is daylight. Both dread and humor "are intended to question our surface evaluations of reality." Hassan clarifies the dichotomy by identifying mystery, violence, suspension of time as aspects of the nocturnal side of narcissus, and literalness and orderly presentation of the story within recognizable areas of space and time as aspects of the daylight side. Hassan lists most of Capote's fiction under one side or the other, but understandably, *Other Voices, Other Rooms* illustrates well the nocturnal side, while *The Grass Harp* and *Breakfast at Tiffany's* represents the daylight side.

Neither Hassan nor Aldridge had the opportunity to consider *In Cold Blood* which, by its very nature as "fiction" could stand as a response to or defense against Aldridge's charge, and as a resolution of the daylight/nocturnal dichotomy in Hassan's analysis—the subject of the book is certainly nocturnal, while the journalistic style in which the story is told is just as certainly daylight.

Peter Christensen's "Capote As Gay American Author," the third of our Overview essays, appeared in 1993, thus had access to the total body of Capote's work. The essay serves a dual purpose in this anthology: it is the most complete examination of the homosexual theme in Capote, and it is a comprehensive survey of the body of criticism devoted to that theme.

Christensen points to *Other Voices, Other Rooms* as the work "most concerned with homosexuality, and . . . the one work on which Capote's reputation as a gay male author will rest." But he also asserts that *In Cold Blood* probably has a homosexual subtext, though Capote denied it; and that *Answered Prayers* depicts "the sordid side of homo- and heterosexuality," while it paints "a very unflattering picture of a writer suggestive of Tennessee Williams."

Among the short stories, only "A Diamond Guitar" openly portrays a gay male relationship. But to some of the critics, the narcissism, the silences, the dichotomies between light and dark all suggest a sort of hidden, secret shame related to homosexuality in all of Capote's work. Christensen cites Steven Adams, for example, who says of *Other Voices* that "the world it creates is animated by characteristics popularly attributed to the homosexual male: freakishness, affectation, and effeminacy. The story of a young boy's discovery of his homosexuality is decked out with all the trappings of gothic melodrama."

Since Christensen covers so completely the critical materials concerned with the homosexual theme which are not included in this volume, it remains only for this introduction to deal briefly with the best of the other overview essays which space and time preclude inclusion.

In *The Short Story in America* (1968), Ray B. West compares Capote favorably with Edgar Allen Poe (a frequent comparison) as an experimenter in the genre of the short story, as one who takes "overt symbolism and atmospheric distortion to an extreme beyond . . . his contemporaries." He praises Capote for his use of symbolism for its own sake rather than "for . . . purposes of examination and discovery"—he praises him that is for the very techniques that Aldridge condemns him for. He couples Capote with Paul Bowles as writers who are leading a revolt against "the 'well-made' short story of our time."

In 1961, two scholars comment on Capote as a Southern writer. Marcel LeMaire ("Fiction in the U.S.A.: From the South") says that *Other Voices* and the early short stories are concerned with a "psychotic" South, but *Grass Harp* and *Breakfast* "are more concerned with the pure-in-heart . . ." who "look for a refuge from the malignance of the world." *Breakfast* is obviously written for the movies: "The dialogue is richly comic; the characters are droll, delightful or grotesque; everything seems to be drawn out of scale." By contrast, Walter Sullivan ("The Continuing Renaissance: Southern Fiction in the Fifties") criticizes Capote as a Southern writer for many of the attributes which Lemoire praises. Capote's work is "contrived." He "does what better writers—like O'Connor—are accused of doing . . . he celebrates the grotesque for its own sake" and for the sake of "his themes of deviation." He is sometimes brilliant, but his works "seem to melt away, leaving no dregs of meaning."

Nona Balakian ("The Prophetic Vogue of the Anti-Heroine," 1962) says that Capote's view of women is "humanitarian;" Holly Golightly inspires "a non-erotic, tender affection" that "ends up strengthening the capacity to love." Jack Ludwig in *Recent American Novelists* (1962) calls Holly Capote's "breakthrough character" who "sums up American confusion" about gay life. But John E. Hardy argues that nowhere in Capote's fiction is there "a sense of the 'normality' of life." Each of his narrators "has something of the character of a sleepwalker." According to Hardy, Capote believes that "the sum of man's experience is the shadow of sense impressions."

In a study more 'scientific' psychologically than Hardy's or Ihab Hassan's cited earlier, Irving Malin (*New American Gothic*) discusses the subject of narcissism as it appears in Capote, Salinger, McCullers, O'Connor, Hawkes, and Purdy. These novelists "explore a world in which characters are distracted by private visions." He devotes three chapters to the subject, one on "self-love," one on "The Family," and one on "Three [Gothic] Images." He concludes that the narcissist is an isolate whose distorted vision of the world destroys familial security "Parent and child . . . stunted by . . . self-love . . . never grow up." The three recurring images are of the haunted castle, the voyage to escape, and the reflection of self. Malin argues that Capote's first three books are best explained in terms of this psychological construct.

During the early sixties, while Capote was working on *In Cold Blood*, a number of important book-length studies of contemporary American fiction appeared. All of them included Capote.

Chester Eisinger devotes a chapter to Capote in *Fiction of the Forties* (1963). He focuses on Capote's use of the Gothic tradition in *Other Voices, Grass Harp*, and *Tree of Night,* and he concludes that *Other Voices* "exists more as a detached art object than as a felt, imaginative experience." Like Moravia, he finds the stories in *Tree of Night* indebted to Poe; "the psychological and moral truths of [Capote's] observations seem to be of less importance . . . than the implications for disintegration" in the situations imagined in the stories. But in *The Grass Harp,* "a parable of innocence and evil," "the gothic element in his other work has been transmuted . . . into mellowed fantasy." Paul West in *The Modern Novel* (1963) concentrates on Capote as a stylist. "The English tradition is short of novelists whose style makes the impossible palatable; there is room for a Djuna Barnes or a Truman Capote." Isolationism in Capote leads to fantasy, but he uses everyday speech, expressing himself with a "rapt, childlike savoring of the physical world." Capote's major weakness results from his fascination with the exotic and the abnormal; his characters lose their reality, and his "view is too myopic for the thorough presentation of large themes."

Walter Allen in *Tradition and Dream* (1964) calls the early fiction Gothic fairy tales, a "censored form of nightmare." Capote is "a delightful and highly original artist" whose fiction represents "a self-contained world which refers to nothing outside itself . . . a toy world" in which style seems to be everything. It is a private, child world "with childhood as a state beyond which lie anticlimax and degeneration with the child as the modern counterpart of the noble savage." And in *After Alienation* (1964) Marcus Klein argues that Capote and Paul Bowles, while appearing shockingly rebellious, actually shocked no one. Their work "had merely the look of danger." American readers had been immunized to the "posture of rebellion," to alienation, and were instead pleased and titillated by the writers' "wickedness."

Louise Y. Gossett in an excellent chapter on Capote ("Violence in a Private World") in *Violence in Recent Southern Fiction* (1965) effectively summarizes and even responds to much of the pre-*In Cold Blood* criticism. She makes a virtue of what others denigrate as Capote's narcissism, seeing nothing wrong or evil in his being "content to stay entirely within his created worlds." She finds that the "violence which Capote portrays" is confined "to the boundaries of his imagination," and, though innocence is always violated by evil, the violence does not transcend the fiction. But the theme of the work, as she sees it, does transcend it. She sees Capote's fiction connoting "the emotional vacuum of life in the twentieth century and the paralysis of will which plagues man." Thus the fiction, "symptomatic of a contemporary malaise," is a commentary upon the world outside itself. But in the end Gossett feels that "technical virtuosity" is far more important than either theme or idea in Capote's work. "His chief art is the creation of external parallels for highly subjective states of feeling." She makes a virtue of what Aldridge would argue are faults: Capote is best when dealing with abnormal personalities, sinister grotesques. And these are virtues because they make Capote's work "more representative of the situation of man in the world as a whole. . . ."

Gossett's book came out during the same year as *In Cold Blood,* therefore, like the other critics discussed so far, she did not have the advantage of that book to try her argument against. But neither did she have the disadvantage of that book's overwhelming influence upon Capote criticism. After 1965, it monopolized most of the critical attention given to Capote, or at least controlled the attention by demanding implicitly that the other work be compared with it. We will get deeper into this issue when we arrive at the section of this anthology devoted to *In Cold Blood.* For the present, I will refer to a couple of post-*Blood* essays which come closest to fitting the pattern of the Overview despite the dominance of *In Cold Blood.*

In 1967, Craig M. Goad published a major essay, "Daylight and Darkness; Dream and Delusion: The Works of Truman Capote," which though its stated purpose is to show that *In Cold Blood* "has more in common with Capote's fiction than his nonfiction," devotes a great deal of attention to an analysis of the other fiction. Goad discusses the characters in terms of light and dark, and argues that "a fusion of style and content occurs in his works." He offers sharp psychological analyses of both "dark" (Joel) and "light" (Holly) characters. The former are destructive, of self and others while the latter "have an influence for good which others may . . . use." *In Cold Blood* contains both, with Capote as 'wizard man' and myth-maker." And Paul Levine ("The Intemperate Zone . . ." 1967) argues that, although *In Cold Blood* "would seem to take neo-realism as far as it could go," it also "resembles the nightmare fantasies of . . . *A Tree of Night.*" "Surrealism has become the new reality."

Chris Anderson in "Fiction, Nonfiction, and the Rhetoric of Silence" (1987) finds as a similarity between Capote's fiction and nonfiction in "his use of authorial silence." Capote silently observes his characters dramatically working out their stories, in concrete detail, but without interpretation or editorializing.

Anderson finds that such silent "concreteness . . . points beyond itself, evokes via association or metaphor something not stated," both in Capote's fiction and nonfiction, though most clearly in the latter. The essay is thus a response to Aldridge's, and to a lesser extent Gossett's charge that Capote seldom expands his work beyond its own horizons. But Anderson's advantage rests in the fact that Capote's nonfiction (*In Cold Blood; Handcarved Coffins*) has a built-in means (fact) which exists beyond the story, and which constitutes its metaphorical end.

STAGE AND FILM

In general, critics and audiences were lukewarm toward Capote's attempts at drama, stage and screen. In 1952, the dramatization of *The Grass Harp* hit the stage to decidedly mixed reviews. Brooks Atkinson called it "a delicate sweet affirmation. . . . Capote believes in the pure in heart and has said so with beauty, humor, and understanding." (*New York Times*, 28 March) Walter Kerr called the play "intellectually idle, emotionally indifferent. If its mood is lazy, its construction is lazier." ("New Play, with Beauty, Style, and Little Drama," 6 April). He is even harder on the revival of the play in Circle in the Square in 1953, saying that "Capote is happiest with tangents, forever . . . darting off into cul-de-sac disquisitions" about irreverancies. (*Herald Tribune*, 28 April, 1953) Unfortunately, most of the "name" reviewers—like Kerr, Eric Bentley, and George Jean Nathan—did not like the play very much, or pointedly disliked it. Bentley called it "ridiculous, trite, inane" and "sentimentality gone rancid." The play is in the "contemporary" school of theatre which expresses revulsion against realism by reaffirming poetic drama. However, in *The Grass Harp,* "the realistic and fantastic elements become the trite and the ridiculous, respectively." Such work is, by its very nature, "negative, vacuous, and contraceptive" ("On Capote's Grass Harp," 1954. Review included here). George Jean Nathan's review of the play is not as eloquently negative as Bentley's, but it is indeed negative. He cites William Saroyan and Tennessee Williams as influences on Capote, but he points out that Capote is far too studiously literary to be a Saroyan, and he does not possess "William's occasional gift for lyric expression." Nathan praises the novel, but finds the play falling far short of the dramatic mark: "Capote is a writer who in another medium has indicated talent, but in that of the stage his name . . . is spelled Kaput" ("The Grass Menagerie," 1954. Review included here).

In addition to Walter Kerr's rather unfavorable review of the revival of *The Grass Harp* at Circle in the Square in 1953 discussed above, there were a number of other reviews, mostly favorable. Harold Churman called the play "valuable"; (*Nation*, 16 May, 1953). Richard Hayes called it "honorable . . . it has all the virtues of minor art." (*Commonweal*, 22 May, 1953).

House of Flowers was staged during the season of 1954, and most of the attention Capote received in 1954 and 1955 focused on that musical drama. Most of the reviews were at best lukewarm; some were hostile. John S. Wilson discusses the genesis of the musical, pointing out that Capote wanted the set "to be like a bird cage that you can see all the way through from any side." He points out that while Capote wrote the story, the play, and the lyrics, Harold Arlen's music and Peter Brooks' direction deserve equal credit ("Building a House of Flowers, 1955). Harold Oberman says that the play is overwritten; it lacks style (*Nation,* 29 Jan., 1955). John Chapman praises the scenery, the acting, the music, but as for the script, he accuses Capote of having "a dirty little mind" (*Daily News,* 1 Jan., 1955). Richard Hayes feels that Capote's version of wickedness does not fit on the Broadway musical stage. His "winking wickedness . . . gradually cracks to reveal merely a simple . . . tale of pure love in . . . a naughty world." The audience is treated to vicarious sexual kicks, "random specimens of smoking-room wit." Capote should return "to the world of serious letters" (*Commonweal,* 28 Jan., 1955. Review included here). Such was the tone of the reviews of the musical, including one in *Theatre Arts* by Maurice Zolotow which pointed out that one of the play's flaws was that Capote knew nothing about prostitutes.

Pauline Kael in a favorable review of the film *The Innocents,* for which Capote wrote the screen play, ("The Innocents, and What Passes for Experience," 1962), credits his dialogue for much of the film's beauty. Her review is not included here because it is only marginally about the script, focusing instead on direction and acting. But a short passage merits quotation: "The dialogue has, at times, the same beauty and ambiguity as the images. I assume that Truman Capote, who is one of the finest prose stylists—as distinguished from writers—this country has ever produced, is responsible" for much of it.

SHORT STORIES

Capote published twenty-nine pieces of short fiction during his career, some of which were stories while some were excerpts from longer works. He collected the early stories in *A Tree of Night* in 1949, a collection which he also included with *The Grass Harp* in 1956. In 1958, he included three others with *Breakfast at Tiffany's,* and he chose a number of them all for inclusion in *Selected Writings.*

A Tree of Night, the only true original collection, received a mixed critical reception, though all critics agreed that the stories exhibited a prodigious talent. Herschel Brickell's comments about *A Tree of Night* were cited above. Newton Arvin includes Capote among the young American writers producing fiction decidedly different from that of the 1920s and 1930s. Capote is "interested in introspection, strangeness, illness, human complexity, rich and evocative prose styles. . . ." ("New American Writers," 1947). And Cyril Connelly warns that Capote is the new young writer whom the publishing world is intent on first making then breaking. They will "smother him with laurels and then vent on him . . . obscure hatred" as a way of bringing him down from his superior perch ("Introduction" to *Horizon* 16, 1947).

Isaac Rosenfeld—ironically one of the young writers whom Newton Arvin defends along with Capote—accuses Capote of simple imitation of Eudora Welty and Carson McCullers in *A Tree of Night*. He has nothing of his own to offer except a superficial sophistication "the disease in which he rots" (*Partisan Review*, July 1949). And Alexander Klein ("Nothing Ordinary," *New Republic* 1949) blisters the stories for lacking substance. Capote seems determined to be memorable only by doing the extraordinary, which means for him the macabre. "His values and equipment as a writer" may be summed up as an "all too fallible delicacy and sensitivity, excellent powers of description . . . a genuine but unselective sense of humor, and an occasional sense for, and (rarely) the discipline of, poetry. . . ."

Among the more favorable reviews, Carlos Baker's "Nursery Tales from Jitter Manor," 1949, asserts that Capote's virtues are a poetical mind, a grotesque humor, and the ability to portray "the outlines of haunted personalities." Iris Barry praises Capote's "gifts of observation, whether of gesture or of atmosphere," and she goes on to say that "he seems to be at once most effective and most perfectly master of his craft," in portraying children. "Children on Their Birthdays" she calls the best story in the collection ("Short Stories of Truman Capote" *Herald Tribune*, 1949).

Leslie Fiedler in a review included in this volume ("Capote's Tale," 1949) seconds Barry's judgment. Only through children, he says, can Capote grasp and convey "a situation at once ridiculous and terrible, creating out of the absurdities of love and death . . . a rich tension." He argues that Capote's "level of achievement," his "peculiar and remarkable talent," are more clearly discernible in these stories than in *Other Voices,* whose excellencies of style and characterization "are more than balanced by poor structure and a general air of padding and pastiche." The stories "are Mr. Capote's essential achievement so far." And Harrison Smith in *Saturday Review* (12 Feb.,1949) in effect responds to the charges of Rosenfeld and Klein that Capote really has nothing of substance to say. Though Capote plays with the "minor theme" of Southern decadence, he does it brilliantly. His "voice alone has been raised in unconscious protest against the monotony of a long series of heavily serious novels . . . of social protest." "We need him and will cherish him, whatever he writes about."

In another essay included in this volume ("Truman Capote: The Revelation of the Broken Image," 1958), Paul Levine returns to the familiar dichotomy of light and darkness in his discussion of Capote's short fiction. "At the heart of

Capote's writing is the dichotomy in the world between good and evil, the daylight and the nocturnal, man and nature." His stories occupy both worlds; the daylight hero is a creative force; the nocturnal hero must come to grips with the destructive power of blackness both inside and outside himself. He searches for identity, and finding it is his initiation. Levine argues that Aldridge is wrong to find Capote's internal metaphors empty and impotent in describing external reality. He finds the metaphors clarifying the dichotomies both within the heroes and their stories and within the reader and his experience.

Irving Malin in an essay also included here ("From Gothic to Camp," 1964) argues that Capote's nocturnal stories weaken our daylight control and disturb the reader "by means of [Capote's] ability to **image** fear." His fiction causes suspension of disbelief, and introduces a "religious" belief in "goblins and witches." The stories "invert Christianity—they are superstitious, pagan, and nihilistic;" but at the same time, they "affirm the **miraculous** danger of life." But the danger in Capote often becomes merely "fashionable alienation;" and the religion he preaches, LOVE, merely "soothes our souls with glittering generalities."

In "Short Fiction: The Ten Dollar Dream," a chapter of his book on Capote cited earlier and unavailable for this collection, Kenneth T. Reed makes a useful division of the stories into "Tales of New York" and "Stories of the South." "The New York stories," he writes, "are those in which a cold, impersonal, and uncongenial environment seems to foster characters who are, in the main, victims of loneliness, alienation, and despair . . . their behavior hovers somewhere between the engagingly eccentric and the certifiably deranged. Generally humorless, the New York fiction lacks some of the occasional warmth and familiarity . . . present in Capote's southern stories."

THE NOVELS

Other Voices, Other Rooms

Capote's first novel appeared in 1948, the year before *Shut a Final Door*, and it immediately attracted great critical attention—more than any other work of his until *In Cold Blood*. And it held that attention. Any discussion of Capote during those intervening years had to focus upon or contend with *Other Voices, Other Rooms*; witness the Aldridge and Hassan essays earlier in this volume. But the immediate first impressions, the reviews, were equally important because they helped to establish the novel's relevance, to gain an audience for it and for the short story collection to be published soon after, and to set forth and define the terms of the critical conflict and point to the direction Capote criticism would take throughout his career.

Of the 60 or so reviews of the novel in 1948-49 (some are little more than passing comments), 18 are unfavorable, 10 are mixed but leaning toward unfavorable, and 22 are clearly favorable. The unfavorable reviews cite Capote's immaturity, his emphasis on style over substance, his distastefully sexual subject matter, and his imitativeness. The opening salvo was actually fired in 1947 by the anonymous pre-publication reviewer for *Virginia Kirkus' Book Shop Service,* who wrote that the novel is "distorted, hallucinatory . . . grotesque, experimental," and that it is recommended only "for a limited audience of initiates."

Carlos Baker ("Deep South Guignol," 1948) cites the novel's lack of "real" characters, lack of control and of structure, and he calls its content "bizarre." John Farrelly in *The New Republic* (1948) accuses Capote of creating "an atmosphere of **things**," including his characters who are essentially "objects." His purpose seems to be to create an effect "deliciously morbid." Elizabeth Hardwick calls the novel "a minor imitation of a very talented minor writer, Carson McCullers." Capote's imitation of Southern fiction writers is whimsical and insincere and "rings a tinkling funeral bell" for that fiction (*Partisan Review* 15 Mar., 1948). In *The Nation* (31 Jan.), Diana Trilling objects to the novel on moral grounds. She finds Joel's passive subjection to deterministic forces simply an excuse for his—and Capote's—irresponsibility.

The mixed reviews acknowledge most of the criticisms of the unfavorable ones, but they find counterbalancing plusses. For example, Walter Allen finds Capote's characters and story uninteresting, but praises "a prose style of exquisite sensibility which make the atmosphere of the story most interesting" (*New Statesman*, 1948). Jacques Barzun praises the novel's evocative style, arguing that it is this ability which will elevate Capote to "high places" in literature, despite the fact that Joel is unreal, a very weak character, "nearly one hundred percent water" ("Delicate and Doomed," 1948). Ralph Habas in the *Chicago Sun* praises the writing by comparing it favorably to "the best of Faulkner" and Proust, but finds the story "morbid," "dull," "sordid," and concludes that the novel is really only "an item of literary curiosa" ("Displays Brilliant Talents," 1948). Like most of the other critics, Orville Prescott praises the prose as poetic, the mood and atmosphere as brilliantly presented but says that the book lacks characterization, reality, direction. It is almost as if the book were "an illusion done with mirrors" ("Books of the Times," 1948).

The favorable reviews of the novel praise it in terms of many of the same qualities for which those less than favorable criticize it. Morton Fineman says that the characters are credible, the structure of the story "is arranged with a cunning, jeweled elegance . . . there is an overall impression of completeness and finality" in the story ("Heir to Terror and Love," 1948). Arthur J. Follows praises Capote's bold "study of adolescence" and "of sexual abnormalies," he compares the "prose poetry" of the novel's style to the verse of Baudelaire and Verlaine ("A Strange First Novel," 1948). Kelsey Guilfoil says that the style "combines a romantic attitude with intense realism of manner." "The people are real" but "the story is otherworldly" ("Exotic Tale . . . ," 1948). W. E. Harriss calls the novel "a fascinating experiment in symbols and images," and he praises Capote's "ability to create a gossamer mood of horror, perversity, and poetic somnambulism" (*Commonweal*, 1948). Lloyd Morris calls the book "the most exciting first novel by a young American . . . in many years. . . ." It "is not only a work of unusual beauty, but a work of unusual intelligence" ("A Vivid, Inner, Secret World," 1948). Finally, Marquerite Young in *Kenyon Review* says that Capote shows "that the abnormal does exist and is therefore valid." The novel "is concerned with the extramarginal . . . symbols interloping among dreams, memories, perceptions . . . the psychic underworld. . . . Character, problem, situation are secondary to these" revelations.

In 1949, in an Italian essay which appeared in English in *Sewanee Review* in 1960, Alberto Moravia contrasts the "subjective fantasy" of Capote with the "objective realism" of Edgar Allan Poe. *Other Voices* belongs to a genre of popular literature in 1949: "the novel of imaginary and fantastic distortions of reality seen through the eyes of a child or adolescent." Two other brief studies appeared in 1949 which dealt with Capote in conjunction with other late-1940s novelists. John Aldridge cites *Other Voices* as a leader in the movement away from World War II fiction. Its weakness is its failure of realism; its strength is in its style as stylistics ("Uneasy Inheritors of a Revolution"). And Richard Gehman resurrects the Rosenfeld/Klein argument, calling new American writing "flat" and "tasteless . . . it reads as though it were written by a group of anxious, precocious children." It fails utterly to deal with contemporary social problems, Gehman asserts—though he adds that *Other Voices* "is by far the most important first novel published in 1948 ("Where Are the Postwar Novels?")

In 1962, in a psychological study published in *American Imago* and included in this collection ("Oedipus Between the Covers"), Marvin E. Mengeling argues convincingly that the theme of *Other Voices* "is Oedipal in nature," rather than narcissistic as Hassan and Malin had argued earlier. Joel is fixated not upon his father but upon his dead mother, and Randolph is accepted by Joel as a mother-substitute, enabling Joel to fulfill his Oedipal desires through homosexual converse with Randolph. In 1967, Frederick Hoffmann (*The Art of Southern Fiction*), sounding like Mengeling, argues that Joel "is forced by the circumstances of his having violated the memory of his mother to turn . . . to Randolph." And Gene Rugh ("The Novelist as Commodity," 1969) interprets this and similar situations in *Other Voices* as "fully in the tradition of Mrs. Radcliffe." Capote attaches the "innocence, acuteness, and inquisitiveness" of her female protagonists to Joel, an effeminate boy. The novel is thus a parody of the gothic novel, an "uncomfortable example of art as serious play"; but is far superior to the "camp vogue led by Susan Sontag." Gothic novels become popular "when sheer physical violence . . . has become so commonplace as to be banal." Hence *Other Voices* harmonizes "not only with its gothic history, but with ours as well."

And in 1970, Dianne B. Trimmier published a "Critical Reception" of *Other Voices,* surveying the critical reactions to the novel from 1948 to 1962. She concludes that, by 1970, the criticism has moved from an adverse reaction "in which the work was obscured by the author's personality," to the current reinterpretation "in which critics admit that the book has faults, but . . . find in it mythical, philosophical, and psychological elements not perceived earlier."

In 1971, Maurice Edgar Coindreau in a "Preface" to *Other Voices, Other Rooms* calls the novel unique as postwar fiction because "in it there is no question of war, nor of ideologies in conflict, nor of race prejudice, nor of social claims." Capote's fantasy characters here and in *Tree of Night,* "are more real, more true, and infinitely closer to us than the soldiers in the . . . war novels. Coindreau's thesis is refined and expanded by Cynthia Ozick ("Truman Capote: Reconsidered," 1973). Ozick recalls and reexamines the reception which her post-war generation gave to *Other Voices, Other Rooms.* They welcomed it as a reaction to war and post war social fiction. It offered escape from the pragmatic values of the post-war college campus—escape into "Capital-A Art," and it became the cult novel of a youthful cult of aesthetics. But now, in 1973, Ozick finds that its generation has moved on, its cult has outlived it.

The Grass Harp

Capote's second novel received less attention than his first, though the attention it did get was much more favorable. *The Grass Harp* is more a whimsical daydream than a dark, spooky nightmare; it doesn't challenge morals and mores in the uncomfortable, almost kinky way that *Other Voices, Other Rooms* does. Most reviewers and critics read it as a relatively harmless, uplifting, though perhaps a bit saccharin, fantasy. As we have seen, it was as a play that these virtues were deemed vices.

John Pendy Kirby in the essay, "Fashions in Sinning," (1952) picks up Ozick's distinction between style and action in modern fiction, arguing that the old-fashioned sociological novel is dead, replaced by a narcissistic "delineation of : . . private spiritual agony . . . of the experience of personal guilt and expiation, and of man's relation to God." But he praises Capote's style for its "delightful humor, delicate poetic perception, and deep human warmth." *The Grass Harp* moves away from the unnatural world of *Other Voices* "into the world of positive ethical values and recognizably normal existence." It is "an echo of the universal human struggle in all ages to maintain the dignity of personal relationships and the integrity of the individual." But H. P. Lazarus ("A Blizzard of Butterflies," 1951, included here) sees *The Grass Harp* as purely oversimplified twaddle. ". . . the ingredients are stale even as they are more than ever pre-digested, dished up with cuteness and a fine artificial flavor."

"Certainly Mr. Capote has abused what talent he has—and perhaps his own fans—in the crassest manner."

Gene Baro on the other hand ("Truman Capote Matures and Mellows," 1951) speaks of the "maturing and mellowing" of Capote, and says that *Harp* "teaches us, through rich humor, eloquent characterization, and symbolic poetry, to accept the strange world of reality." The book "offers us more than a fair measure of delight and wisdom." Richard Hayes (*Commonweal,* 1951) calls *Harp* "a masterpiece of passionate simplicity, of direct, intuitive observation." "Capote has sunk a shaft more deeply into human experience" [than he had in *Other Voices*], and his vision now encompasses greater variety and flexibility." In a similar comparison Granville Hicks ("A World of Innocence," 1951) says that while both novels are about private worlds, *Harp* has rejected Gothic elements, choosing to be "extravagant rather than bizarre."

Orville Prescott (*New York Times,* 2 Oct., 1951) says that though "*The Grass Harp* is not a powerful or important novel, it is an extremely well-written one," for Capote "is a genuinely gifted writer who has developed intellectually and artistically in the last three years." Oliver La Farge calls *Harp* Gothic, but says that "It is a light, skillful, delightful story." He continues that Capote's sense of and control over his style helps him to avoid "the sweet sentimentality of Robert Nathan, the treacherously soft, green pastures of Saroyan" ("Sunlit Gothic," 1951). But Katherine Gauss Jackson in *Harpers* (Nov. 1951) calls the novel "a weird mixture of inferior Carson McCullers and Robert Nathan, with a touch of Saroyan thrown in."

The passage of time served to reinforce Jackson's critical harshness. Thus, Louis Rubin in "The Curious Death of the Novel . . ." (1966) attacks Capote's fiction as meaningless. *Other Voices* is "nothing more than a great deal of lush atmosphere. . . ." And "*The Grass Harp* was a skillful little exercise in calculated nostalgia and quaintness." Rubin goes on to attack *Breakfast at Tiffany's* as "popular magazine froth," and says that the newly published *In Cold Blood* has no "meaningful pattern," and will be forgotten in ten years. And Frederick Hoffman in *The Art of Southern Fiction* (1967) says that though *Harp* deals "with the fact of innocence," making it a part of a long literary tradition in America, it remains an "inferior" work on any terms.

But the passage of time also seemed to open critical eyes to a more sophisticated, though no less obvious, interpretation of the novel than the earlier critics could perceive. Thus, Charles I. Glicksberg ("The Lost Self in Modern Literature," 1962) finds the theme of homosexuality to be at the heart of *The Grass Harp* as it was, more overtly, at the heart of *Other Voices.* "At odds with himself and his society, the invert retreats into fantasy, unable, as in the work of Truman Capote and Tennessee Williams, to come to terms with social reality." The socially maladjusted homosexual copes with social reality by climbing into a tree. And Roger Austen in *Playing the Game: The Homosexual Novel in America* (1977) discusses the homosexual content of the first two novels, arguing that though Capote skirts the issue of homosexual commitment in both, the events and the situations and the characters in both novels are those with which gay readers identify.

Breakfast at Tiffany's

Breakfast at Tiffany's got a much more favorable critical reception than *The Grass Harp*. Alfred Kazin (*Reporter*, 13 Nov., 1958) calls the story "sentimental when it is no longer clever;" he cites Capote's "emphasis . . . on Holly as a town character and Holly as a Southern waif—never as Holly as a woman." But "the purely external side of Holly's character . . . is skillfully done. Capote has caught perfectly the professional accent of New York, the trigger-tenseness of a speech that is always excited, declamatory, on the make. Miss Golightly alone seems to keep cool." But Capote either presents social detail wittily, "or he collapses into tender and mawkish details that are really private symbols," and the novel loses "the tone of actuality."

William Goyen ("That Old Valentine Maker," 1958) accuses Capote of relying too much on whimsy; he writes without "full imaginative control." Though he has a talent "for catching the off-beat nature of people," he writes "as though he were delivering a midnight monologue." Gordon Merrick ("How to Write Lying Down," 1958) compares *Breakfast* with *The Great Gatsby*; both are written in "a prose of the utmost clarity and precision," but while Fitzgerald was constantly digging below the surface" revealing the horror and emptiness below, for Capote, the surface is everything." F. E. O'Gorman (*Best Sellers*, 1 Nov., 1958) calls the novel "a truly superb piece of workmanship," although "Capote is sketching too close to life at times." Oddly, he finds the book "shockingly vulgar in a few spots," himself betraying a shocking unsophistication if not a shocking unawareness of the fiction of the fifties.

Paul Darcy Boles (*Saturday Review*, 1 Nov., 1958) calls the work "outstanding," and says that Capote's voice "cool even when exasperated, never more sure of itself than when amazed, sounds through every sentence." John K. Hutchens (*Herald Tribune*, 4 Nov., 1958) says that Capote "has definitely come out of his macabre, isolated world of shadowy characters in flight from sundry terrors."

Irving Howe says that, in *Breakfast,* Capote finally displays a "genuine interest in . . . **someone else's** character, for its own sake." He cites Capote's "brilliantly feline sensibility," though he argues, in contrast with Kazin, that "his style is annoying in its Broadway familiarity," and he criticizes Capote's reliance on "dimestore exotica" (*Partison Review,* Winter, 1959*).* Norman Mailer predicts that "*Breakfast at Tiffany's* will become a small classic" though Capote doesn't seem to be serious "about the deep resources of the novel." He is not social critical enough; he relies on the "saccharine" rather than the serious, especially in the short stories (*Advertisements for Myself,* 1959).

Walter Allen (*New Statesman,* Dec., 1958), along with numerous other critics over the years, finds Sally Bowles in Holly Golightly, though, says Allen, Capote "is rather less of the camera-eye than Isherwood, and much more a comic turn."

Paul Levine (*Georgia Review,* Fall, 1959) compares Holly to Salinger's Holden Caulfield and Bellow's Augie March, the three of whom embody "the vestigial moral consciousness of a society alarmed by everything except indifference." The theme of the novel is whether "the private world of love and imagination can invest life with beauty, joy, and meaning." In the novel, Capote is speaking more freely, more convincingly than he ever has before about the central quest in post-war fiction: the search for love." Levine concludes that "Like good whiskey . . . Capote seems to mature with age."

In his perceptive study of Holly Golightly, ("Birth of a Heroine," 1959, collected here) Ihab Hassan compares her to Joel in *Other Voices* and Collin in *The Grass Harp* on the grounds that they all "stand for knowledge through dream, love, and free action." They all represent "the new type of hero in American fiction, and whether we call him saint or criminal, rebel or victim, rogue or picaro, his heart, though not entirely pure, is in the right place." Joel however represents the "nocturnal" aspect of Capote's style, Holly the "daylight," and her aspect is characterized by humor, by "her quixotic ideas of hope, sincerity, truth," which qualities Hassan identifies as "peculiarly American." In the case of all three rebels, while we might disapprove of their rebellion, "we cannot in good conscience ignore the truth their proud faith so urgently implies."

Answered Prayers was by far the most critically disappointing of all Capote's fiction, largely because he hyped it so recklessly and irresponsibly in interviews and essays. It was to be a Proustian **roman a clef** that would be three times as long as all his other work combined. He published four excerpts from the work in *Esquire* which intrigued and titillated his audience. But when his novel appeared, posthumously, readers discovered that the "excerpts" were all that existed and that one of them, "Mojave," was deleted for appearance in *Music for Chameleons,* leaving three. It might be said kindly that Capote died before he could finish the work; but the fact is that he wrote nothing between 1976 when the last piece appeared and 1984 when he died.

Terrence Rafferty, whose review/essay we include here, (*The New Yorker,* 21 Sept., 1987) says the book "seems merely to have got stuck in time, arrested at a shockingly early state of development," like Cousin Randolph in *Other. Voices* "whose great secret is that he doesn't really exist." Neither does Jonesy/Capote of this book who, in "trying to produce a true self-portrait . . . seems terribly alone, unable to imagine himself." Rafferty compares the characters in *Answered Prayers* unfavorably to the "typical outcasts, losers, children, and the childlike old" of Capote's early work; contrasts the middle aged rich bitches of "La Côte Basque" to the "graceful, delicate literary effects" of *Breakfast at Tiffany's* which gave us the "buoyant young gold-digger Holly Golightly." The novel "was a fulfillment of his early fiction's prophecies of the terrifying emptiness of maturity." And finally, Capote "just turned into Cousin Randolph and disappeared, and *Answered Prayers*, broken, with cold winds howling through its deserted rooms, achieved its inevitable, its perfect form."

FACT INTO FICTION

In Cold Blood

In Cold Blood is a full-fledged attempt to turn recognizable, identifiable fact into fiction, into what Capote, in a 1966 interview with George Plimpton, called a nonfiction novel, "narrative reportage." It is the one book by which, most critics concur, in all likelihood Capote will be remembered. It was an immediate bestseller garnering over two hundred reviews in 1966 alone, and it has continued to attract serious critical attention both pro and con. We have tried to exemplify and summarize the critical response to the book, and we have chosen from amongst the many examples four selections which we feel represent well both the pros and the cons of that response.

The first reviews of *In Cold Blood* appeared at the end of 1965. There were only a handful, and of those, only the anonymous review in the *Times Literary Supplement* (25 Nov.) which calls the book a prime example of the current movement away from imaginative fiction toward reportage in the *New Yorker* image "with its elegant hygienic style. . . ." and the *Virginia Kirkus' Service* review (9 Nov.) which calls the book "a magnificent job" with "incomparable Capote touches" are worthy of mention here.

The truly major reviews began to appear early in 1966. Walter Allen in a "London Letter" in the *New York Times Book Review* (10 Apr.) reports on the British reviews, in which he finds that *In Cold Blood* is "the book of the day here," prompted by a gigantic "fanfare of publicity." The most perceptive review, Allen says, is Tony Tanner's in *Spectator* (18 Mar.). Tanner calls the book "a black fable from contemporary reality" particularly relevant to current society and "the deep doubleness in American life." Tanner notes that behind Capote's dispassionate objectivity lurks "the excited stare of the southern-gothic novelist with his febrile delight in weird settings and lurid details." *Time* (15 Apr.) claims that the book "drains an event of its content as few events have ever been emptied before," and *Newsweek* (24 Jan.) cites Capote's technical and esthetic triumph: "he has given form to the sloppy, disastrous and tragic patternings of life itself." The book "is the perfect anti-novel" which constructs "a brilliant shapeliness out of the most sorrowful, shapeless and loathsome material." The *Economist's* (19 Mar.) reviewer praises the first part of the book as "gripping as anything appearing in crime fiction;" but he finds that, in the final third of the book "Mr. Capote the novelist gives way . . . to Mr. Capote the journalist and observer," and the book degenerates "from a 'nonfiction novel' to a well-told documentary." The *TLS* reviewer lauds the "narrative skill and delicate sensibility that make this re-telling of a gruesome murder story into a work of art." (17 Mar.) But during the same year James Bannerman (*MacLean's,* 5 Mar.) accuses Capote of "treating the murders and their consequences as a sort of exercise in pop art," while Lee Bayandall argues from the Marxist position (*Studies on the Left,* 6 Mar.) that Capote is dealing seriously with social reality. He "is aware . . . of social bases for the murder," and "one gets from Capote a more concrete sense of barely concealed violence in our social order than from many novelists."

Evan Connell (*This World,* 16 Jan.) considers *Blood* "bland. It goes down the gullet like custard." Citing numerous clichés, he finds "the prose so bad that it invites disbelief," and structurally, the book "is put together with no more subtlety than a house of dominoes." However, F. W. Dupee (*New York Review of Books,* 3 Feb.) believes the book "is the best documentary account of an American crime every written." It is "a striking response to . . . the tendency . . . among writers to resort . . . to super-creative reportage." Also on style, Stanley Kauffmann calls the book "residually shallow." Capote is unable "to write straightforward English," he is "the most outrageously overrated stylist of our time" (*New Republic,* 22 Jan.). Dwight MacDonald says that the book lacks "documentary truth." "The very qualities that make the book such a remarkable **tour deforce**—the author's intelligence, his sense of form, and the strength of his personality—play an ambiguous role" (*Esquire,* April). Phillip Tompkins in *Esquire* (June) goes to the court transcripts and interviews for verification of the factual truth of events as presented in the book. He finds Capote's facts frequently wrong because he got too close to the killers, especially to Perry Smith. Capote's claim that every word in the book is true does not hold up under investigation.

The three best essay-reviews of *In Cold Blood* which appeared in 1966 were by George Garrett, Diana Trilling, and Kenneth Tynan. Garrett's favorable review (*Hollins Critic,* Feb.) is concerned with form, with the "innovative arrangement" of the details and facts in the book. The murder scene is withheld from the reader until after the killers have been caught and confess, for the sake of the suspense necessary to fiction. Though Capote makes use of thematic and characterization techniques found in his earlier fiction, here he is far less conservative in technique. ". . . though he has created a rich gallery of interesting and memorable characters in his fiction, he has never until now displayed such ability to handle a large number of characters, all of whose lives and fortunes are intricately and subtly inter-related, and to treat them with depth and understanding. . . . Before this he had seemed content to offer a kind of fan dance, showing only glimpses [into his characters] and then chiefly by the allusive method of signs, clues, hints, and symbols. Here the characters are stripped. . . . It is exactly the kind of thing he seemed to be sidestepping in his other work."

Diana Trilling, in her unfavorable review included here (*Partisan Review*, Spring) argues against calling the book a novel because Capote is too objective. She maintains that he does not rely on his subjective response to the people about whom he writes, as does James Agee in *Let Us Now Praise Famous Men*. The book merely produces "a sensationalism proportionate to the horror of the actual events . . . being described," and therefore it lacks literary merit. Capote refuses to be morally involved with the story; his objectivity is used "as a shield for evasion." Trilling finds this "objectivity, this subjection" of personal involvement, morally objectionable and "prideful" in the extreme.

Kenneth Tynan (*Observer*, 15 Mar. included here) praises the book as "by any standards a monumental job of editing and a most seductive piece of writing" and "certainly the most detailed and atmospheric account ever written of a contemporary crime." He too finds the book morally lacking, but for the reason that Capote refuses to try to help Perry and Dick, not because he refuses to involve himself with their story. "For the first time an influential writer of the first rank has been placed in a position of privileged intimacy with criminals about to die, and . . . [has] done less than he might have to save them." Tynan argues that Capote betrayed Perry and Dick's trust; that he should have gotten them psychiatric help. And he concludes, sounding very much like Trilling, that "the blood in which this book is written is as cold as any in recent literature."

Critical attention remained focused on *In Cold Blood* in 1967. Jean Mouton in an essay in French (*Nouvelles Litteraures*, 12 May) defends the book as realistic; it allows the reader to experience reality accurately because it leaves so little to the imagination. He compares the book to *Robinson Crusoe*, to Stendhal's *Red and the Black*, and he compares Perry Smith to Roskalnikov and Camus' Meursault. And William Wiegand in an essay included here ("The 'Nonfiction' Novel," 1968) centers his discussion on the art of *In Cold Blood*, asserting that Capote fulfills a long history of attempts to merge journalism and fiction, "wages total war with journalism and its conventions by his conscious intention to keep the instinct to inform and discuss subordinated to the novelistic objective throughout." Thus, he creates a new form, be it called nonfiction or documentary novel. Concentrating on structure, Wiegand argues that *In Cold Blood,* "shows there can still be a connection between the artist, practicing his art to the full, and the random event which verifiedly happened and has this implication, this texture, this raw core."

Also in 1968, Irving Malin published *A Critical Handbook* to *In Cold Blood*. Jackson Bryer attached an extensive though not annotated bibliography to the collection. Most of the essays were reprints and have been covered in their original form elsewhere in this Introduction. But three important essays were

wr   *dbook.* The first, by Melvin J. Friedman aims "to
pro   aditional writer." He has "consistently turned base
me   own writing gently holds up the mirror to what is
bei   , by Faulkner, O'Connor, Styron, and the French
nou   He is adept at using "the devices of cinema,
pho   to great advantage" ("Towards an Aesthetic:
Tru   ces"). The second original contribution to the
Har   y's "Why the Chickens Came Home to Roost in
Hol   Galloway calls *In Cold Blood* "a social document of
undeniable significance" whose major theme is "the metamorphosis of dream
into nightmare." Capote "reconstructs not just the lives of six people, but a
microcosm of the world in which we all live," a world in which America is
"both killer and victim, turning the shotgun against herself." Robert K. Morris in
the third original essay shows that there is a continuity between the characters in
In Cold Blood and those in Capote's early fiction. They "share similar patterns
of behavior, their acts differing . . . in kind, but carried on with a like intensity."
Capote's settings consistently serve as "metaphors of loneliness and isolation."
Morris discusses also the consistent "obsessive" images in Capote's work:
windows, mirrors, grotesques, and grotesqueries.

Two interestingly conflicting analyses appeared in 1969. Grigor Pavlov, a
Soviet critic, published a lengthy study of class conflict in Capote's work
through *In Cold Blood.* It is worth examining his total argument here. According
to Pavlov, in his early stories Capote is chiefly interested in evoking the "foul
atmosphere of stagnation and depravity in the South." To accomplish this aim,
Capote "poses the problem of decay in abstract terms, severing it from the social
experience of the American South." But with *Tree of Night*, he begins to explore
"the depths of the bourgeois individual's" alienation, of his "trackless
existence." The theme of *The Grass Harp*, Pavlov says, is "revolt against the
humdrum existence in a small Southern town." Capote argues for "the moral
superiority of the innocent, sensitive, and quixotic person over the practical
money-minded business figure in American life." And *Breakfast* gives us an
even deeper exploration of the theme of alienation. But *In Cold Blood* is final
proof "the artist has come of age." It "is a chilling comment on the irrelevance
of the so-called American Dream and on the . . . violence and destruction
modern American society has let loose." Class conflict is at the heart of the
novel; the Clutter family is "the symbol of a class manipulating and perverting
other human lives."

On the other hand, Marion Truesdale ("Reality and Illusion in the Theatre")
charges Capote with manipulating facts in *In Cold Blood*, in order to impose
"the sense of myth upon the events." By such manipulation, Capote enables
himself to "comment upon the moral implications of an outrageous act." But he
is dishonest, because "he does not admit of contradictions in fact" or in

"interpretations of those facts." Such dishonesty visits upon the facts "an order, a consistency, and hence a significance that [they] did not have" in reality.

In 1970, William Nance published a book-length study of Capote's work through *In Cold Blood* (*The Worlds of Truman Capote*). His basic premise is that Capote's work has grown from inner to outer experience. In the early stories, the protagonist "is always and essentially a victim." He tends to move inward deeper and deeper toward a revelation at the core of his being. The later protagonists outface the monsters of their childhood, seeing them "in truer perspective and with proper detachment" exposing them for the monsters they are. Nance finds that *In Cold Blood* "is a factual echo of Capote's earliest fiction" with the monsters externalized rather than internalized.

In 1971, in "Faction . . ." an essay in a German book on American literature in the twentieth century (there is an English summary), Dietmar Haack discusses *In Cold Blood,* John Hersey's *Algiers Motel Incident*, and Mailer's *Armies of the Night* as nonfiction novels. He declares that it is Capote who brings the issue of the nonfiction novel into focus. But Capote's work is flawed in its total rejection of imaginative concerns.

J. U. Jacobs by contrast ("The Nonfiction Novel," 1971) argues that "Capote is essentially a mythopoeic artist," and finds that *In Cold Blood* contains most of the elements of art to be found in great fiction. He goes on to discuss the theme of the book as disenchantment with the American Dream "resulting from its betrayal in terms of American history." "But we must never lose sight of the true nature of [Capote's] fable," writes Jacobs, "which is a factual representation of fiction . . . and not a fictional representation of fact."

Alfred Kazin ("The World As Novel: From Capote to Mailer" 1971) agrees that *In Cold Blood* is "ultimately a fiction in the form of fact." But he goes on to argue that Capote's sympathy for real people makes the book too personal for fiction." Still, his art makes it possible for the reader "to realize and possess and dominate this murder" in the way that only fiction makes possible.

But Tony Tanner, also in 1971 (*City of Words*) says that "By juxtaposing and dovetailing the lives and values of the Clutters with those of the killers, Capote produced a schematic picture of the doubleness in American life." But by objectifying his vision, Capote prevents himself from offering psychological insights into the lives of his characters, and, argues against Kazin, the citizens of Holcomb "tend to be caricatured, and the forlorn, dangerous criminals sentimentalized (particularly Perry Smith)." "Overall," he concludes, "Capote's illusory objectivity seems to falsify its evidence by seeking to hide all reportorial bias and disposition."

The novel continued to attract critical commentary throughout the seventies and eighties. John Hellman calls it "a wedding of allegory to fact"—an allegory journalistic in subject matter, realistic in form. Capote "portrays factual events as unfolding in an overall allegorical pattern" ("Death and Design in *In Cold Blood,* " 1980). He reverses the usual artistic process by using fact to emphasize symbol. Capote, Hellman concludes, "has repeatedly forced the reader to view events as manifestations of recurring, timeless patterns," and he cites three sources for the pattern in this book: the Book of Genesis, classic American literature, and the formula detective story, of which the first and the third are strongest (apparently Capote knew less about American literature than he did about the Bible and detective fiction).

Jack De Bellis' "Visions and Revisions" (1979) is concerned with the revisions Capote made in *In Cold Blood* from publication in *The New Yorker* to book form. De Bellis devotes the first two sections of the essay to a largely statistical analysis of those revisions. On the basis of this analysis, De Bellis concerns his essay with 1) the factual accuracy of *In Cold Blood*, and 2) the "distractions" which kept the book from being absolutely accurate. In the former, he finds that Capote made many errors in transposing from magazine to book, even to carrying obvious errors, which had been pointed out to him by his sources, over from one to the other. The major distraction, De Bellis finds, is that Capote saw Perry Smith as his own doppelgänger, reflecting his own life and character. In this argument, Kansas becomes the South, Smith—in real life a proto-typical Capote outsider—becomes Capote, and, with further twists of the evidence, the novel becomes Capote's revenge upon the South for having spawned him.

And finally, in an essay from 1986 which we include in this collection ("Real Toads in Real Gardens") David Galloway implicitly contradicts both Diana Trilling and Kenneth Tynan by crediting Capote and *In Cold Blood* with significant help in abolishing the death penalty in the United States, "however we read the moral implications of the author's detachment." Galloway prefers the term "Documentary Novel" to "Nonfiction Novel," though the book does not follow the linear mode of documentary reportage—Capote rearranges chronology, uses flashbacks, manipulates point of view—in the pursuit of "Creative Reconstruction." Most importantly, Galloway argues that *In Cold Blood* "helped to redraw the map of American fiction;" it was "the catalyzing experience" behind Tom Wolfe's *Electric Kool-Aid Acid Test* and *The Right Stuff.* And although Norman Mailer protested documentary fiction as "'the bleeding heart of TV land,'" he used it himself in *Armies of the Night* (and later in *The Executioner's Song).*

ANTHOLOGIES: *THE DOGS BARK* AND *MUSIC FOR CHAMELEONS*

In his "Preface" to *The Dogs Bark* (1973), Capote writes that *Local Color* (1950) and *The Muses Are Heard* (1956)—both reprinted in *Dogs Bark*—were "the initial thrust of an interest in nonfiction writing." He goes on to say that he believed "that reportage could be as groomed and elevated an art as any other prose form." And in the "Preface" to *Music for Chameleons* (1980), he amplifies that argument, saying that during the fifties, he had been "drawn toward journalism as an art form in itself" because it seemed to him that nothing "truly innovative had occurred in prose writing . . . since the 1920's," and further, that "journalism as an art was almost virgin territory . . . very few literary artists ever wrote narrative journalism," except as "travel essays or autobiography."

These arguments motivated him, he suggests, to spend six years researching and writing *In Cold Blood*, and another four years gathering together the materials for *Answered Prayers* which he began writing in 1972, and which is not "any ordinary roman a clef," for his intentions are "to remove disguises, not manufacture them."

Much of *Answered Prayers* appears in *Music for Chameleons*, as does *Handcarved Coffins,* a short nonfiction novel. Both novels, Capote insists, are evidence of his development and refinement of journalistic technique into an art form, superior even to *In Cold Blood.* He felt that he had found what he called his "framework," and he hung *Answered Prayers* and *Handcarved Coffins* upon it.

Both *Local Color,* a travelogue of "youthful impressions" as Capote called it, and *The Muses Are Heard,* further youthful impressions of Russia and Russians garnered while Capote accompanied the America touring company of *Porgy and Bess,* received some critical attention upon first publication as thin volumes. Edward Parone ("Truman in Wonderland," 1950) calls *Local Color* "prose poetry," and says it is "a between books book" with "nothing very trenchant or brilliant in it." And Mary McGrory (*Sunday Star,* 17 Sept. 1950) says that Capote "is still precious, still precocious; but he can write." "Metaphor after metaphor rings with absolute aptness." And the anonymous reviewer of *Muses* for the *Times Literary Supplement* (5 July, 1957) calls it frothy, superficial, "a fantasy ready made for a Ronald Firbank novel." "Capote says little about the Russian people except to point out the drabness of their dress and their social life." Interestingly, another English scholar, John McCormick (*Catastrophe and Imagination . . .* 1957), like the anonymous reviewer for *TLS,* also compares Capote to Ronald Firbank. Indeed, he argues that Capote, Welty, McCullers, and other Southern writers imitate Firbank in "writing with taste and sensibility of children, madmen, and homosexuals." They "share with Firbank a taste for excessive stylization, an adolescent desire to shock," and "a fondness for exotic paraphernalia. . . ." But Alfred Kazin (*The Open Forum,* 1961) calls *Muses* "one of the shrewdest analyses we have of daily life in the Soviet Union." He praises Capote's ability to capture the "personal **style** in people . . . with affectionate irony."

But it is as part of *The Dogs Bark* that we are considering *Local Color* and *Muses*, as it is as part of *Music for Chameleons* that we are considering *Handcarved Coffins* and the excerpts from *Answered Prayers*—and for that matter, any other of Capote's previously published material which is included in these two anthologies.

Neither anthology was widely reviewed, and what reviews there were were decidedly mixed. Willy Morris (*New Republic*, 3 Nov., 1973) uses a passage in "Muses" to focus on Capote's "attention to style, to the extraordinary pull of places, to all the fleeting wisps of the past that give this volume a durability far beyond" the ordinary between-books book. It is "a self-charting of a courageous literary life, a life of stamina . . . of considerable solitude." Capote, he concludes from *The Dogs Bark,* "is among our best" writers, "and surely the one who most defies a category."

On the other hand, in his review of *Music for Chameleons*, (*New Republic*, 6 and 13 Sept. 1980), Stanley Kanfer says that "Everything is displayed in this crow's nest of a book: insights and snuff-movie outlines . . . old jokes and fresh wit." When Capote thinks "he is like nobody else—a lapidary craftsman, master of nuances and detail. When he babbles, he is a nobody. *Music* displays the thinking Truman." His "powers derive from his weaknesses: fussiness becomes exactitude; gossip, acute dialogue; snobbism a form of confession. . . . There is, in fact, nothing new in Capote's new book, except Capote."

We have included as part of this collection two substantial essays to represent considered critical opinion beyond reviews.

John Waldmeir, in an essay written especially for this collection, cites Capote's long interest in and use of religion as a basis for comparing and contrasting these two collections. He points out that religion figures in all of Capote's writing from the inscription from Jeremiah in *Other Voices*, through the quote from St. Theresa which gives *Answered Prayers* its title. In between, are the many gothic tales with religious overtones (also mentioned by Irving Malin, above) and the stories which are concerned with religious or quasireligious holidays. Waldmeir finds that *Dogs* "introduces the topic in a number of selections including the piece that opens the volume, 'A Voice from a Cloud,'" and that *Music* "refers to the topic consistently. . . . All 14 works employ a terminology . . . best interpreted as religious." But despite these superficial similarities, Waldmeir finds distinct differences between the attitudes toward and presentation and use of religious materials in the two books. In *Dogs*, Capote "cites religious practices from a variety of traditions" but he "rarely develops his thoughts or integrates them into the worlds he depicts." In *Music,* however, he uses religious words and images "in ways that seem to offer critical commentaries on [religion's] social role." The text from the Sermon on the Mount in "A Lamp in the Window," for instance, "informs the entire story as it asks readers to ponder the religious meaning of hospitality."

Waldmeir goes on to say that "religion as a topic . . . shapes other literary conventions such as theme and style," and he devotes a significant portion of his essay to the relationship between topic and convention, and to a careful analysis of Capote's style as it develops in these two books. The objectivity, the distancing which characterizes his attitude toward religion in *Dogs,* is replaced in *Music* by a tendency to introduce himself personally and biographically into the text of many of the pieces by way of illustrating "religious" convictions and practices in a social sense.

Waldmeir relies substantially for his evidence on *Handcarved Coffins,* the "nonfiction account of an American crime" in *Music for Chameleons,* and in so doing he cites Jack Hicks' discussion of that work, which appears next in this collection ("Fire, Fire, Fire Flowing Like a River, River, River" 1990). Like Waldmeir, Hicks too examines stylistic devices in Capote's prose, the "interrupting commas, ellipses, and dashes" that "highlight disjointed thought rhythms undercutting plain language" and illustrate the conclusion that, in *Coffins,* "the role of the narrator" has been expanded "considerably." Hicks, however, treats the piece almost purely as fiction rather than nonfiction and argues that it is most profitably read as one text in a postmodern genre that includes works by John Barth, Kurt Vonnegut, Jerry Kosinski, and Thomas Pynchon.

CAPOTE AND OTHERS

While David Galloway cites the influence of *In Cold Blood* upon the nonfiction fiction of Tom Wolfe and Norman Mailer, and Cynthia Ozick credits the early Capote with leading young post-war writers away from sociological fiction back toward "Art," many more critics have cited the influence of other writers upon Capote. They focus upon other Southern writers from Poe to Faulkner, and find especially the influence of Southern women writers like Eudora Welty and Carson McCullers and Flannery O'Connor.

J. Douglas Perry in an essay included in this collection ("Gothic As Vortex: The Form of Horror in Capote, Faulkner, and Styron," 1973) defines gothicism in terms of its "three structured principles" concentricity, predetermined sequence, and character repetition. Perry goes back to Mary Shelley and "Monk" Lewis, Poe and Melville, to define his terms, then he moves into the body of the essay: a comparison of the gothicism of Capote, Faulkner, and Styron. The three authors "use the gothic form, with its denial of final absolute affirmation, tragic or otherwise, to capture the irony of our twentieth century existence: the conviction that the search for self-awareness may not only be fatal, but fruitless, because it is equivalent to self-negation . . . that self-awareness and self-destruction are one and the same . . ." In Capote, Perry focuses primarily on *Other Voices, Other Rooms*, with passing reference to *In Cold Blood* as "the archetypal horror machine of time. . . ."

Blake Almendinger ("The Room Was Locked with the Key on the Inside," 1987) argues that while Capote denies the influence of other writers, his texts contradict him. Almendinger finds he was heavily influenced by women writers, and that he felt anxious about it, and his anxiety is reflected in his fiction. Most of the essay is devoted to the influence of Eudora Welty's "Why I Live at the

Post Office" on "My Side of the Matter." The central theme of "My Side" is "female influence and the denial of it." Women in the story dress and behave like men, thus acknowledging their inferiority. But men win only in a physical sense (they are stronger) and by isolating themselves from women.

Frank Baldanza compares Carson McCullers and Capote in some detail ("Plato in Dixie," 1958). They are alike, basically, in sharing "distinctly Platonic theories of love," if you love one thing, you can love all things. He surveys much of McCullers focusing especially on the short story "A Tree, A Rock, A Cloud," comparing her work most directly with Capote's *Other Voices* and *The Grass Harp*. He concludes that, while love in McCullers is often unreciprocated, in Capote it is more often fulfilled.

While Almendinger cites Capote's debt to Welty, and Baldanza to McCullers, Jon Tuttle points out Capote's debt to Flannery O'Connor. Tuttle demonstrates in detail that "A Good Man Is Hard to Find" influenced *In Cold Blood* ("Glimpses of 'A Good Man' in *In Cold Blood*," 1988), and although he does not object to the influence *per se*, he does remind readers that Capote refused to acknowledge them. Tuttle quotes Gore Vidal, who claimed that Capote, ruthlessly and unoriginally, "plundered Carson McCullers for *Other Voices, Other Rooms* [and] abducted Isherwood's Sally Bowles for *Breakfast at Tiffany's*."

In another essay included here, William L. Nance offers a psychological study of how the neoplatonic dream of paradise exists in the works of Capote and Katherine Ann Porter ("Variations on a Dream . . ." 1969). The argument is similar to Baldanza's. Nance finds Porter's vision of an ideal world "seems only to confirm a feeling of captivity, [while] Capote's use of a similar kind of dream seems to have been for him a means of liberation." Unlike Porter, Capote blends acceptance and relinquishment with the support of a Platonic philosophy of love. In Porter as in McCullers the philosophy seems to reflect despair.

Some comparisons are made between Capote and other writers not on the basis of influence but on the basis of circumstantial similarity in subject matter and/or approach.

Donald Pizer ("Documentary Narrative As Art," 1971) compares Capote with William Manchester as documentarians, rating Capote far superior. "Unlike Manchester, who fails to convince us of any significance in *The Death of a President*, Capote has led us to dwell on the social and ethical problems present in the death of a murderer [in *In Cold Blood*]." The essay concentrates on Capote's use of various documentary devices—direct quotation, sequential narrative, "present-time event [used] primarily as a means of exploring the past," shifts away from chronological order "to maintain suspense" and to show motivation, and on his use of irony as a thematic device. According to Pizer, it is this final point more than any other which distinguishes Capote's work from Manchester's.

John J. McAleer ("Turning Case History into Art," 1972, included here) compares Theodore Dreiser's *An American Tragedy* and *In Cold Blood*, largely to the detriment of Capote, who "seems to have mistaken craft for art." McAleer explores the parallels between the two books, though he does not argue direct influence. Capote, he says, is reluctant "to make functional use of his facts, save at the most literal level." "The pursuit of the American Dream" is behind the murders in both books, but Dreiser explores the cause, and Capote does not, largely because he lacks or rejects insight into human behavior. "As a documentary novelist, Capote was shackled by" facts, permitting him little lateral movement away from them. He is "footloose amid the lovely lawns of his lyricism. To see facts wholly, to be enveloped in verities that are real, we still must go to Dreiser."

BIBLIOGRAPHY

The bibliographical section of this book begins with an original bibliographical essay written for us by Peter Christensen. It is intended to update Robert J. Stanton's indispensable annotated bibliography of primary and secondary materials (1980) and to augment and expand this Introduction. For these reasons, we have asked Christensen to give us an essay rather than a simple chronological listing. There have been numerous checklists and mini-bibliographies since the publication of *In Cold Blood*, most notably by Jackson R. Bryer (1968) and by Kenneth Starosciak (1974). But only Stanton and Christensen flesh out the entries in a manner most useful to the categorizer and anthologizer.

This section also includes a selected bibliography of works about Capote focusing primarily on the materials covered in this Introduction and in Christensen's essay.

I wish to thank each of the contributors to this volume, with special thanks to Peter Christensen and John Waldmeir (also my coeditor) for writing original essays, and to Leslie Fiedler for revising his review of the short fiction.

Joseph J. Waldmeir
East Lansing, MI

I

OVERVIEWS AND INTERVIEWS

Plate du Jour: Soul Food: Truman Capote on Black Culture

CECIL M. BROWN

In the fall of '74, I was sent by *Rolling Stone Magazine* to Key West to interview Tennessee Williams, and during the week that I was there I met Truman Capote. Drawing on our Southern background for running off at the mouth, shooting the breeze, as the folks back home call it, we became instant friends. At the end of each day, we would sit outside beneath the Southern skies, sipping B&B and swap lies. Truman was famous for it; so I did a lot of listening. Of course, catching a whiff of the laughter, others would join us: writers Jim Harrison and Thomas McGuane, who at the time was shooting a film from his novel, and Annie Liebowitz, photographer for *Rolling Stone* and so forth.

So delightful was Truman on almost any subject, that I decided to test his perspicacity on such profound matters as Black culture, which, as it turns out, he knew a lot about. Still, his witty insight, as he schmozzled over touchy areas like the tensions between Jews and Black intellectuals, was very much intact and, all in all, it made for very interesting listening. I now present it to you with this one precaution: it is three o'clock in the morning and we have just left a big bash with Tennessee Williams, and hundreds of other people; yet Truman is still going strong! . . . Uh, what was that? Black culture? . . . sure I know a lot about it . . . take Bianca Jagger, for example . . . Here we go!

ME: What is Bianca Jagger like?
TRUMAN: An original. A completely totally self-invented person. The kind I like best. She is bright, intelligent, and has told herself a lot of untrue things but she has convinced herself of them, and they are all parts of her character.

She has tremendous style; when I first met her she was having an affair with Jimi Hendrix. Before that she was having an affair with Billy Bertson . . . Now,

Quilt, 1 (1981): 36-42.

there's somebody *Rolling Stone* should do a piece on, a truly original person, he has a kind of aura about him. His mother was a lady called Eleanor Lander. And his father was a guy called Seymour Bertson, *New York Daily News* editor; Bertson cut a very wide swath and then cut out, and now lives in a commune in Northern California. Bianca was in love with him, but theirs has subsided.

An extremely fashionable lady was having a dinner party for six or seven people, and Bianca was one of the guests, but she kept getting up from the table and dialing this telephone number. "I have a friend coming to pick me up," she told the host. "Do you mind?" At eleven o'clock when we were preparing to leave, Jimi Hendrix comes in. He was very . . . well, not like anything he was subsequently. He was polite, subdued, shy, and stayed about half an hour. It was obvious Bianca was madly in love with him.

Then later that winter they were around in New York. I guess their relationship just must have broken up. The next time I saw her was at the home of a great friend of some friends of mine in Paris. They told me she was the daughter of the Ambassador of Nicaragua. I knew she wasn't but she had transformed herself. Her mother and father ran a shop in Nicaragua in the marketplace. Was she wealthy? Not at all! She arrived in grand style at this grand house of Monsieur and Madame Carreau. I didn't say anything when she said she was the daughter of an ambassador. I was highly amused. Seeing as it had only been a year ago that I met her in New York with Jimi Hendrix.

She is a real adventuress. She is a good friend of a girl called Sue Mengers, and they are inseparable. I love Sue and think she is one of the finest girls I have ever met in my life, and she is really a great wit.

The next thing I knew Bianca was married to Mick. Not too long ago, she said to me: "Do you know Michael York?" I said yes. She said, "Do you think he's attractive?" I said I did, but I hated his wife. She's a stupid bitch. Bianca: "Oh, I think he is yummy." Oh? But what about Mick? "Oh, I think Mick is super, but do you think I could make it with Michael York? Do you think I can?"
ME: Let's talk about Saul Bellow.
TRUMAN: Saul Bellow walked up to me at a literary and cultural symposium and said, "Well, now, what is your opinion of the Jewish Literary Mafia?"

I said, "Saul, I'm not the victim of the Jewish Literary Mafia—*you are!* They created you and they can destroy you. They can't touch me! I'm totally outside of it. They think they created you—which in fact they did. They think they can destroy you and they will. I'm not your enemy, Saul. I think you are a very gifted and extraordinary person. So, don't tell what *I* think of the Jewish Literary Mafia. They will destroy you." I said that to Saul Bellow and then I just walked away.

And it is true; they created him and they will destroy him, just like they created Philip Roth. It is the very nature of the Jewish Literary Mafia.
ME: But why?

TRUMAN: They create a thing which can't be what they want it to be, and then they destroy it.
(Annie Liebowitz begins to sing, for some odd reason, "America the Beautiful!")
ME: When did the JLM start?
TRUMAN: After the war . . . started with Irwin Shaw, Saul Bellow. Look what they did to *Shaw!* They tossed him on the old heap pile and called him a hack . . . and Norman Mailer! The great Norman Mailer! And now they have turned against him . . . and James Baldwin . . . whom they took up as a surrogate Jew. Now James Baldwin is a big pile of shit to them! Norman Podhoretz was given a terrific build-up by *Commentary*, and Mailer, Bellow, and Lionel Trilling— now Norman Podhoretz is a monster! Norman Podhoretz just happens to be the number one prodigy of Lionel Trilling! But suddenly Podhoretz is an absolute nothing: a stupid shit! *(followed by a great deal of laughter)*

These people! You can't be any part of a group . . . that's why I always wanted to be alone . . . *(sadness in his voice)* I never wanted to be a part of any kind of anything, because all of those people are a bunch of bullshitters. . . .
ME: Any publishers that go beyond the Jewish analysis?
TRUMAN: No.
ME: They all abandon you?
TRUMAN: Anybody will abandon anybody.
ME: Richard Wright?
TRUMAN: Richard Wright was a dear friend of mine. I had a big discussion with Saul Bellow about Richard Wright. I said, Richard Wright was a good friend of mine, and do you know what Saul Bellow said? He said, "Huh! Well, Wright just became a victim of these heavyweight intellectuals. I used to see him carting around books on Wittgenstein. He was becoming convinced he was an intellectual." I thought that was very sad and pathetic. It certainly wasn't true. I remember once I took Saul Bellow to dinner at Wright's apartment. At that time Saul Bellow was a nothing; had published only one thing, something called *Dangling Man.* In light of all this, it was certainly stupid of him to say what he said about Wright. Bellow was saying that Wright had a vitality which had become subjugated to a pose by the European intellectual, totally alien to his nature. Now, I knew Wright from 1955 to his death. I didn't know him well but I knew him *quite* well. He was a wonderful person. He did get a little confused, but in a way that one could understand completely. He had published *Native Son,* and he had moved to Paris because he felt he couldn't live the sort of life that was sympathetic to his family situation, for his wife was white. He had a nice apartment in Paris. So for Saul Bellow to say Richard was a kind of sell-out, that he had become a victim, that he was a lightweight that had been turned into a heavyweight—a primitive into a sophisticate—is totally absurd.
ME: Do you think it has anything to do with Bellow's Jewish heritage?
TRUMAN: I think there is a terrific tension—and God knows that it came out in the symposium the other day—an extraordinary tension between Black

intellectuals and Jewish intellectuals. Because Jews can't believe, can't accept the fact that Black intellectuals are not totally indebted to them. The Jews feel, "But my God! We did all the groundwork; we are the people who said that the Black intellectuals can do this and can do that! Why are you turning against us?" But they totally ignore the fact that Jewish intellectuals have exploited the Black intellectuals in a totally commercial way.

ME: At that time, nobody else was helping the Blacks?

TRUMAN: The point is there is one thing Jewish intellectuals do ignore. All Black ghettoes—all of Harlem was exploited by the Jews. There is between Jewish and Black intellectuals a real genuine thing! Having been at that conference and seeing the real animosity and the *high* sort of feelings, I think that there is an irritability between them. Well, you know Jewish people have done much in actual cultural support—more culture for blood. Especially in theatre. No question about it. But Black people have a genuine right to feel that they have been ripped off in all kinds of creative areas but mostly especially in music. God. That was the rip-off of the century! I think that Black people have given and contributed more to the original things in America than anybody else. They have contributed things that were not borrowed—from song lyrics, dance, theater—everything! It's been borrowed, stolen. What I really feel about it, I really truly believe to one hundred percent it will balance itself off.

ME: You feel it will eventually come out in the open?

TRUMAN: When all the chips are down, the Jewish people don't have that much influence. When it all comes to an end.

ME: As an example of a Black artist obviously influenced by Jewish philanthropy, what do you think of LeRoi Jones?

TRUMAN: I only knew LeRoi Jones early in his career. But he is a person for whom I have no respect at all. And I'll tell you why. He was married to a white girl, and had two children; he was accepting grants. I said to myself, if LeRoi Jones is so anti-establishment why did he take a Guggenheim Foundation Fellowship? You can't have it both ways. I mean why take foundation fellowships and turn right around and say that this organization is despicable, that Harlem is all run by Jewish landlords, when that entire Guggenheim Foundation is both capitalistic and Jewish. Don't you agree? I couldn't see how he could do it. He had a very nice wife. He used to go around with white intellectuals. Then all of a sudden, overnight, he did this *vont face,* left his wife, his children—and announced, he was not into the black thing! It was the greatest piece of hypocrisy you could ever conceive of. He just wasn't real— you know, he wanted—he was following the fashion. I could have said, "Okay!" I would have accepted this *if* he hadn't taken the Guggenheim. You can't denounce the very thing and everything it represents—capitalism, white power structure, etc.—and then accept money from the same people. That doesn't make sense, does it? If he hadn't done that I could have had respect for him. But you can't have respect for anybody who denounces on the left hand and on the right hand is grabbing a check.

ME: Several important people have noted this curious subtlety of Black behavior—such as Carl Van Vechten.

TRUMAN: Van Vechten was a real friend of the Black. A real pioneer. That's why I said the other day when people brought up Billie Holiday, that Carl Van Vechten should be there. He was one of the first to recognize the whole truth of the matter. I think that about 60% of everything in America originated entirely with Black culture. That's why I get so absolutely furious with the whole cult of modern music—starting with practically anybody, because it's *all! all! all!* taken from Black people! I can't think of anybody in America, who isn't ripping off Black people. Really, I can't think of any.

ME: Not only in music. Look at literature and the *Confessions of Nat Turner* by William Styron?

TRUMAN: I know Bill. He was terribly upset when the book came out and the Black intellectuals attacked it, but he was trying, I feel, to buy sympathy and acceptance. You know I never read that book. I don't know why, but I started to read it, you know how you read 25 pages, then you stop, then you forget where you were and then you start again but never really get into it? Somehow or other, I never finished it.

ME: It received the National Book Award.

TRUMAN: Oh, they campaigned for it. The whole thing was a big mistake, I thought.

ME: Black film is another imagery of that progress.

TRUMAN: Your view is not incorrect. But what the producers of exploitation films found out is they could make a lot of money out of these films. People only produce films to make money. One thing you get to admit—even with Gordon Parks—they do make money. Gordon Parks—somebody I really respect—entered that whole business with that detective film, *Shaft*. I liked *Learning Tree*. But I don't see why he did the *Shaft* film. Maybe he just wanted to direct a big vulgar film. It was a curious thing for somebody with his sensibility to do. Maybe he thought it was a good film; if he did, I can see his reasoning.

ME: Do you see a possibility of a new Black film esthetic?

TRUMAN: I watch five or six of the exploitation films with primarily Black audiences, and their enthusiasms, their identification with the characters in the film was unbelievable! Therefore I think there is a point about them; it's just too bad they are always so violent and negative. I went to see *Death Wish,* which is not a Black film but contains the elements that will make my point. *Death Wish* is the kind of film you must see with a large audience. It's about a man— Charles Bronson—whose wife is raped and killed by three white youths. He sets out to get this revenge by killing muggers and people like that. In the course of the film, six of the nine victims are Black. Half of the audience is Black. When the man was about to set up the murder, the audience cheered for him madly. And the Black people shouted, "Get that motherfucker!" It was interesting that they were cheering for him to kill Black people. There were no differentials in their psychology.

ME: Is this because of the demoralizing results of exploitation films?

TRUMAN: Absolutely.

ME: Do you see the beginning of a Black art film movement?

TRUMAN: It is coming, sure. You take *Sounder*. . . . Never would have been financed ten years ago. I think that it's stupid that people think it's a good film. It's bad, it's so terrible it makes you *cringe!* But the point is that ten years ago they would never have gotten the money to make it at all. But the film revolution is coming because making films is going to be less and less expensive. People think it's going to be more and more expensive but it's not. Because of technological development, it will become less and less expensive to do, and anybody will be able to make a reasonably sound film with not so much money. I have a theory that film is going to take over totally novel writing. The people who write novels will take over films and for a relative little money they will make films. That day is almost here. But you gotta admit that the audience taste level is still so low that it doesn't make a difference to distinguish between film quality nowadays. All of them are done so poorly.

ME: Do you see the intervention of politics as an aid to the film artist, or the fiction artist for that matter?

TRUMAN: What I think is this. Simply this. It's got nothing to do with anything but itself. Art has nothing in the world to do with groups, people, commerce, with nothing—it's just *you!* Somewhere in Henry James, there is a nice quote: "We live in the dark, we do what we can. Our passion is our strength, the rest is the madness of art." I think it's an extraordinary simple statement about the position a creative person is in. It's all up to you, it's all up to me—it has nothing to do with politics. Politics is something else. It doesn't have anything to do with art. You can have very strong politics, but there is a great danger; for if you mix art with politics, you will end up with bad politics and bad art.

The Metaphorical World of Truman Capote

JOHN W. ALDRIDGE

On the face of it, Truman Capote would seem to be just about the most promising new writer we have in America today. Not only is he the most precocious of the group of younger novelists whose first books began attracting attention right after the war, but he has already displayed an idiosyncrasy of vision and temperament which has ended, literarily, in the creation of a world unmistakably his own and, publicly, in the creation of a mythical personality of considerable charm and color. When compared with his contemporaries, Capote at once seems remarkable for his rigid adherence to his personal bias, his refusal merely to be in style. In fact, if one can set aside Jean Stafford, Walter Van Tilburg Clark, and Mary McCarthy as belonging to an older literary group and Shirley Jackson and Howard Nemerov as existing somewhat apart from the group that came out of the war, it is possible to say that Capote is the only writer of the new war generation who has remained clear of the journalistic tradition and explored a genre that does not depend simply on the reportage of social manners or of events of strictly topical interest.

Having said this much, I hope I shall not seem to be taking it back if I direct attention to certain elements in Capote's work which, while they may well be attributable to the accident of his precocity, do not seem to promise for him the kind of growth beyond precocity which up to now we may have had reason to expect of him. I think first of what seems to me most distinctive of all that he has written—its quality of isolation. I do not mean the sort we ordinarily associate with Joyce, laboring in Paris to reconstruct his youth in Dublin, or even with Proust, laboring in his cork-lined chambers to reconstruct a past for himself that would justify the death with which he was about to climax it. For both these men isolation was a necessary phase of the creative act. It enabled them to retreat momentarily from the literal business of life so that they could get down to the imaginative business of reentering life through art. The

Western Review 15 (Summer 1951): 247-60.

important thing was that they were performing a task of synthesis and interpretation. They had always before them the image of life as they had lived it; in isolation and through a kind of suffering we cannot hope to understand they elevated that image to the highest level of artistic creation.

In Capote one feels not that life has been lived and then laboriously achieved but that life has somehow been missed. Capote's world seems to be a concoction rather than a synthesis. It has a curious easiness about it, as if it has cost nothing to make, as if, really, the parts had all been made separately at some anonymous factory and might have been put together by just anyone. Its purity is not the purity of experience forced under pressure into shape, of painstaking selection and rejection amid a thousand possibilities. Rather, it is the sort that seemingly can be attained only in the isolation of a mind which life has never really violated, in which the image of art has developed to a flowerlike perfection because it has developed alone.

II.

This quality is revealed in the failure of Capote's work to achieve true symbolic realization, a failure which is evident throughout his novel *Other Voices, Other Rooms* and the stories in his collection *A Tree of Night*, but which in the latter, because they are stories, takes a somewhat different form than it does in the novel. One can say of the figures in the novel that, if they are not, in the true sense, symbols, they are at least metaphorically related to one another and that, within the limits of this relationship, they illuminate one another. But one can also say that, for such illumination to occur, figures of this sort must share a common context in which they may actively carry out their relations and, through a process of mutual enhancement, become part of a single structure of meaning. When they are transplanted to a series of short stories, each of which represents a distinct and separate context, they, therefore, must necessarily lose their metaphorical function and become, at best, merely images and, at worst, merely ghostly abstractions.

In such a story as "Master Misery," for example, we encounter in the figure of the sadistic buyer-of-dreams the familiar devil-god of Capote's world. Like Randolph in the novel, he is intended to represent a sort of power of universal evil to which the will-less individual is hypnotically compelled to give his soul, as Joel is compelled to give up his manhood. We cannot say that either he or Randolph properly symbolizes such a power. But Randolph's plausibility as at least a manifestation of this power is enhanced by the metaphorical support which Idabel, Miss Amy, and Mr. Sansom, as well as the whole haunted world of the Landing itself, are able to give him. At every stage in the development of the narrative, their accumulated meaning serves to fortify his and, finally, to give it a context from which it can never be disengaged for analysis. Master Misery, on the other hand, is eternally isolated by the form in which he is presented. Outside the novel context, with its multiplicity of characters and its thick fabric of interacting themes, he is deprived of metaphorical support and revealed as merely the inert projection of a horror whose namelessness is all too analyzable.

The same is true of the terrible little girl named Miriam. She is another stock Capote type—the witch-child whose behavior is horrifying because it has behind it both the innocence of the very young and the awful cunning of a brilliant demented adult. Thousands of readers have been enchanted by Miriam as well as by her prototypes Miss Bobbit in "Children on Their Birthdays," Appleseed in "Jug of Silver," and D. J. in "The Headless Hawk." They have derived such a delicious sensation of evil from her that they have willingly mistaken it for the precise schematization of evil which she is intended, but clearly fails, to become. A soberer reading discloses no evidence to indicate that she is anything more than the momentary aberration of a lonely old woman.

It is interesting to see to what a large extent the power of Capote's stories depends upon the clever use of supernatural and aberrational devices and how quickly that power is dissipated as soon as one becomes conscious of them as devices. In the title story of the collection, for example, a college girl, returning to school by train, finds herself sharing a coach seat with a pair of carnival performers. The woman is a hard-drinking, crazy-eyed witch; and the man is a professional zombie and hypnotist who lives in a perpetual trance. As the story progresses, the woman plies the girl with cheap gin and fantastic stories of carnival life; while the man, with appropriately obscene gestures, keeps holding out to her a love charm in the form of a shellacked peach seed. Finally, although she struggles frantically to escape, the girl succumbs to the evil spell which the couple have cast upon her and, as the story ends, looks helplessly on while they take away her purse and pull her raincoat "like a shroud above her head."

Here the devices are used to give shock value to material which is without inherent dramatic or symbolic value. We know nothing about the girl beyond the fact that she becomes the victim of some hallucinatory intrigue; and we know nothing about the perpetrators of the intrigue beyond the fact that they are grotesque. But to have the sort of visceral reaction to the story which we are compelled to have if we are to have any reaction at all, these two facts are all we need to know. The girl's plight becomes a substitute for a fully motivated, truly meaningful experience; and the grotesqueness of the couple becomes a substitute for an incisive portrayal of a truly meaningful criminality.

III.

The theme of *Other Voices, Other Rooms* is a boy's search for a father; but it is not Telemachus's search for Ulysses, Stephen Dedalus's for Bloom, or even Eugene Gant's for W. O. It is literally and permanently Joel Knox' search for one Edward R. Sansom or, as it turns out, for some suitable substitute. If we are prepared to accept this fact at all, then we shall be prepared to accept the novel for what it is and for all that it is and not for what we should like it on every page to become. For there can be no doubt that, viewed within these limits, the novel comes alive with metaphorical suggestiveness; and it is possible to appreciate the skill with which Capote has expanded his theme through metaphor rather than through symbol into a complex pattern of psychological and moral action.

Joel's search for Edward Sansom, the blood-father whom he has never seen, is a parallelism of his struggle to grow out of the dream-world of childhood and to enter the real world of manhood. His discovery of Sansom, lying paralyzed in the center of the paralysis of Scully's Landing, and his subsequent rejection of Sansom as unreal, as literally not existing, is a parallelism of his rejection of the real state of manhood and prepares the way for his acceptance of Cousin Randolph as a homosexual father-substitute. Randolph, with his nightmare history, his obsession with dolls and dead blue-jays, and his female impersonations, is as unreal as the fantastic creations of Joel's dream-world— Mr. Mystery and Annie Rose Kuppermann. But once he has rejected his true father as unreal, Joel is left with no alternative but to accept Randolph, and through him homosexuality, as real.

The novel is divided into three parts, each part corresponding to a crucial phase in Joel's development toward the moment of this acceptance. Part I has to do with his arrival at the Landing and his efforts to escape its influence; Part II with the gradual reduction of his power to escape; and Part III with his surrender to Randolph. In each part the change being effected in Joel is demonstrated in terms of concrete events; and all the parts are tied together with key metaphors that define the various shifts in theme and setting. Thus, when in Part I Joel takes leave of the real world, represented by the garishness of *Noon City,* and enters the unreal world of the Landing, the transition is shown to be from daylight to darkness, with Joel falling asleep in the back of Jesus Fever's wagon and entering the house as if in a dream. Then in Part III, after Joel has tried and failed to escape, the process is reversed; he loses his sense of the unreality of the Landing while lying in a coma; and when he awakens he discovers that the unreal has become the real. The transition this time is from darkness (the night of the Carnival episode) to daylight (morning in the sick room several weeks later).

The bluejay which Miss Amy kills in Joel's room on the morning after his arrival functions in much the same way. As it flutters against the window in an effort to escape, it becomes a metaphor of Joel struggling to shake off the influence of the Landing. And by the time it reappears, at the end of Part II, as merely a lifelike arrangement of feathers on Randolph's worksheet, Joel has arrived at a point where he is no longer capable of escape. Like the bird he has been changed from a living thing with a free existence in a real world into a dead prisoner in an unreal world.

A similar device is the old bell that lies in the garden outside the house. At the end of Chapter II Joel catches his first glimpse of Randolph standing at an upstairs window in his disguise of the beautiful lady. In his astonishment Joel staggers back against the bell; and it emits "one raucous cracked note" as if in derision at what is taking place. Then at the end of the book while Joel is waiting in the same spot in the garden, he sees the figure of the lady once again, knows it for what it is, and responds to its beckoning. This time there is "a sound as if a bell had suddenly tolled, and the shape of loneliness, greenly iridescent, whitely indefinite, seemed to rise from the garden. . . ." Now the sound of the bell is imagined; but it seems loud and serious, as if it were tolling the news of a victory; for Joel has finally put the real world and his hope of manhood behind him and accepted the comfort and love of Randolph.

The events of the narrative naturally form a literal record of all that happens to Joel. Yet most of them function at the same time as figuratively as these other devices. In fact, so thoroughly is the material of the novel suffused with thematic meaning that it becomes impossible, and probably pointless, to separate figure from event. In Part I, Joel's struggle to escape the Landing is centered in three events, each of which has a figurative significance.

The first occurs during Jesus Fever's Sunday service shortly after Joel's arrival at the Landing. As the excitement of the ceremony reaches a climax, Zoo, who has been dancing, discards the red ribbon she wears around her throat and reveals the scar left by Keg Brown's razor.

> It was as though a brutal hawk had soared down and clawed away Joel's eyelids, forcing him to gape at her throat. Zoo. . . . He leaped off the stump, and made for the house, his loosened shirttail flying behind; run, run, run, his heart told him, and wham! he'd pitched headlong into a briar patch. . . .

Joel's identification of himself with Zoo is important for two reasons: he sees in her an intimation of what is to happen to him if he remains at the Landing (they are both destined to be its victims), and because of his fright at seeing the physical evidence of her suffering he is rendered less capable than he might have been of taking action to free himself.

The second incident occurs on the evening of the same day as Joel is questioning Randolph and Miss Amy about the ghostly lady he has seen at the window. Miss Amy, knowing of Randolph's penchant for this particular disguise, is on the verge of giving away the secret when Randolph kicks her under the table. The effect on the neurotic woman is instantaneous and, to Joel, terrifying. . . .

> Joel went all hollow inside, he thought he was going to wee wee right there in his breeches, and he wanted to hop up and run, just as he had at Jesus Fever's. Only he couldn't run, not this time. . . .

After the nightmare events of the day Joel is too paralyzed to move. Already he has begun to slip into that state of passive receptivity which is later to send him to Randolph; although at this point he is still able to distinguish between the real and the outlandish.

The third incident is a logical development of the first two: as they have paralyzed Joel emotionally, so this one makes it clear that he is paralyzed physically. He has written letters to his Aunt Ellen expressing his hatred of the Landing and asking her to help him get away. He has put the letters in the mailbox and then gone to visit Idabel and her sister. Upon his return he stops at the box and discovers that the letters are gone. The postman has not taken them because the postage money is lying in the dust under the box. Joel realizes for the first time that he is being kept a prisoner at the Landing and has been cut off from all contact with the real world outside. As he starts back to the house, he hears the sound of gunfire as someone shoots at the chicken hawks circling overhead. Like the bluejay and himself, they are free beings who must be drawn down into the paralysis of the Landing and destroyed. They are also, like his letters, potential agents of interference which constitute a threat to the security of those who depend on the imprisonment of others.

In Part II the emphasis shifts from Joel's struggle to preserve himself from the Landing to his struggle to preserve his masculinity. Interestingly enough, although it is in this section that his masculinity becomes identified with the idea of his father and its loss with his rejection of his father, Joel's conflict is really with the tomboy Idabel. With an evil innocence comparable to that of Henry James's terrible children, she begins to undermine the confidence on which Joel's manhood rests some time before he brings himself to commit the act of paternal denial that is to release him to Randolph.

The process begins shortly after Joel has seen his father for the first time and realized that the hopelessly paralyzed invalid can be of no help to him. As if to erase the shock of the encounter from his mind, he goes with Idabel to fish and swim in the creek. There, as they lie in self-conscious nakedness on the bank, Idabel confesses her loneliness; and Joel suddenly sees that her tough exterior is merely a defense and that beneath it she is really very much like himself. Overcome with tenderness for her, he kisses her on the cheek. Instead of responding to his mood, Idabel reverts at once to her old self, grabs him by the hair, and throws him on the ground. As they struggle together, he falls back on her dark glasses and crushes them. At this Idabel's anger quickly subsides; and when she speaks again, it is as if nothing had happened. "And, indefinably, it was as if nothing had; neither of course would ever be able to explain why they had fought."

The reason is obvious, however, if we relate the incident to all that has led up to it. Idabel has fought to regain the defenses which she let down in her moment of confession and which she must have if she is to dominate her environment and survive within it. Joel has fought to regain his masculine position which was threatened, first, by Randolph, second, by the paralysis of his father, and now by Idabel. The breaking of the glasses ends the struggle for Idabel because the glasses have been an essential part of her defenses—"everything looks a lot prettier" through them—and she is temporarily lost without them. It ends the struggle for Joel not only because the broken bits of glass have cut him but because he realizes that, by having caused the breakage, he has somehow seriously wronged Idabel and, by having fought with her, has somehow defeated himself.

A similar incident occurs a short time later. Joel is reading to his father when he hears Idabel whistle for him to come outside. Although he is supposed to go on reading, he has become so convinced of his father's unreality—"Certainly this Mr. Sansom was not his father. This Mr. Sansom was nobody but a pair of crazy eyes."—that he leaves him and, stopping just long enough to buckle on the sword Zoo has given him, hurries down to Idabel. Perhaps because she has lost her glasses, Idabel seems oddly feminine—"all the rough spirit seemed to have drained from her voice. Joel felt stronger than she, and sure of himself as he'd never been with the other Idabel, the tomboy." With her defenses gone, she has lost her dominion over her environment: at home she has had trouble with her sister Florabel; and her father has threatened to shoot her dog Henry because "Florabel . . . says Henry's got a moral disease. . . ." As they walk toward the creek, she proposes that they run away; and Joel is struck once again by the change in her—"if it had been anyone but Idabel, Joel would've thought she was making up to him." For the first time their relationship seems almost normal; and Joel has a sense of masculine power he has not had since just before their fight on the creek bank. But it is to last only for a moment. As they start across the creek on an old board with Joel leading the way, they suddenly see directly in front of them a huge snake lying coiled and ready to strike. Once again Joel is too paralyzed to move. He stands there wavering, holding his sword helplessly in his hand, the imagined sting of the snake's bite already hot on his body. But Idabel acts. She pulls the sword out of his hand, swings it, and "the cottonmouth slapped into the air, turned, plunged, flattened on the water: belly up, white and twisted, it was carried by the current like a torn lily root."

The scene is important for several reasons. It is, first of all, another instance of humiliation for Joel. Secondly, it makes explicit the identification of his manhood with his father: the snake's eyes are like Mr. Sansom's; and it is because of this that Joel is so frightened, for the eyes remind him of his sin. He has deserted his father to come with Idabel; and he has gradually come to deny the existence of his father as his attraction toward Randolph has grown stronger. Thirdly, there is the metaphorical use of the sword and snake images. Because of his failure to use the sword, Joel has disgraced not only his own manhood but that of his ancestor, the original owner of the sword. And because Idabel has killed the snake in the midst of his fear, she has figuratively killed his manhood, his father, and, as is later evident, all maleness in her world.

Viewed in these terms the climaxing scene of the novel—the Carnival episode and the encounter with Miss Wisteria—can be taken as a dramatic presentation of the sexual paralysis Idabel has induced in Joel. The Carnival itself, with its whirling ferris-wheel lights and bursting rockets, is a nightmare catalyst that destroys Joel's sense of reality and prepares him to accept as real the world of the Landing and Randolph; while the midget Miss Wisteria is the embodiment of female temptation, Joel's last chance to find reality in a normal sex relationship. Significantly, it is his vision of Randolph standing beneath the ferris-wheel that prevents Joel from responding to Miss Wisteria's advances; just as it is the violent rainstorm coming a moment later that separates him from Idabel and prevents their escape.

In the deserted house in which he has sought shelter from the storm, Joel has a brief insight into his predicament. It is not Randolph alone that he fears, he tells himself, but Randolph in the person of "a messenger for a pair of telescopic eyes." Once again it seems to Joel that the eyes of his father are everywhere, accusing him of shameful desertion and even, perhaps, of patricide. But what he does not realize is that his fear of Randolph as a "messenger" and his sense of having, at least mentally, destroyed his father are one and the same thing. The very fact that it was the image of Randolph and not the image of his father who came to him is evidence that Randolph has won out over his father in the struggle for Joel's love. And because Randolph has won, because Joel has *chosen* him to win, he must appear as a messenger of his father's anger; for his appearance is made possible only after the father has been forsaken.

And now that he has finally accepted Randolph, Joel finds it impossible to respond to the pathetic entreaties of Miss Wisteria as she searches for him through the rooms of the empty house: ". . . he dared not show himself, for what she wanted he could not give: his love was in the earth, shattered and still, ..."

To Joel the door leading to the real world, to manhood and the love of woman, is closed forever. He has been arrested in childhood, led back into the secret "other rooms" of the Landing, where the unreality of dream-life and the reality of life lived in a dream merge and become indistinguishable.

The awakening of Joel from a coma induced by the Carnival experience opens Part III and prepares us for two discoveries that have ironic bearing on his development through the preceding episodes. The first is that Zoo, the daughter of the ancient Negro Jesus Fever, who had left the Landing right after her father's death to find a new life in Washington, D.C., has returned during Joel's illness. When he sees her again, he hardly recognizes her for the gay and optimistic person who was kind to him when he first came to the Landing. "How small she seemed, cramped, as if some reduction of the spirit had taken double toll and made demands upon the flesh. . . ."

Zoo, during her brief excursion into the outside world, has had an experience as destructive and humiliating as Joel's with Idabel and Randolph. On her way to Washington she was stopped on the road by several men and brutally raped. Like Joel, she has been crucified at the very moment of salvation; and all the hope and illusion that sustained her while she waited for her father to die has been crushed out of her. Now she too has come back to the Landing and accepted its paralysis as the only possibility left to her.

The second discovery is that Idabel has succeeded in escaping to freedom. In a postcard to Joel she says:

> Mrs. Collie ½ sister and hes the baptis prechur Last Sunday I past the plate at church! papa and F shot henry They put me to life here. why did you Hide? write to IDABEL THOMPKINS.

But Joel doesn't believe her: "she'd put herself to life, and it was with Miss Wisteria, not a baptis prechur." This, then, is the supreme irony. Like Joel and Zoo, Idabel has fought for freedom; but even though she, alone of them all, has actually found it, she has allowed herself to become imprisoned in a relationship with Miss Wisteria that is as unnatural as that between Joel and Randolph. Joel in his search for manhood has become pervertedly feminine; Idabel in her search for a dominant womanhood has become pervertedly masculine; and Zoo in her search for the normal love of men has been pervertedly violated by them.

The really important event in Part III, however, is Joel's and Randolph's trip to Cloud Hotel, the home of the hermit Little Sunshine. The hotel, with its fantastic, haunted history and picturesque decay, is a microcosm of the entire world of the Landing. Like Randolph's house, which is slowly sinking into the earth, it represents the way of life to which all the characters, either willingly or unwillingly, are committed. Randolph, Miss Amy, Mr. Sansom, Jesus Fever, and Little Sunshine have nearly always belonged. Years before they turned away from the real world of the present and found refuge in the phantasmal world of the past—Randolph in his lost love for Pepe Alvarez, Miss Amy in the baroque manners of a dead culture, Mr. Sansom in the literal cessation of time that accompanies paralysis, Jesus Fever and Little Sunshine in misty memories of their years of aristocratic service. Joel, Idabel, and Zoo have all learned or been forced to belong. The Landing has conquered them as decay has conquered the hotel. It has even turned their struggles for freedom to its own advantage, so that they have not only been imprisoned but maimed in the process.

And as Joel follows Randolph and Little Sunshine through the hotel, seeing the crumbling furniture—"Swan stairs soft with mildewed carpet curved upward from the hotel's lobby; the diabolic tongue of a cuckoo bird, protruding out of a wall-clock, mutely proclaiming an hour forty years before, and on the room clerk's splintery desk stood dehydrated specimens of potted palm."—imagining the scenes of long ago when the huge old rooms were alive with "the humming heel-clatter of girls, the bored snores of fat fathers . . . the lilt of fans tapped in tune, and the murmur of gloved hands as the musicians, like bridegrooms in their angel-cake costumes, rise to take a bow," it seems to him that the moment which all his experience at the Landing has prepared him for has finally arrived. . . .

The last of his resistance has now slipped away; the struggle for freedom has ended; and the Landing and the hotel have become the world, all the world there will ever be. And when, after they return to the Landing, Randolph appears once again at his window in the disguise of the beautiful lady, Joel is waiting to respond to his beckoning:

> She beckoned to him, shining and silver, and he knew he must go;
> unafraid, not hesitating, he paused only at the garden's edge where,
> as though he'd forgotten something, he stopped and looked back at
> the bloomless, descending blue, at the boy he had left behind.

IV.

I suggested earlier that Capote's achievement, for all its brilliance, is an achievement in the skilled use of metaphor rather than symbol; and I implied that such an achievement is necessarily of smaller scope than, for instance, Conrad's in *Victory*. It seems to me that we have a right to ask of a novel that it stand in some meaningful relation to recognizable life; we have a right, that is, to ask that the characters resemble or in some way illuminate human beings and that their situation in some way connote or enlarge upon the human situation. It is, of course, true that Capote's novel is, by its very nature, the product of the disappearance of those common assumptions of value by which writers have traditionally been able to get such illumination into their books. It is no longer possible for a writer to take it for granted that his audience will share his view of life or even that his audience will comprehend his view of life. But it was beginning to be no longer possible when Conrad write *Victory,* Joyce wrote *Ulysses,* and Forster wrote *A Passage to India.* Yet these men were able to infuse their novels with a significance that persistently transcended the specific characters and situations about which they wrote. We read *Victory* and we read a chapter from the moral history of modern man; we read *Ulysses* and we read an ironic satire on the petty heroism of modern man; we read *A Passage to India* and we read a tragedy on the evil that is in all men; and we are reading, at the same time, the stories of Axel Heyst, Leopold Bloom, and Dr. Aziz. It was not black magic that enabled these writers to get such meaning into their books. It was the highly organized use of symbolism upon material specifically created to be symbolically suggestive. And it is the absence of such material in *Other Voices, Other Rooms* that renders it simply the metaphorically reinforced story of Joel Knox.

We cannot say that Conrad, Joyce, and Forster were appreciably nearer to value than Capote is; but we can say that they were infinitely nearer to life, and that, being nearer, they were able to make full use of all the equipment they could muster to give it meaning. All of them had to create a private world just as Capote has had to do; but they took great pains to see that it did not remain private, even if, to make sure, they had to go back in time to ancient Greece or as far from contemporary London and Paris as Chandrapore and Samburan.

Their achievement, founded on the deepest insight into life and thus fortified by myth and distance, communicated insight into life and took on the universality of myth; while Capote's achievement, founded on a technical skill largely divorced from insight, communicates no insight beyond that which it affords into its own parts.

The difference between the two is essentially the difference between symbol and metaphor. A symbol ordinarily refers to a thing, a person, or, most often, an idea that exists in a context other than its own, as do the symbols in *Victory*. A character in a novel may symbolize mankind, evil, sin, or death; but he may not symbolize another character in the same novel. He may, however, serve as a metaphor of another character, and through ironic juxtaposition or contrast, enrich or enliven that character as he in turn is enriched and enlivened. A metaphor, this is to say, functions only within a given context; its meaning spreads horizontally through the area in which it is created, not vertically above or beneath it; and it remains in action as a live agent of meaning only so long as the material of which it is a part is in the process of carrying out and completing the idea or theme which originally set it in motion. Once the immediate requirements of the narrative have been satisfied, it ceases to function. A symbol, on the other hand, only begins to fulfill its true function after the action has ceased. It begins, then, to build outward and downward toward all those varieties of meaning which the action in its passage has suggested.

As I have attempted to make clear in my analysis, the characters in *Other Voices, Other Rooms* repeatedly function as metaphors of one another. Idabel, Zoo, and Miss Wisteria are metaphors of Joel; Jesus Fever and Little Sunshine of Randolph and Miss Amy; Jesus Fever and Idabel's father of Mr. Sansom; and, of course, in each case the relationship is reciprocal, so that the metaphor and the person metaphorized are mutually enhanced. The various other devices such as the bluejay, the hawks, the snake, the hanged mule, and Cloud Hotel are also metaphors. The first four are like *Joel:* they demonstrate his predicament. Cloud Hotel is *like* the Landing and the people of the Landing: it is a physical representation of the decayed past to which Randolph, Miss Amy, and the others are dedicated.

But even though, taken together, the characters and the devices produce a world, they do not produce a world of external significance. They belong to the special illusion Capote has created; outside it, they do nothing and are nothing. If we refuse to accept them on these terms, if for a moment we shake off the dream and open our eyes, then the spell is broken and the real world rushes in upon us. The real world should, by rights, be part of the illusion; but it is not and cannot be. The tennis balls, the beautiful lady, the hanged mule, the bluejay, the dwarfed Miss Wisteria, the neurotic Idabel are the phantasmal contents of the nightmare in which, for a little while, we allow ourselves to be lost. But having once awakened and looked about us, we see that, really, for all its intensity and horror, the thing was never there at all.

Capote is, of course, by no means alone in his use of this kind of deception. Shirley Jackson in a great many of the stories in *The Lottery* and Paul Bowles in his novel *The Sheltering Sky* repeatedly resort to it. It is simply one method of making fiction possible in a time when writers are finding it increasingly hard to give dramatic and symbolic importance to human behavior in social and moral terms. Miss Jackson's daemon lover James Harris is undoubtedly a compensation of the lack of a suitable means of making mere earthly love presentable; and certainly the bizarre violence of Mr. Bowles's Africa serves in the novel to replace the motivation which Bowles could not find in Kit and Port Moresby. By presenting characters in the grip of some supernatural spell, one is able to suggest that the motives behind their behavior are unknowable, irrational, and, hence, irrelevant; and by presenting them in the grip of violence, one is able to divert the reader's attention from the inadequacy of their motives to the shocking circumstances which surround them.

But Capote cannot be absolved of blame simply because he shares it with his time and some of his contemporaries. The truth is that his great dependency on these devices is indicative of one of his gravest limitations as an artist. He is capable of evoking a world of mystery and fantasy and of endowing it with grotesque creations of true imaginative splendor. But he has so far shown himself incapable of endowing it with the kind of significance which one expects to find in literature of the first order.

The Daydream and Nightmare of Narcissus

IHAB H. HASSAN

The name of Truman Capote is already legend, and the picture of his boyish face—the famous bangs, the wide, mysterious eyes—is on the cover of all his books to give the legend credence. To some, Capote is the sprite with a monstrous imagination, the lonely child—"I had the most insecure childhood I know of. I felt isolated from all people"—living with his aunts in Alabama, painting flowers on glass and tap dancing on the Mississippi boats. To others he is simply the ephebic purveyor of Gothic extravaganzas, the fashionable opportunist of a mid-century madness. Whatever the faults of Capote may be, it is certain that his work possesses more range and energy than his detractors allow—witness the clear ring of *The Muses Are Heard*, the crackling impressions of *Local Color*, the crazy humor of his filmscript, "Beat the Devil"—and is equally certain that no faddish estimate of his work can suggest his real hold on the contemporary imagination.

Yet it is, of course, as a Southern and Gothic writer that we insist on knowing Capote. Southern he is by accident of birth more than natural affinity; he once said, "I have lived in many places besides the South and I don't like to be called a Southern writer." He is right. We are quick to sense that the elemental quality in the fiction of Faulkner, Warren, or McCullers is consciously poeticized in his fiction, and their loving adherence to the manners of Southern life often vanishes before the surrealist appearance of his romances. Romance, as practiced by Capote and defined by Henry James, is "experience liberated . . . experience disengaged, disembroiled, disencumbered," and as such it remains open to the Gothic impulse which is one of its elements.

The idea of romance, about which Richard Chase has ably written, is informed by the modern techniques of symbolism and analysis, and defines the general character of Capote's work. We begin to perceive the specific concerns of Capote's fiction when we note the division between his "daylight" and

Wisconsin Studies in Contemporary Literature, 1 (Spring-Summer 1960): 5-21.

"nocturnal" styles, and when we understand both as developments of a central, unifying, and self-regarding impulse which Narcissus has traditionally embodied. The impulse brings together dread and humor, dream and reality, insight and experience. The difference between "Miriam" (1945) and "House of Flowers" (1951), between *Other Voices, Other Rooms* (1948) and *The Grass Harp* (1951) distinguish the two styles of Capote; the chronological development suggests a deepening awareness of the tensions between self and world, a redistribution of love between ego and object, a movement towards light which retains the knowledge of darkness. *Breakfast at Tiffany's* (1958) carries these developments a step farther, and though it appears to elude some of the distinctions we make, it confirms the emergent patterns of Capote's work.

The nocturnal style of Truman Capote—and it is the style we are likely to identify with his achievement—makes the greater use of uncanny trappings and surreal decors. The sense of underlying dreadfulness, which Tennessee Williams called the black root of all modern art, compels the style to discover "the instant of petrified violence," the revelation which only the moment of terror can yield. In stories like "Miriam," "The Headless Hawk," "A Tree of Night," or "Shut a Final Door," fear seems to take the characters by their entrails and reduce them to that curious condition of insight and paralysis which is the best expression of their predicament. "All our acts are acts of fear," Capote writes in the last story, and so man is consigned to perpetual solitude, not so much because he cannot love or be loved—these are merely the symptoms—but because his dreams must remain unsharable and his night world must rise continually against his daily actions. It is this recognition of the unconscious, and all that it holds of wish and terror, that specifies the nocturnal mode of Capote's writing. The recognition is impelled by a force which D. H. Lawrence noted in Poe's work: the disintegration of the modern psyche. Like Poe, like Carson McCullers, Truman Capote shows, in his nocturnal mood, that his image of the modern psyche is preeminently isolated and Protestant. Hence Capote's interest in the theme of self-discovery—Narcissus may have been the first Protestant—and in the technique of character doubles or alter egos—"Miriam," "Shut a Final Door," etc. Hence also the omnipresence of dreams in Capote's fiction. Dreams in the earlier stories do not only constitute a private and self-sufficient world, and do not only contain the destructive element of our psyche ("it is easy to escape daylight," Randolph says in *Other Voices, Other Rooms*, "but night is inevitable, and dreams are the giant cage"); dreams also reveal, in the later stories, the creative element of the unconscious, and permit that release of the imagination which, as Capote implies, is the prerequisite of love. "But a man who doesn't dream is like a man who doesn't sweat: he stores up a lot of poison," Judge Cool tells Verena in *The Grass Harp* when the latter derisively calls his marriage proposal to Dolly, his confession of love, a dream. If Capote's darker style seems uncanny, it is precisely because uncanny effects are produced, as Freud knew, "by effacing the distinctions between imagination and reality," by seeing, as Rimbaud did, a mosque at the bottom of a lake.

But in effacing the distinctions between reality and imagination, the nocturnal style does not only evoke the shapeless world of our dreams; it evokes, no less, the fabulous world of myth and fairy tale. In our age, alas, dream, myth, and fairy tale are no longer allowed to drowse in their separate corners. Freud has noted the occurrence of material from fairy tales in dreams, and Geza Roheim has argued, in *The Gates of the Dream*, that myth, animistic thought, and in fact culture itself, find a common source in oneiric phantasies. In Capote's work, the familiar figure of the Wizard Man partakes both of dream and archetype, and it is there to remind us that our archaic fears must be forever conquered, our childish past reenacted. Such fabulous evocations must reclaim the universal symbols of human experience. Yet it is wise to remember that Capote once said, "All I want to do is to tell a story and sometimes it is best to choose a symbol. I would not know a Freudian symbol as such if you put it to me." In the end, the nocturnal style of Truman Capote appeals to the qualities which Henry James found essential to all fiction of the supernatural, appeals, that is, "to wonder and terror and curiosity and pity and to the delight of fine recognitions, as well as to the joy, perhaps sharper still, of the mystified state." Of these qualities, and of the human failings which these qualities silently criticize, the supernatural element in Capote's fiction is a metaphor.

But if the supernatural defines the nocturnal mode of Capote, humor defines his daylight style. The style, evident in "My Side of the Matter," "Jug of Silver," "Children on Their Birthdays," *The Grass Harp,* and *Breakfast at Tiffany's* assumes the chatty, first-person informality of anecdotes. It also specifies character and admits the busy-ness of social relations more than its darker counterpart. And the scene which it lights upon is usually the small Southern town—not the big city which witnesses in abstract horror the so-called alienation of man from his environment. (The one notable exception, of course, is *Breakfast at Tiffany's*.) Now it is true that *humor*, like the *supernatural*, must finally rise to universal implications. But if one may judge from the differences between Twain and Poe, between the American tall tale and the native ghost story, humor is always more of this earth; it is apt to individualize rather than generalize; and it can rise to universal meanings but gradually. Humor has also a social reference. Humor—which may be called a catholic if the supernatural can be called a protestant impulse—binds rather than separates: it is as much a mode of communion as the Gothic is a mode of self-isolation.

I have suggested that *humor* and the *supernatural*, metaphors of the daylight and nocturnal styles of Capote, reflect the central and unifying motive of his fiction. The motive will be understood when the relation between the two elements which express it is further clarified. In his essays "On Narcissism" and "The Uncanny," Freud has some interesting things to say on the subject. The uncanny, Freud believes, derives from an animistic conception of the universe occasioned by a narcissistic over-estimation of the self. Freud also characterizes humor as a triumph of the pleasure principle, and "of narcissism, the ego's victorious assertion of its own invulnerability." His essays make it evident, however, that a humorous comment, while it begins by recognizing the threat of reality—and to that extent we are justified in seeing humor as a movement towards objectivity—ends by refusing to meet the threat. Humor, therefore, is like the uncanny in that both suggest a reactionary or regressive impulse towards the security of the narcissistic state.

This may sound more simple than art should be allowed to sound. A more sensitive observation is made by Wylie Sypher when, taking his cue from Bergson as well as Freud, he says, "The comic gesture reaches down toward the Unconscious, that dim world usually assigned to tragedy, the midnight terrain where Macbeth met the witches. The joke and the dream incongruously distort the logic of our rational life." The bulk of Capote's work persuades us, in the same way, that both humor and the supernatural are acts of the imagination intended to question our surface evaluations of reality, and indeed to affirm the counter-reality of phantasy. The prevalence of dreams, the interest in childhood, the negative conception of adolescent initiation, the concern with self-discovery, the emphasis on homo-eroticism, and the general statis of the mythic world of Truman Capote—all these must confirm the central narcissistic impulse of his fiction, an impulse which serves both as a critique and a crooked image of American reality. Ancient paradigm of the Artist, the Lover and the Dreamer, Narcissus must also reconcile appearance and reality within the scope of romance, that "neutral territory," as Hawthorne said, "somewhere between the real world and fairy-land, where the Actual and the Imaginary may meet, and each imbue itself with the nature of the other." This is the aesthetic burden of Narcissus. His moral burden in the contemporary world, which Tate's "Ode to the Confederate Dead" presaged some decades ago, is still self-transcendence in the moment of action or love. The former seems to us now irrecoverable, the latter, it appears, our only hope. But there is always Holly Golightly to reckon with, and the peculiar image of freedom she invokes.

The contrast between the two styles of Capote can be observed in his stories, of which the best are included in *A Tree of Night and Other Stories* (1949) and can be even more sharply discerned in his two novels, *Other Voices, Other Rooms* and *The Grass Harp*.

The peculiar mixture of phantasy and reality in Capote's first novel begs for allegorical interpretation. Carvel Collins has suggested the quest of the Holy Grail as a possible framework for the action, pointing out numerous parallels between the details of Joel Knox's story and those to be found in Jessie Weston's account of the Grail myth. John Aldridge, on the other hand, has seen Joel's story essentially as an archetype of the Boy in Search of a Father. Both views correspond to genuine analogues of the narrative. But Joel Knox is not only a miniature Dedalus-Telemachus in Dublin-Ithaca, or Parsifal-Galahad at the Chapel Perilous. He is also a smaller model of Castorp-Tannhauser at Davos-Venusberg, and Narcissus sitting by his pool. Above all, he is simply Joel Knox who, no matter how much or little he may resemble Capote, is still a character in a work of fiction.

Joel is in search of an image which reflects darkly his own identity, his reality, and, ironically, which becomes available to him only when reality is dispelled in the palace of pleasure, the secret house of dreams. (To call *Other Voices, Other Rooms* a story of initiation is to recall how shrunken the range of initiation has become since Huck Finn bounced down the Mississippi on his raft.) What Joel elects is what the enchanted world of Skully's Landing forces upon him, and what he finally accepts is beyond good and evil, as dreams are, which alone are real. Love, which used to be an anchor of reality, is set adrift in the darkness of the human heart—"The heart is deceitful above all things, and desperately wicked. Who can know it?" is the epigraph of the novel, taken from Jeremiah. Love returns upon itself as the mirror image turns to the beholder and absents itself with his absence. The search for the Other, who may be god, sweetheart, or father, ends in the discovery of the Self, and initiation to the world amounts to regression to the world of infantile phantasy in which the father is also a lover. Such is the apotheosis of the love between Joel and Randolph at the spectral Cloud Hotel towards the end of the novel.

The novel begins with Joel's arrival at Noon City, an oasis in the busy world, less pre-Civil War than legendary, near which is the even more legendary mansion of Skully's Landing, where he expects to meet his father for the first time. He is glad to leave Aunt Ellen's house behind: "It was as if he lived those months wearing a pair of spectacles with green, cracked lenses, and had wax-plugging in his ears, for everything seemed to be something it wasn't, and the days melted into a constant dream." But Joel does not see his father, Mr. Samson, for a long time. He roams the wild, incredible garden of the Landing which, like some lost ruin, is haunted by the enfabled past; and, true to Capote's vision, he perceives in an "instant of petrified violence," the apparition of a strange lady in a window. This is his first glimpse of Randolph, of his own fate. Randolph, prototype of the Evil Magician, the artist, the teacher, and the criminal, whose eloquence and learning are like echoes of a spectral chorus, is the genius who dominates the Landing. Exquisite in his cultivation and irrelevance, at once languid and sinister, lucid and depraved, Randolph has all the "unpredictability and perverted innocence" which qualify him for becoming the mentor and lover of Joel. Whether he is exposed to the half-pagan Sabbath ceremonies of Jesus Fever and His daughter Zoo, or the primitive magic of Little Sunshine, the wizened Negro hermit who haunts the Cloud Hotel, or the talcumed world of invalids, lunatics, and perverts who inhabit the Landing, Joel's sense of reality is constantly subverted by his environment. Like Little Sunshine, who acts, together with Randolph, as father-substitute, Joel is drawn to the terrible Cloud Hotel: "for if he [Little Sunshine] went away, as he had once upon a time, other voices, other rooms, voices lost and clouded, strummed his dreams." The progressive attenuation of external reality is evident as Joel moves from Aunt Ellen's to Skully's Landing to the Cloud Hotel; the movement is indeed a descent into Hades, a journey, in various stages, towards the darkest unconscious, or perhaps towards the womb of death. Dreaming of the Cloud Hotel, Joel realizes that it was not and never had been a real hotel: "this was the place folks came when they went off the face of the earth, when they died but were not dead." And dreaming of his journey through its rooms, he sees himself "in the dust of thorns listening for a name, his own, but even here no father claimed him."

The second part of the novel opens with a climactic incident. Joel finally meets his father, and finds him a paralytic with two glinting eyes, who can only communicate with the world by dropping red tennis balls. Meanwhile, we are apprised in a grotesque tale of love and violence that Randolph is responsible for Samson's condition. Joel's resistance to Randolph, and to all that he stands for, receives its first check when Joel discovers that his real father is nearly a zombie. His resistance is further weakened when his relation to Idabel Tompkins fails to confirm his groping manhood. When Joel attempts to kiss Idabel on a fishing trip, she fights him off viciously and overpowers him; and on their excursion to a decayed mill, it is she who kills the water moccasin with Jesus Fever's old Civil War sword. The snake has the eyes of Joel's father, and the boy fails equally in asserting his manhood with Idabel as in conquering the phantom of his father with the ceremonial symbol of the past. Thus it is in *failing* the traditional ordeals, which in overcoming he might have earned his manhood, that Joel makes himself eligible to the insidious knowledge of the Cloud Hotel. Three further incidents clinch Joel's failure, and therefore clinch his regression, the form that his initiation takes. An appeal he sends to Aunt Ellen in the form of a letter is intercepted by Randolph. When Idabel and Joel decide to run away, they encounter in the woods two Negroes making passionate love. The scene reawakens Idabel's hostility towards Joel; it is a firm intimation that between them no stable relation can obtain. A little later, both find themselves at a fair, and they strike up an excited companionship with a wistful midget, Miss Wisteria. They all ride a ferris wheel. . . .

On the ferris wheel the vision of love, loneliness, and mutability is suddenly illuminated in Joel's mind, and it is in the name of love that he renounces the willfulness of sexual possession. At the same instant he glimpses Randolph staring fixedly at him from the ground underneath.

The discovery of reality and the search for fulfillment in heterosexual terms fail. Zoo, who dreams all her life of journeying to Washington after her father dies, does not get very far. She is raped by three white men and a Negro driving a truck and returns to the Landing crushed, her dream desecrated. Even Idabel, who makes good her escape, winds up with Miss Wisteria as a companion. With

Idabel away—she and Randolph, like images of day and night, are never seen together in the novel—Joel can only turn to Randolph.

Part Three opens with the return of Joel to the Landing. He returns in a coma, his world contracted, appearance and reality altogether fused, and when he recovers from his illness, he is finally at peace, fully attuned to the enchantments which await him: "lo, he was where he'd never imagined to find himself again: the secret hideaway room in which, on hot New Orleans afternoons, he'd sat watching snow sift through scorched August trees." It is with Randolph, not Idabel, that he finally visits the Cloud Hotel, while Aunt Ellen looks for him in vain. But for Joel there is no going back to the old realities; like Randolph, like Little Sunshine, he finds at last his Other Room in the Hotel—with a hanged mule in it for effect. And strangely enough, the last acts of Joel indicate not surrender but liberation. Faithful to the Jungian archetype of the Descent into Hades, Joel re-emerges somewhat healed, possessed of a dangerous and ambiguous knowledge. "'I am me,' Joel whooped. 'I am Joel, we are the same people,'" he shouts exuberantly on his way back from the Cloud Hotel. And he is suddenly wise enough to see "how helpless Randolph was: more paralyzed than Mr. Samson, more child-like than Miss Wisteria, what else could he do, once outside and alone, but describe a circle, the zero of his nothingness?" At the end of the novel, when Zoo overturns the cracked, moss-covered bell with which the old plantation owners used to summon their slaves, ancient symbol of a vanished order, and when Randolph appears in a window, beckoning in his female attire to Joel, we are not sure whether it is in triumph or defeat that Joel responds to this mute appeal. We can only sense that the traditional modes of behavior are no longer in command of life.

Mr. Aldridge has objected to the self-contained quality of evil and guilt in the novel, to the failure of the book to "stand in some meaningful relation to recognizable life," and to the feeling that Capote's world "seems to be a concoction rather than a synthesis," its purity "not the purity of experience forced under pressure into shape" but rather the "sort that can be attained only in the isolation of a mind which life has never really violated." The objections appear serious; but as usual, the impatience of Mr. Aldridge is not entirely justified. We need to remember, however, that Capote's work is, in its intentions, at least, a novel-romance, and that it attempts to engage reality without being realistic. Evil and guilt in it are self-contained only in the sense that they are defined by the individual consciousness without reference to an accepted social or moral order. Evil, in other words, is mainly poetic and archetypal; its moral issue is confined to the predicament of the victim without visible oppressor, and of the beloved almost without a lover. The result is a sharp, narrow focus, a reflexive vision seeking constantly to penetrate the arcana of personality. "They can romanticize us so, mirrors," Randolph says to Joel, "and that is their secret: what a subtle torture it would be to destroy all the mirrors in the world: where then could we look for reassurance of our identities? I tell you, my dear, Narcissus was no egotist . . . he was merely another of us who, in our unshatterable isolation, recognized, on seeing his reflection, the one beautiful comrade, the only inseparable love." Experience is limited to what a mirror reveals of the beholder, and if the novel sometimes appears to be a concoction rather than a synthesis, it is perhaps because the job of dramatic resolution is surrendered to ambience and verbal magic. Here is the context of Joel's final revelation at the Cloud Hotel:

> (He looked into the fire, longing to see their faces as well, and the flames erupted an embryo; a veined, vacillating shape, its features formed slowly, and even when complete stayed veiled in dazzle; his eyes burned tar-hot as he brought them nearer: tell me, tell me, who are you? are you someone I know? are you dead? are you my friend? do you love me? But the painted disembodied head remained unborn beyond its mask, and gave no clue. Are you someone I am looking for? he asked, not knowing whom he meant, but certain that for him there must be such a person, just as there was for everybody else: Randolph with his almanac, Miss Wisteria and her search by flashlight, Little Sunshine remembering other voices, other rooms, all of them remembering, or never having known. And Joel drew back. If he recognized the figure in the fire, then what ever would he find to take its place? It was easier not to know, better holding heaven in your hand like a butterfly that is not there at all.)

The recognition of Joel is, to a large extent, the event upon which the dramatic unity of the novel depends. It is characteristic of Capote's nocturnal mode that the event should be presented in the guise of a trance or hallucination, a verbal *tour de force*, and that its moral effect should be muffled by "atmosphere."

Of his first novel Capote has recently said, in *Writers at Work,* "I am a stranger to that book; the person who wrote it seems to have little in common with my present self. Our mentalities, our interior temperatures are entirely different." The remark accentuates our transition to Capote's second novel, *The Grass Harp,* which is indeed a different story. That the book contains much autobiography is evident from a later story Capote wrote, "A Christmas Memory," in which the prototypes of Collin and Dolly are shown to be, in words *and* picture, young Capote (then an urchin with a happy, toothless grin) and his elderly female cousin. The narrative, written in the "daylight" style, is told in the first person by young Collin Fenwick. The story is not "strummed in dreams," as in *Other Voices, Other Rooms*; it is strummed by the wind on a field of Indian grass adjoining a cemetery—the Grass Harp. To be sure, the contrast between the two novels is not as striking as if Poe had taken up residence at Walden Pond, but it suggests, nevertheless, a welcome restoration of reality to the surface of things, and an expansion in social awareness. *The Grass Harp*, at any rate, sings the story of all people, as Dolly Talbo says, people alive and dead, and to sing one needs more space than the Cloud Hotel affords.

The "initiation" of Collin Fenwick results less in a regression to the oneiric fastness of childhood than in a nostalgic awareness of past innocence and lost love. Collin is an eleven-year-old orphan when he comes to live with Verena and Dolly Talbo, two elderly cousins of his father. The two women are as dissimilar as cactus and violet. Verena, who represents the ruthless, practical world, is shrewd, grasping, and masterful. Her single weakness, the memory of a liaison with a certain Maudie who leaves Verena to get married, enhances her apparent toughness. Dolly, on the other hand, is shy and retiring—her "presence is a delicate happening." She lives in a tender, wistful world, gathering herbs for her dropsy cures, feeding only on sweets, and extending her sympathy to all created things. Her devout friend, Catherine, and old Negro who claims to be of Indian descent, calls her Dollyheart, and calls Verena, That One—the Heart, the Self, versus the Other, the World. With Dolly and Catherine, Collin enters into a spiritual sisterhood dedicated to preserve everything frail, lovely, and unique.

But the trouble comes when Collin is sixteen. The world, in the person of Verena, decides to ask the unworldly trio to account for itself. Verena bullies Dolly to obtain from her the formula of the dropsy cure which has commercial possibilities. When force and persuasion fail, Verena humiliates Dolly by reminding her of her uselessness and dependency. The trio takes to the road, finding refuge in a tree-house, "a raft floating in the sea of leaves," up an old chinaberry tree.

The tree-house, of course, is the last refuge of innocents abroad. But though it is unlike Huck's raft in that it offers limited opportunities of experience, it is not so much a vehicle of escape, Capote would have us believe, as a harbor of lost values. For Dolly teaches Collin that the tree-house is a ship, "that to sit there was to sail along the cloudy coastline of every dream." At peace in the tree, the two women and the boy feel at one with their surroundings: "we belonged there, as the sun-silvered leaves belonged, the dwelling whippoorwills." But most important, they feel at one with one another, and with the two "outcasts" from town whom they attract, Riley Henderson and Judge Cool.

Inspired by the enraged Verena, and led by a brutal sheriff, the representatives of Church and State attack the tree and are repulsed time and again in hilarious scenes of impotent fury and gentle mockery. The spirit of the chinaberry tree, the presence of Dolly, the insight into their separate predicaments, unite our five refugees as the sheriff's posse can never be united. "I sometimes imagine all those whom I've called guilty have passed the real guilt on to me: it's partly that that makes me want once before I die to be on the right side," the Judge, who is the voice, as Dolly is the heart of the group, says. He continues: "But here we are, identified: five fools in a tree. A great piece of luck provided we know how to use it: no longer any need to worry about the picture we present—free to find out who we truly are." As usual, the search for identity in Capote's work precedes the discovery of love. But here, for the first time, both the reflexive and the outgoing impulse are caught in a single vision.

The outgoing impulse, the burden of love, is defined when Judge Cool says to Riley—and his message is identical with that of the hobo in Carson McCullers' "A Tree, A Rock, A Cloud,"—"We are speaking of love. A leaf, a handful of seed—begin with these, learn a little what it is to love. . . . No easy process, understand: it could take a lifetime." At which Dolly with a sharp intake of breath cries, "Then . . . I've been in love all my life." Yet Dolly is not so out of touch with reality that she can accept the world, like Polyanna, on immitigable faith. The persecutions of Verena, the fact that her friend Catherine is "captured" and thrown into jail, force her to ask Collin—and how ironic that an old woman should ask an adolescent question about the world—force her to ask him in pain and perplexity, "Collin, what do you think: is it that after all the world is a bad place?" Collin is wise enough (almost too wise) to reflect: "No matter what passions compose them, all private worlds are good, they are never vulgar places: Dolly had been made too civilized by her own, the one she shared with Catherine and me, to feel the winds of wickedness that circulate elsewhere."

We are never quite sure whether the novel portrays the disenchantment of an elderly woman or the initiation of a young man. But of this we can be more certain, that Dolly in renewing her powers of universal sympathy by drawing constantly on the resources of her inner world strikes a parable of the artist who, secure in the freedom of his imagination, reaches out to free ours. In this sense, the healing powers of Dolly can be said to extend, through the medium of the Grass Harp, not only to the fictive community of tree-dwellers but also to the real community of book-readers. The idea of the artist as healer is, of course, quite ancient. What makes the idea interesting in the works of such contemporary authors as Salinger and Capote is the particular form it acquires. In both writers the concern with lovelessness seems to have allied itself with a criticism of the new philistinsm, the implication being that the poet and lover, to leave out the lunatic, are of one imagination compact. Hence Salinger's interest in Zen and haiku poetry, which bring the aesthetic and spiritual to meet at a still point, and Capote's interest in Narcissus whose adoration of beauty may be considered an act both of love and cognition.

The reaction against a grim and unlovely world, which insists that all private worlds are good *and* beautiful, tends to perpetrate the myth of the Noble Unconscious. It may also lead to the myth of the Noble freak. Of this Dolly is an example, and Sister Ida, with her revivalist tribe of fifteen children all sired by different fathers, is another. Ida's wandering brood, whose slogan is Let Little Homer Honey Lasso Your Soul For the Lord, brings into the novel a good deal of bustle and folksy humor. They also reveal a certain outgoingness, an attitude which, in its vigor and acceptance, qualifies the pathos of Dolly. But the impression remains that though Dolly and Ida have suffered much, their idea of freedom is undoubtedly romantic and the form of their rebellion extravagant.

Nothing is very extravagant about the denouement of the novel. Verena, robbed and deserted by the infamous Dr. Ritz, is utterly broken. In a candle-lit, tree-house scene, while rain pours and thunder rages, Verena, who had actually climbed the china tree, confesses to Dolly: 'Envied you, Dolly. Your pink room. I've only knocked at the doors of such rooms, not often—enough to know that now there is no one but you to let me in."

Dolly's "pink room" is a place for Collin to start from: Joel's "other room" at the Cloud Notel is a place to which he can and must return. When Dolly dies, it is as if a ceremony of innocence and beauty had come to an end, and behind each character the Garden of Eden had clanged its gates shut. But life continues. Riley Henderson goes on to become a public figure, and Collin journeys north to study law. Reality does not surrender to the dream: it is merely redeemed by it. The childish self-absorption of a Joel yields to the wider horizon of a Collin. Seen in retrospect from Collin's point of view, the novel still appears as a pastoral elegy to irrevocable innocence. But the elegy is also mythicized; it is sung by the field of Indian grass, "a grass harp, gathering, telling, a harp of voices remembering a story." The elegy is present and continuous; it may even affect the future. Yet Collin confesses, as Huck would never confess, that "my own life has seemed to me more a series of closed circles, rings that do not evolve with the freedom of the spiral."

The nocturnal style of Capote revealed a sea-green world of silence and sudden violence; characters vanished and appeared in mystery; things happened, as it were, intransitively: connectives of motive as of syntax were omitted; time was suspended; and the liquid, dreamy density of sentences absorbed the shock of action and thrust of sense. Against the former mode, the daylight style commits itself to the autobiographical stance: it feigns literalness, personal authenticity; it seeks to clarify temporal and spatial relations; and it acknowledges the external claims of reality by yielding to a kind of humorous naiveté. Here is Collin's moment of illumination to stand against the witchery of Joel's vision at the Cloud Hotel:

> Sister Ida chose a place on the bank from which she could supervise the bathing. "No cheating now—I want to see a lot of commotion." We did. Suddenly girls old enough to be married were trotting around and not a stitch on: boys, too big and little all in there together naked as jaybirds. It was well that Dolly had stayed behind with the judge; and I wished Riley had not come either, for he was embarrassing in his embarrassment.
>
> *   *   *   *   *
>
> Those famous landscapes of youth and woodland water—in after years how often, trailing through the cold rooms of museums, I stopped before such a picture, stood long haunted moments having it

recall that gone scene, not as it was, a band of goose-fleshed children
dabbling in an autumn creek, but as the painting presented it, husky
youths and wading water-diamonded girls; and I wondered then,
wonder now, how they fared, where they went in this world, that
extraordinary family.

The contrasts between the two passages, style and context, are obvious. Joel is
led to his insight by departed spirits, once the guests of the Cloud Hotel; Collin
is led to his meditation by naked children bathing in the sunlight. Joel ends by
choosing "a butterfly that is not there at all," by embracing a qualified autism;
Collin ends on a note of "objective sympathy," wondering about the fate of "that
extraordinary family." In short, the earlier passage looks inward, the latter
outward. Narcissus, having plumbed his ultimate shallowness, harks once again
to Echo.

Capote As Gay American Author

Capote's forty-year career was divided among fiction, journalism, and drama and filmscript writing. One could tabulate in several ways the number of novels Capote wrote. Everyone would agree that *Other Voices, Other Rooms* (1948) and *The Glass Harp* (1951) are novels. Some would go further and say that after 1951, at age twenty-seven, he failed to develop his early talent as a novelist. At times, Capote thought of the lead story of his collection *Breakfast at Tiffany's* (1958) as a short novel and of *Handcarved Coffins* in *Music for Chameleons* (1980) as a novel. Between them, chronologically, we have the "nonfiction novel," *In Cold Blood*, his longest sustained work, and, finally, the incomplete and presumably never completed *Answered Prayers*, published in installments in *Esquire* in 1976 and then in book form in 1986. Of these works, *Other Voices, Other Rooms* is the one most concerned with homosexuality, and it is the one work on which Capote's reputation as a gay male author will rest. In addition, some readers have seen homosexuality as a subtext of *In Cold Blood*, a suggestion that Capote denied in detail (perhaps because he did not feel it would help gay people) but that requires further investigation. *Answered Prayers*, known for its depiction of the sordid side of homo- and heterosexuality, contains a very unflattering picture of a writer suggestive of Tennessee Williams. Of the short stories, only "A Diamond Guitar" from *Breakfast at Tiffany's* has a gay male relationship at its heart, although "The Headless Hawk" from *A Tree of Night* features as protagonists a man and woman who have previously experienced same-sex love.

Other Voices, Other Rooms appeared in 1948, the same year as Gore Vidal's much more explicit novel *The City and the Pillar* and the limited edition of

Tennessee Williams' first short-story collection. *Other Voices, Other Rooms* is a boy's coming-of-age story in a small Southern town in the 1930s. Joel Harrison Knox, a thirteen-year-old, comes to Noon City to live with relations and is introduced into a world of eccentric and grotesque characters. At the end of the novel he decides to leave the outer world behind and take up life with his withdrawn gay cousin, Randolph. *Other Voices, Other Rooms* has been given several pages of discussion in four of the standard books on male homosexuality in American fiction: Georges-Michel Sarotte's *Like a Brother, Like a Lover* (French original 1976, English translation 1978), Roger Austen's *Playing the Game* (1977), Stephen Adams's *The Homosexual as Hero in Contemporary Fiction* (1980), and Claude J. Summers's *Gay Fictions: Wilde to Stonewall* (1990). The first two of these critics are more sympathetic to Capote's novel than the last two. Sarotte finds the novel to be about a boy's recognition of his homosexuality, and he concludes that the novel endorses the idea that one should be true to one's "basic nature against the ideals of a hostile society" (48). Austen notes that "[a]lthough in tone and atmosphere this book may be regarded as gay, in actual fact Capote avoids having the main character come to grips with the problem by keeping his thirteen-year-old safely prepubescent" (114). In other words, he "remains sexless within the terms of the novel," even though we assume that he will grow up to be gay. Furthermore, the adult gay character, Cousin Randolph, speaks of his love for the prizefighter Pepe in a way that can be considered as a generalized plea for human love as much as a statement of specifically gay male feelings (115).*

In marked contrast, Stephen Adams stresses the nonliberational nature of *Other Voices, Other Rooms*. He feels that "the world it creates is animated by characteristics popularly attributed to the homosexual male: freakishness, affectation, and effeminacy. The story of a young boy's discovery of his homosexuality is decked out with all the trappings of gothic melodrama" (57). Through "Joel's identification with Randolph, Capote implies that homosexuality is a failure of manliness—an 'ugly room', yet one which fantasy can prettify" (58). Adams compares Capote's treatment of homosexuality unfavorably with that of Carson McCullers and James Purdy, for whom the failure of love rather than homosexuality itself is the source of problems.

Again, in Claude J. Summers's evaluation, Capote is a less interesting and perceptive author than McCullers. He writes, "Truman Capote creates in *Other Voices, Other Rooms* a world of Gothic romance reminiscent of *The Ballad of the Sad Cafe,* but one that lacks the philosophical seriousness and sure vision of McCullers's work" (131). Cousin Randolph is less bizarre than several of the other characters in the novel; nevertheless, "[r]ather than engaging life and challenging or at least defying the world's cruelty, Randolph relishes his victimization" (132).

Since the mid-1970s, the treatment of homosexuality has become the central issue for critics of *Other Voices, Other Rooms*. We can see this phenomenon from the articles just considered and from that of Annette Runge's Lacanian study (1988). An overview of the criticism from the period before the blossoming of gay studies can be found in the 1970 review article by Dianne B. Trimmier, which treats the critical reception up to 1962, including studies by John W. Aldridge, Nona Balakian, Paul Levine, and Marvin E. Mengling. Craig M. Goad's entry on Capote in the *Dictionary of American Biography* (vol. 2, 1978) is also relevant. Goad (83) notes positive views of the novel by Carvel Collins, Frank Baldanza, and Ihab Hassan against the negative view of John W. Aldridge. Objections to the novel on the basis of its intense inferiority may mask antigay prejudices in the sense that the experiences of gay youth are often not of interest to society as a whole.

Critical reaction to the slightly later "A Diamond Guitar" has not gone very far, although the story is skillfully written. This is a tale of two men in a Southern prison camp set in a pine forest. An older inmate named Schaeffer, who has been in the camp for some time, is attracted to a young Cuban knifer named Tico Feo, who arrives with a diamond guitar. It is clear that they fall in love, but there is no overt sexual interaction between them. They plan an escape, but only Tico makes it, and Schaeffer is returned to the camp for the rest of his life. He himself starts to play the diamond (actually "paste") guitar.

In her book on Truman Capote, Helen S. Garson notes that Tico Feo never had wanted Schaeffer to escape. The younger man is a liar, a thief, and a betrayer (93). Nevertheless, in her evaluation, Tico Feo does bring Schaeffer back from the ranks of the emotionally dead. In contrast, Kenneth T. Reed (62-64) in his book on Capote does not point out this element of betrayal. Nor does Ramón Garcia Castro in his book on Capote (120-21). One suspects that the mainstream critics are sometimes reluctant to deal with themes of gay betrayal. In contrast, William L. Nance notes that "the story is a rather explicit rejection of the homosexual option that Joel accepted" (74). Although one should not overstress a story that appeared as far back as November 1950, it does seem typical that Capote is unable even at a later date to imagine a story in which the love of two adult men would lead to mutual salvation or even help.

In *In Cold Blood* male bonding produces violent results. The book recounts the brutal murder of four members of the Clutter family by Perry Smith and Richard Eugene ("Dick") Hickock in Holcomb, Kansas, in November 1959. The murders took place at night, and, as they were out-of-towners and not even acquaintances of the Clutters, the two killers almost got away with it.

In 1966 George Plimpton asked Capote if there was a sexual attraction between Perry and Dick. Capote answered that there wasn't any. He considered that Dick was totally heterosexual and that Perry had little sexual interest: "Yes, Perry had been in love with his cellmate Willie-Jay in the State Prison, but there was no consummated physical relationship. He was not in love with Dick" (Inge 60).

Despite Capote's denial of homosexual attraction between the team of murderers, here we have a chilling example of men who exert what is perhaps a fatal influence over each other in the course of their bonding. It is also clear that by the end of their lives they have had a major falling out. The novel could benefit from an analysis that foregrounds a gay studies point of view, particularly one concerned with the break between the homosocial and the homosexual in American society. In a sense, the novel deals with issues related to repression and sublimation, but as they are not the focus of the novel, interpretation of them remains difficult. Indeed, one set of readers have seen it as a story in which violence substitutes for sexual expression.

Perry himself mentions homosexuality. Reflecting on his experiences as a sixteen-year-old on a boat, he states, "I never minded the work, and I liked being a sailor—seaports, and all that. But the queens on ship wouldn't leave me alone. . . . A lot of queens aren't effeminate, you know" (156). Before the main part of the story opens, Perry, a bodybuilder, has a homoerotic attraction for his cellmate, a person to whom he reveals the anticipated murder. We are told: "Dick's literalness, his pragmatic approach to every subject, was the primary reason Perry had been attracted to him, for it made Dick seem, compared to himself, so authentically tough, invulnerable, 'totally masculine'" (27). Perry had "no respect for people who can't control themselves sexually" (230). When Perry and Dick try to escape in Mexico, they become temporary guests of an openly gay man.

At another point in the novel it is hard to figure out where Capote's reflections end and Perry's begin: Capote writes, "[N]or did [Perry] care to chance the loss of a manila envelope fat with photographs—primarily of himself, and ranging in time from a pretty—little—boy portrait made when he was in the Merchant Marine" (169). If we consider the famous "pretty boy" photograph of Capote on the dust jacket of *Other Voices, Other Rooms,* it is possible to find a projection of the author himself here. Indeed, one of the most disturbing episodes of Capote's life was his unsuccessful attempt to keep the two men at an emotional distance from himself, especially when Perry began to realize Capote's interest in him would not keep him from execution. Capote avoids direct commentary in *In Cold Blood,* and his lack of evaluation appeared shallow to some reviewers, such as Diana Trilling (Malin 107-14). In any case, it remains difficult to determine his actual feelings on a case in which he was perhaps debilitatingly involved.

Late in the novel, a Dr. Jones makes a report in which he contextualizes the personalities of Perry and Dick against those of four other men convicted of apparently unmotivated murderers. He found that to "all of them, adult women were threatening creatures, and in two cases there was overt sexual perversion" (336). In addition, all had been considered "sissies" in their youth. Despite what seems to be Capote's attempt to point out the violent effects of the unjust and bigoted repression of same-sex attraction in America, it is easy to leave the novel confused about where Capote stands in relation to the Freudian-derived views of sexuality that surface in the novel.

Because Capote's veracity in his novel has been questioned and because this issue intersects with Capote's attitude toward the two men, readers may wish to consult two other essays, one an "as-told-to" article that claims to give Hickock's account and another by Philip K. Tompkins that is a direct refutation of Capote's claims to accuracy. Both of these can be found in the critical casebook (along with several important reviews) on the novel edited by Irving Malin in 1968. In 1990 a second "casebook" appeared in *Contemporary Literary Criticism* (vol, 58: 84-136), including lengthy excerpts from many of the reviews in Malin's book, plus the texts of the Capote-Tynan debate, relevant interview material, and parts of four more recent articles. One of these is a discussion by Jack De Bellis (originally 1979) of the changes in the text from the *New Yorker* articles to the Random House edition and their relationship to the book's claimed truth-value. Other statements on this issue can be found in Clarke's biography and Donald Windham's memoir.

Donald Windham's *Lost Friendships: A Memoir of Truman Capote, Tennessee Williams, and Others* (1987) is the only one of the memoirs to give insight into Capote's work as an author and as a gay man. He discusses both the journalism and the fiction. Windham, a novelist and playwright, gives a piercing view of Capote as an irresponsible weaver of fictions about himself and others, using several of his writings as examples.

Windham challenges Capote on his memories and treatment of gay men such as André Gide. He notes that in *Observations,* a text/image collaboration with the photographer Richard Avedon, Capote describes a last meeting between Jean Cocteau and André Gide at Taormina in the spring of 1950, an encounter that he supposedly witnessed (48). Windham maintains that Cocteau was not in Sicily in 1950 and that Cocteau had written in 1951 that his last encounter with Gide was at Seine-et-Oise in February 1949 (48).

Considering that so much has been written on *In Cold Blood* as a nonfiction novel, Windham's evaluation bears attention. He claims that Capote got at the facts mostly by discounting the stories of Hickock and Smith when they were different and crediting them when they were the same. So, for Capote the true story "was the unagreed-upon versions they both told him" (79). Since the book could not be published until the execution of the two men, when "the book came out, the only living authority for the factualness of much of the narrative was Truman himself" (79). Windham admires the novel, but he thinks that we should scrap the categorization that Capote impertinently and uselessly created for it.

As Capote's most openly gay short story is "A Diamond Guitar," it is worth noting that Windham claims that he gave Capote a copy of his novel *The Dog Star* in 1950 and that this work influenced Capote's later story. He feels that although the events and characters of "A Diamond Guitar," written shortly after, are not taken from his own book, the "assembled properties of his story come from my novel: the emblematic guitar, passed on as an inheritance, the glass jewels; the blondness of the guitar player; the settings—a prison farm, a creek in the woods; the repeated images of sunlight on a woman's hair" (81). He indicates that Carson McCullers also kept track of Capote's borrowings from her, such as a passage in *The Grass Harp* that she matched up with "A Tree. A Rock. A Cloud" (81).

Windham warns us not to take *Answered Prayers* as either a truthful roman à clef or factual reportage. For example, he tells us that even when Montgomery Clift is depicted under his real name in the story "Kate McCloud," there is "no veracity in the incident depicted" (118). Not only does Capote attribute Clift's erratic behavior to a time before it had commenced, Capote's rendition of his meeting with Tallulah Bankhead in the story makes little sense, as they had acted together in *The Skin of Our Teeth* in 1942. Again, we are left with the complicated issue of judging Capote's work both for its literary quality and for its regard of truth-value.

The absence of full-length literary studies on Capote's work since his death is probably an indication that his work is seen as essentially finished by 1966 and that *Answered Prayers* does not add anything to it.

* * * *

Even as late as 1985, evaluations of Capote's life and work may fail to mention Capote's homosexuality, as is the case with the three-page entry by Thomas Bonner Jr., in Rubin's *History of Southern Literature*. Nevertheless, in the case of Truman Capote we cannot say that homophobia lowered the overall critical reception of Capote's work. In fact, to some extent the opposite is true because of the notoriety he gained. Furthermore, he had champions among nongay critics who promoted Southern literature or fiction about American family life. Post-Stonewall evaluations are likely to see Capote as a relic of the closeted age in which happy futures for gay characters and positive evaluations of deep male bonding are relatively unimaginable.

Although there were some initial hostile reviews of *Other Voices, Other Rooms* because of its subject matter, Capote was able to ride them out and to promote himself to a far greater extent than more talented writers of his time. The hostile reaction to *Answered Prayers* can not be attributed to homophobia either. The vulgarity of the published fragments tends to reinforce stereotypes of gay male bitchery, especially in the treatment of the figure inspired by Tennessee Williams. If *In Cold Blood* continues to be studied in terms of the nonfiction novel rather than through a gay-studies approach, we must remember that Capote himself attempted to set criticism along these lines.

Several directions of research are left open. Considering that *Other Voices, Other Rooms* has been treated by many critics as an example of "Southern Gothic," it is worth de-emphasizing the Southern aspect and asking how Capote relates to a tradition of same-sex-oriented writers who, since Horace Walpole, have been prominent practitioners of "Gothic." On another note, we may examine "A Diamond Guitar" in the context of gay men's prison literature. The Smith/Hickock murders in *In Cold Blood* could be related to treatments of the Leopold/Loeb murders in journalism, fiction, and film.

Truman Capote provokes strong emotions to this day as both author and personality. Like his contemporary Andy Warhol, Capote created a public personna for himself, and the comparative strategies of these two men would be worth evaluating in tandem. An in-depth study of the complex web of literary networking among American gay authors and artists could provide new materials for study of Capote as well.

As it stands now, with the academic establishment caught up in debate over the boundaries and comparative strategies of literature and fiction, Capote will be remembered for some time to come mostly as the author of *In Cold Blood,* not as the author of "gay fictions." For those interested in descriptions of childhood, Capote has a respectable place with *Other Voices, Other Rooms, The Grass Harp* and his autobiographical family stories. Indeed, as we attempt to reach out to the thwarted lives and opportunities of gay youth, *Other Voices, Other Rooms* may prove of interest to gay male teenagers (despite Cynthia Ozick's exaggerated claim that the book is "dead and empty" [80-89]). However, Capote's achievement as a revealer of adult feelings is considerably less; and if we take his desire for comparison to Proust seriously, we can only be disappointed.

II

GENRES AND INDIVIDUAL WORKS

STAGE AND FICTION

On Capote's Grass Harp

ERIC BENTLEY

At first blush Mr. Capote's play is simply ridiculous: it is about living in trees; but it is saved from the ridiculous by the trite when, late in the evening, the conclusion is announced: "We can't live in trees, maybe some of would like to, but none of us can."

It is true that the arboreal fable of *The Grass Harp* is meant to symbolize an escape from humdrum reality, that Mr. Capote's real theme is the search for one's real self, and that such a theme is not to be stigmatized as trite merely because it is traditional. It has the effect of triteness in this play because it is in no way rendered active by Mr. Capote's art: when he has finished it still belongs to tradition, he has in no way made it his own. When his people speak we hear only other voices echoing in other rooms. On occasion this may be partly blamed on the actors. In the large part of the bad but subsequently repentant sister, Miss Ruth Nelson, makes Mr. Capote's spread-eagle prose sound even more awkward than it need; as the Wise Southern Judge, Russell Collins adds an actor's unctuousness to an author's. Yet the one performer who contrives to remain real (by remaining herself) is forced to call attention to ham writing by making us feel she only speaks *those* lines because she has to. This is Mildred Natwick, without whom the play would have no adult existence.

The triteness is in the conclusions and at the core; in the premises and at the periphery all is ridiculous. Since the ridiculous is acceptable when it is funny and unpretentious, one can readily accept such minor characters as (in order of merit) Buster the goldfish; the daft, if somewhat overacted, barber of Mr. Sterling Holloway; the headlong cosmetician of Miss Alice Pearce, and several other villagers who might be described as *by* Robert Lewis *out of* Charlie Chaplin. On the level of wise-cracking Broadway farce—on which the large part of the servant, acted by Georgia Burke, is played—Mr. Capote reveals a surprising talent.

From *The New Republic* 126 (14 April 1952): 22-23.

If only he would stay on that level! Instead he follows what seems to be the dominant contemporary "school" of theatre in pursuing the ridiculous high into the intense inane. Negatively described, this school is the latest revulsion against realism. Positively, it is usually presented as a rebirth of poetic drama or at least as an assertion of charm and theatricality over brute facts. Disparate authors come together to produce a somewhat coherent total result. Here the Eliot of *The Cocktail Party* joins hands with the Huxley of *The Gioconda Smile* to relieve the rich of sexual guilt by belief in a higher reality. Eliot and Huxley keep the framework of the drawing-room play; Anouilh and Fry, even when they present a drawing-room, make sure that the place is filled with the fauna of a rococo fancy even if it is not actually decked with the flora of the new stage design. The new school in stage design is the counterpart of the new school in dramaturgy: fancy, effeminate, lush, and in the best of taste. The father of the school is the late Christian Bérard. He was a great designer but a highly specialized one. His specialty was costumes, so much so that his sets appeared to be costumes for the stage itself: the stage was a lovely woman.

The Grass Harp has sets by Cecil Beaton, the English Bérard, who is quite literally a costumier turned stage designer. His work dominates the evening at the Martin Beck largely because it is content to be what it is. It "is" the new style. It is what Mr. Capote and, I should judge, Mr. Robert Lewis aspire to and only partially, ambiguously, half-heartedly achieve. For example: there is nothing of the spirit of the South in Mr. Beaton's work, and why should there be? Art is a holiday, is itself, is silk shawls and luscious colors, is upholstery. Mr. Beaton is happy in the realm that I have called the ridiculous; he does not need the trite. But Mr. Capote has to use words, can't get by with color and form, can't help being involved with life even if he is incapable of shaping it. It is almost as if he started with a realistic play and later tried to transform it into a fantasy. In combination the realistic and fantastic elements became the trite and the ridiculous, respectively.

Mr. Lewis is one of the finest talents in our theatre. Had he hewed to either line, realistic or fantastic, he might possibly have made something of Mr. Capote's play. As it is, the directing is non-committal and unsure without being discreet or unobtrusive. Mr. Lewis tries to cover up the ambiguity of the play, on his own ambiguous feelings about it, with apparatus: the Beaton costumes and decor, Virgil Thomson's music, and his own directorial gimmicks. Of the gimmicks the most showy and fatuous is the shining of flashlights in Miss Nelson's face when she wishes to make a pronouncement to the tree-dwellers; a shot is fired, everyone wonders who is hit, and the flashlights pick out the wounded man with magical unanimity. One could perhaps put up with this sort of thing had not the simpler scenes been so neglected by comparison. The opening and closing scenes of the play could never be convincing, but they might have been interesting had Mr. Lewis helped the actors to bring a reality from themselves which the author had not managed to give them in his script.

At present, the domestic scenes are as wooden as the table which they revolve around. Where something human might have been shaped and defined, Mr. Lewis fled into triviality and ostentation.

Admittedly no one would wish to banish triviality from the theatre, its traditional home. Ostentation, too, is of the theatrical essence. What one protests against in the trivial, ostentatious work is its pretentiousness. The reason why *The Grass Harp* is so far out of tune is more fundamental. It is *decadent*—not, it is true, in the life depicted but in the spirit of the depiction.

Although in *The Grass Harp* there is none of the scandalous subject-matter for which writers like Mr. Capote are known, and we are, on the contrary, in the company of virginal old ladies, innocent schoolgirls, and wistful widowers, this author's interest in innocence seems more extravagant than his interest in vice. Here is a form of sentimentality which is simply the reverse side of unpleasant sophistication. It has all the defects of pure sentimentality plus those of sentimentality gone rancid. Ostensibly we are presented with simplicity yet everything is slightly off—off color, off center, off key.

Why should all the organization, expenditure, work and talent that go to the making of such a show stop short of creating a living work of art, or even a few living moments? Deliberate charlatanism will perhaps partly account for it, yet in the end I would withdraw such a charge, not out of generosity, but because the failure seems to me to be more desperate and involuntary. It is a failure to be sincere, to be human. Not intentionally or accidentally, but of its very nature, such work is negative, vacuous, and contraceptive.

The Grass Menagerie

GEORGE JEAN NATHAN

In *The Grass Harp* the joint influence of William Saroyan and Tennessee Williams on Truman Capote, its author, is as manifest as the influence of Joe Mielziner on Cecil Beaton, its scene designer, and as the influence of all three on its producers, Saint Subber and Rita Allen. The script combines an attempt at Saroyan's whimsicality and eccentric humor with an attempt at Williams' lyricism, or what passes for it, just as the stage settings combine Mielziner's scrim curtains with his fanciful mixture of dreaminess and realism. And the producers, evidently admirers of the trio, have swooned over what they doubtless viewed as a tripled threat.

I am afraid, however, that my own equilibrium remains undisturbed, except for Beaton's successful scenic patterning and Virgil Thomson's incidental music, which is independently expert. The reasons are several. Though Capote tries for the Saroyan flavor, he has none of the latter's devil-may-care blood in his pen and rather gives off the impression of a more studiously "literary" writer. His imagination, furthermore, is infinitely more constricted and contained than the Armenian bad-boy's and hasn't the latter's often winning wildness and surprise. Taking much the same basic idea that Saroyan frolicked with in his *Sweeney In The Trees,* he corsets it out of any easy, carefree flight and the result is a fantasy that remains largely literal and close to the ground. His humor, in addition, is mostly of a conventional and worn cut; it lacks the boozy wings that Saroyan's has and is much the kind we usually get from a Broadway revue skit author.

Nor has he Williams' occasional gift for lyric expression; when he essays it, little more comes from his ink than something that resembles one of the slightly better Tin-Pan Alley sentimental ditties. I speak, of course, solely in respect to this play; in both his novels—*The Grass Harp* is derived from one of the same title—and his short fiction he demonstrates much greater facility. But in his first

Theatre Arts, 36 (June 1952): 17-19.

effort in the dramatic form the virtues are absent, largely because he has deemed it necessary, with his limited experience, to remove the bloom from his prose and make it conform to what he believes or has been led to believe is the stage's always arbitrary demand for barer, skeletonized expression. The consequence is a play that, while it purports to be fantasy, is too frequently nothing but realism with colored ribbons in its hair. The settings and incidental music may deceive some into seeing a touch of poetry in the play, as others such have deceived many into seeing an even greater touch in Williams, but if the play itself is listened to with a reading ear there is found to be no more real poetry in it than in the average Broadway show.

The story, as in the earlier Saroyan exhibit mentioned, is essentially of a person, in this instance a spinster, who to get away from conniving and irksome humanity goes to live in a tree. Capote discourages those critics who are fond of discerning symbolism in something otherwise so scant that they can't believe it possible a playwright would conceivably write anything so simple without meaning a lot more by asserting that there is no symbolism whatsoever in the play and that it merely aims to say that one cannot run away from people but is inevitably part of them. Thus, the spinster who makes a move to escape from a sister bent on swindling her out of a patent medicine formula that promises riches eventually returns to her and lives out her life, for good or ill, with her. To the treatment of his theme, the author brings an infrequent fancy and, truth to tell, a very feeble and crippled fancy at that, and the end product suggests only a potentially fanciful script written in prosaic ink and given over into the keeping of a scene designer and composer entrusted with the job of working a little imagination and poetry into it.

The acting company, directed by Robert Lewis, who also has worked himself into a sweat in the enterprise of trying to inject some lyric quality into the script, is in addition scarcely of the sort to vein the exhibit with any melody. The performances are here and there accurate enough but mostly of a recalcitrant literalness, due to the personalities of the players. Fantasy, or anything that aspires to it, calls for actors who, aside from their competencies, have the personal appearance, air and spirit to accommodate themselves to drama above the mundane, and the play for the major part has been cast instead with the kind who, while they would suit a different kind of drama, seem as out of place in this kind as Claude Rains would in drawing-room comedy or Carol Channing in Maeterlinck. Georgia Burke suffices in the low-comedy role of a Negro servant who polkas around the edges of the play and delivers herself of saucy cracks, and Russell Collins serves satisfactorily as the retired judge who joins up with the spinster's tree party. But the rest, including Mildred Natwick as the spinster, Ruth Nelson as her sister, and Jonathan Harris as the sister's swindling accomplice, give one the feeling, for all their sincere efforts to adapt themselves to the business of the evening, that they would be much more comfortable in something by Elmer Rice.

Capote is a writer who in another medium has indicated talent, but in that of the stage his name, at least on this occasion, is spelled Kaput.

The Stage: House of Flowers

RICHARD HAYES

Mr. Truman Capote's scented fable, heavy with the fragrance of bougainvillea and hibiscus, unquestionably flourishes with a great and seductive beauty on the Caribbean shores of Oliver Messel's décor; the sadness is that the first trade wind of taste or reality can wither so much of its bloom. Indeed, the new musical at the Alvin—for which Harold Arlen has written the score—celebrates a most exotic misalliance: the union of Mr. Capote's slender, sophisticated version of primitive with the hard, gross, pushing resources of the Broadway musical stage. The marriage is possibly one of convenience, certainly one of mutual distemper: the warring interests of both parties are never reconciled, and their sudden temporary concessions, each to the other, give the enterprise a flavor signally hybrid. Thus the elaborate panoply of winking wickedness—so explicitly invoked and slyly insinuated—gradually cracks to reveal merely a simple cautionary tale of pure love shining like that good deed in oh! what a naughty world! The ambiguous "innocence" of the new sensibility—its luxurious self-deceit—has not, I think, previously been exposed in such naked and incriminating vulnerability, for here we see the offensive spectacle of a vicarious enjoyment of all the pleasures of sexuality with no recognition of their human, spiritual risks.

Specifically, there are excellences in "House of Flowers"; generally, the mood is one of ennui. Mr. Capote's random specimens of smoking-room wit—the libretto cannot really be said to consist of anything else—are graceless and ill-bred; the gentleman is not a tramp, and how painfully green seem his efforts to compete in this league. Mr. Arlen's score explores every variety of calypso: they are few. (Yet a paradox here, for "Bamboo Cage" seemed to me a little masterpiece of musical local color.) To the Negro dancing, I shall concede energy, and a ruthless exploitation of sensual response, in the meanwhile noting crossly that I am not at all partial to these emasculated parodies of native

Commonweal, 61 (28 January 1955): 454-55.

civilization—rather a bit too much hoodoo-voodoo, as Miss Anna Russell observed in one of her more sibylline moments.

Pearl Bailey and Juanita Hall—supremely imperious, insolent, knowing—are Mr. Capote's distinguished ladies of uncertain virtue. They animate these Southern languors with a richness of personality quite impossible to suppress; their characterizations, one might note, are the only ones the script does not subtly patronize, and their performances suggest again how much *essential* contemporary dramatic talent has been lost to cabaret. Mr. Capote's own loss— temporary, we must hope—to the world of serious letters is altogether another affair, and to be contemplated, I should think, with decidedly less sanguine an eye. (*At the Alvin.*)

SHORT STORIES

Capote's Tale

LESLIE FIEDLER

This collection contains one extraordinarily good story plus three or four others less good but still memorable that should help redeem Truman Capote, the writer, from that other Capote, the creature of the advertising department and the photographer. Risen from the couch that adorned the jacket of his last year's novel, he leans for this volume, epicene among lush blossoms—very tender, very young. The boy author has been a standard feature of our literature ever since the beginnings of romanticism, and I suppose our generation is entitled to one of its own, but surely Capote deserves better than being fixed in that stereotype.

True, his work shows the occasional over writing, the twilit Gothic subject matter, and the masochistic uses of horror traditional in the fiction of the boy author ever since the eighteen-year-old Lewis wrote his *Monk* 150 years ago. But Capote has, in addition, an ability to control tone, an honest tenderness toward those of his characters he can understand (children and psychotics), and a splendid sense of humor—seldom remarked upon. In the best of his stories, "Children on Their Birthdays," he grasps a situation at once ridiculous and terrible, creating out of the absurdities of love and death among children a rich tension lacking in his other stories, even such successful performances as "The Tree of Night" and "Miriam." On the whole, the level of achievement of these shorter pieces of fiction seems to me a good deal higher than that of Capote's novel, *Other Voices, Other Rooms*, whose occasional triumphs of style or characterization are undercut by poor structure and a general air of padding and pastiche.

Mr. Capote is not yet ready to sustain a novel, but as a teller of tales he has a genuine and peculiar talent. He has, however, certain disturbing faults even in the shorter forms, most notably an inability to **hear** and reproduce common

The Nation, 168 (2 April 1949): 395-96. Revised by the author.

speech; so that when he tries occasionally to tell a whole story through the mouth of a simple or vulgar character ("My Side of the Matter"), he fails dismally. But in his hands the fairy tale and ghost story manage to assimilate the attitudes of twentieth-century psychology without losing integrity by demanding to be accepted as mere fantasy, or explained as mere symbol.

The bogeyman, though he fades sometimes into the delusion of the paranoiac, remains a **real** bogeyman still. He is indeed scarcely ever absent from these stories, reappearing in various guises, as a constant antagonist: the buyer of dreams who is also Master Misery in the story of that name, the old man in "Miriam," Mr. Destronelli in "The Headless Hawk," Lazarus the Man, Who is Buried Alive in "A Tree of Night," a voice on the telephone in "Shut a Final Door." These are not symbolic representations of evil but genuine spooks: what the child, having learned in the whispered tale, finally believes in, but what the adult absurdly denies and is destroyed by.

> I call him Mastery Misery on account of that's who he is, Master Misery. Only maybe you call him something else: anyway, he is the same fellow, and you must've known him. All mothers tell their kids about him: he lives in hollows of trees, he comes down chimneys late at night, he lurks in graveyards, and you can hear his step in the attic. The sonofabitch. . . .

In Capote's stories the fairy world, more serious than business or love, is forever closing in upon the skeptical secure world of grown-ups. But his children—and the natural allies of children, clown or lunatic—are competent to deal with the underground universe of the incredible. Consequently they are Capote's most credible characters; especially the *Wunderkind,* the precocious child, sometimes flesh and blood, real if not quite canny, like Appleseed or Miss Bobbit, sometimes fading into a haunt like the title character in "Miriam."

Mr. Capote writes not merely of children but from their side; his stories are the kid's imagined revenge upon maturity. Adults find neither mercy nor tenderness in these tales; for to have denied childhood or to have lost faith in its terrors—by simply growing up, is such a loss and denial, that, except for the mad—it invites the nemesis which Capote's children, as the bearers of this mystery, never have to endure.

Only in "Children on their Birthdays," the most complex and satisfying of these tales, is there an ironical reverse, when the astonishing Miss Bobbit, the little girl who has shocked, cowed, and bullied a whole town of grownups, is killed, at the point of leaving for Hollywood (the child's paradise), by the six o'clock bus, blind on its adult business. This story alone is enough to make the volume worth reading, but there are rewards too in the other pieces, and it is a pity that fewer people will read it than have read *Other Voices, Other Rooms,* since it represents Mr. Capote's essential achievement so far.

Truman Capote: The Revelation of the Broken Image

PAUL LEVINE

The inclusion of Truman Capote in any discussion that pretends to be at most scholarly and at least literary is usually frowned upon by the more sternfaced of our critics. The mention of his name conjures up images of a wispish, effete soul languishing on an ornate couch, emitting an ether of preciousness and very little else. The reaction to the amazing success of his early books, *Other Voices, Other Rooms* and *A Tree of Night*, has relegated Capote to the position of a clever, cute, coy, commercial, and definitely minor figure in contemporary literature, whose reputation has been built less on a facility of style than on an excellent advertising campaign. Even an earnest supporter would have to admit that Capote's stories tiptoe the tenuous line between the precious and the serious.

Yet the attacks on Capote seem more personal than literary. Critics like John Aldridge—whose essay appears in *After the Lost Generation*, a book that generally has little good to say about anyone (except Mr. Aldridge)—have blatantly confused the author's private life with his literary ability. The notion—as fantastic as any of Capote's stories—that Capote's style comes too easily is an excellent example. Not only is the banner of the tortured writer rather tattered by now but in Capote's case the charge of a "natural style" is false. His first stories—"These Walls Are Cold" and "The Shape of Things"—are written in the painfully realistic prose associated with those young writers in transition from the *Saturday Evening Post* to the *New Yorker*. Moreover, Capote is really no more precocious than a number of our outstanding writers. J. D. Salinger published his first story at twenty-one and Carson McCullers had written two novels before she was twenty-four. As with the legend surrounding Fitzgerald, critics have a difficult time discerning Capote from his work, a slight not only to the author but to the critic. Mr. Capote is no more an *enfant terrible* than Mr. Aldridge is.

Virginia Quarterly Review, 34 (Autumn 1958): 600-17.

Perhaps the most frequent criticism leveled at Capote's work is that he is limited in scope and remote from life. While it is true that Capote writes fantastic and grotesque stories, it is not necessarily true that these stories, because of their genre, must be remote from life. In many ways, Capote has chosen the most universal medium in which to present his thematic material, because the genre of the fantasy, evolving from the daydream, the fairy tale, and the tall tale, is among the oldest and most elemental of fictional forms.

While we must acknowledge Capote's admission that "style is the mirror of an artist's sensibility—more so than the *content* of his work," we must also recognize that there is no dearth of content in his work. To understand that content fully we must first posit some very elemental points, because Capote is to a great extent an erudite writer about primal things. At the heart of his writing is the dichotomy in the world between good and evil, the daylight and the nocturnal, man and nature, and between the internal and external manifestation of things. As Harry Levin has pointed out in a different context:

> This takes us back to the very beginning of things, the primal darkness, the void that God shaped by creating light and dividing night from day. That division underlies the imagery of the Bible from Genesis to the Apocalypse, and from the word of life to the shadow of death. It is what differentiates the children of light from the children of darkness in the Dead Sea Scrolls.
> . . . But all religions, in accounting for the relation of the earth to the sun and for the diurnal and seasonal cycles, seem to posit some dichotomy, such as the Yin and the Yang of the Orient or the twin paths of the Bhagavad-Gita.

The dichotomy of good and evil exists in each Capote character just as the dichotomy of daylight and nighttime exists in the aggregate of his stories. We might almost say that Capote's stories inhabit two worlds—that of the realistic, colloquial, often humorous daytime and that of the dreamlike, detached, and inverted nocturnal world. This double identity must be viewed with a double vision because Capote's stories can be interpreted either psychologically or as an expression of a spiritual or moral problem. In either case, whether the story be realistic or fantastic, the central focus is on the moment of initiation and the central character is either adolescent or innocent.

One way to distinguish the daylight from the nocturnal tales is to note the hero's position in relation to his private world and the public world. In the daylight stories the movement is out towards the world while in the darker tales the hero tends to move away from the world and in towards his inner *Id* or soul or imagination. In the daylight variety, there is a tension between the hero and his society which resolves itself often in a humorous and always in a creative or imaginative way. All these stories are told in the first person but none of them tries to move into the character's psyche or soul. The focus, instead, is on the surfaces, the interest and humor deriving from the situation and the action.

The realism in these daylight stories seems to evolve from Capote's early pieces, printed in Decade Magazine. But the warmth, humor, and ease of style lacking in these surface stories is picked up in "My Side of the Matter," which closely resembles Eudora Welty's "Why I Live at the P.O." in its colloquial use of language. This slim tale of a minor skirmish between a young, beleaguered hero and his querulous in-laws is slight in comparison to the later "Jug of Silver" and "Children on Their Birthdays." Both of these stories are markedly similar in that they are concerned with extraordinary, almost supernatural children. The hero of the first story, Appleseed, is blessed with a kind of extrasensory power for determining the amount of money in a jar filled with silver: a power acquired from being born with a caul over his head.

Similarly, the heroine of Capote's most perfect story in the daylight genre, "Children on Their Birthdays," is a precocious child with an uncanny power. Like Cousin Lymon in Carson McCullers' "Ballad of the Sad Cafe," Miss Bobbit comes to a new town and disrupts its whole pattern of living with her awesome brand of animal magnetism. From her first appearance, grotesquely made up like an adult and sporting a parasol, Miss Bobbit impresses as a fantastic mixture of innocence and experience, morality and pragmatism. She sings like Sophie Tucker, dances like Gypsy Rose Lee, and possesses the business acumen of a Polly Adler. Miss Bobbit doesn't go to church because she finds the odor there offensive but she adds:

> "I don't want you to think I'm a heathen, Mr. C; I've had enough experience to know that there is a God and that there is a Devil. But the way to tame the Devil is not to go down there to church and listen to what a sinful mean fool he is. No, love the Devil like you do Jesus: because he is a powerful man, and will do you a good turn if he knows you trust him. He has frequently done me good turns, like at dancing school in Memphis. . . . I always called in the Devil to help me get the biggest part in our annual show. That is common sense; you see, I knew Jesus wouldn't have any truck with dancing. Now, as a matter of fact, I have called in the Devil just recently. He is the only one who can help me get out of this town. Not that I live here, not exactly. I think always about somewhere else, somewhere else where everything is dancing, like people dancing in the streets, and everything is pretty, like children on their birthdays. My precious papa said I live in the sky, but if he'd lived more in the sky he'd be rich like he wanted to be. The trouble with my papa was he did not love the Devil, he let the Devil love him. But I am very smart in that respect; I know the next best thing is very often the best."

It is necessary to distinguish here between the hero in the two worlds of day and night. Notice that the *mana*-laden child is the hero in the stories discussed so far, while this same figure becomes the shadowy antagonist in Capote's nocturnal stories. Instead, the protagonist becomes an impotent Prufrock, a character to whom things happen. Yet the relationship between the antagonist and the protagonist is ambiguous: one seems the alter ego of the other. The uncanny power in the daylight hero is a creative force—the manifestation of the imagination. In the nocturnal stories the hero is forced to come to grips with the destructive element—the power of blackness which resides in each of us. The confrontation of the psyche leads to the exposure of the constructive and destructive elements: the wish for death and the wish for life.

In Capote's nocturnal stories the movement out into the world becomes simultaneously the movement into the self. John Aldridge has compared Capote's novel *Other Voices, Other Rooms* unfavorably to Joseph Conrad's *Victory*. The comparison between the two writers is a just, almost obvious one when used in a different context. If we juxtapose Conrad's *Heart of Darkness* with any Capote twilight story, it becomes immediately apparent that the structures are the same. In Conrad's story, Marlowe moves into the heart of the dark continent at the same time he moves into the heart of his own subconscious or soul. In reality, the two movements are the same. The same idea occurs in Paul Bowles' *The Sheltering Sky,* in which two Americans move into the primitive Arab world and the primal inner world simultaneously. Similarly, each Capote nocturnal hero must face a fiendish form of *mana,* an external force, and his inner guilt. The relationship in all cases is the same: there is an inescapable fascination with the outer and inner faces of evil. The moment of initiation, the shock of recognition, comes when the hero discovers that the two are the same: the *mana* which confronted him was an external manifestation of his inner identity. The dichotomy then is not only between the two worlds but between the two faces of each world: the constructive and the destructive.

The story of initiation is the search for identity. For instance, in *Master Misery,* one of Capote's favorites by his own admission, his heroine, Sylvia, is caught between the outside world represented by her insensitive girlhood friend, Estelle, and the impersonal, mechanical Santa Clauses in store windows, and the personal world of her own dreams. In an attempt to escape the outside world, Sylvia sells her dreams to the anonymous Master Misery, only to discover that she has not escaped the outer world but only lost the inner.

Sylvia is befriended by Oreilly, a used-up clown with no more dreams to sell, who squints one eye and says: "I don't believe in Jesus Christ, but I do believe in people's souls; and I figure it this way, baby; dreams are the mind of the soul and the secret truth about us." When Oreilly leaves her with a smile to go "traveling in the blue" where *"the best old pie is whiskeyberry pie"* and not *"loveberry pie,"* Sylvia is left completely alone, having lost her dreams and her friend:

> I do not know what I want, and perhaps I shall never know, but my only wish from every star will always be another star; and truly I am not afraid, she thought. Two boys came out of a bar and stared at her; in some park some long time ago she'd seen two boys and they might be the same. Truly I am not afraid, she thought, hearing their snowy footsteps following after her: and anyway, there was nothing left to steal.

In no other nocturnal story is the reader as conscious of the tension between the individual and society. Sylvia, in attempting to escape from society, discovers that the destructive element comes from within. Master Misery is himself a bogey man that "all mothers tell their kids about": a force outside the self and yet an extension of the self. Sylvia's surrender at the end of the story is not to society but to the dark side of her soul, the destructive element which dominates when the creative imagination is exhausted. In this lies the idea that the creative imagination of the dream world is the one *thing* by which the individual is identified; the surrender of identity and of the creative force is the acquiescence to the death wish.

The differences between the lighter and darker sides of Capote's writing come out more clearly in one of his most famous stories, "Miriam." In it, an old woman, Mrs. Miller, is haunted by a striking and uncanny child who is her namesake——Miriam. The story shows how Miriam moves in and takes over Mrs. Miller's home, person, and life. The plot is similar to "Children on Their Birthdays" and "Jug of Silver": an uncanny child upsets the equilibrium of the drab routine of living. Miriam is in many ways similar to Miss Bobbit and we may almost think of her as that remarkable child's darker sister. But in "Miriam" there are some significant differences from the daylight stories, most important of which is the withdrawal from the outside world, a movement from the relationship of self to society to a confrontation of the self by the self in which Miriam becomes an uncanny device—a result of *mana* and projection. In fact, Miriam stands as the primal alter ego to Mrs. Miller: an extension of her destructive, unconscious instinct. The withdrawal from the outer world is accompanied by a complementary shift in style; the clarity and realism of "Children" is replaced by a filmy and surreal style in which Miriam's fingers "made cobweb movements over the plate, gathering the crumbs."

The hero's encounter with, and surrender to, *mana* is perhaps most richly stated in the inverted story, "The Headless Hawk," in which an extraordinary young girl, half child, half adult, innocent, experienced, demented, homicidal, naïve, and primitive, invades the sterile life of a young failure on the fringes of the art world. Vincent is "a poet who had never written poetry, a painter who had never painted, a lover who had never loved (absolutely)—someone, in short, without direction and quite headless. Oh, it wasn't that he hadn't tried— good beginnings, always, and bad endings, always . . . a man in the sea, fifty miles from shore; a victim, born to be murdered, either by himself or another; an actor unemployed." Vincent falls under the spell of a demented young girl, D. J., whose painting of a headless hawk hovering over a headless body—a vivid symbol of his own disconnectedness—forces on Vincent "a note of inward recognition." Vincent takes the girl as his mistress because she recalls from his past his incurable fascination with carnival freaks and because "it was true that about those he loved there was always a little something wrong, broken." D. J. thus becomes a mirror of his own disconnected self into which he can retreat. He shuns all his old friends because he does not know how to explain his relationship with the grotesque young girl.

However, Vincent's immersion in D. J. takes a sharp turn when he discovers her obsession with a Mr. Destronelli, a shadowy figure out of her past who she is sure will kill her. When Vincent discovers her dementia he knows he must betray her in favor of his old life, just as he had betrayed his other lovers, just as "he'd betrayed himself with talents unexploited, voyages never taken, promises unfulfilled . . . why in his lovers must he always find the broken image of himself?" He soon turns her out of the house and on the same day symbolically stabs the headless hawk in her painting as he is trying to catch a butterfly. But, of course, he has not escaped her. D. J. hunts him night and day, convinced that he is Destronelli. Vincent, returned to his old world which he now finds "sterile and spurious," discovers that he is held by "a nameless disorder . . . a paralysis of time and identity." Vincent's fascination with D. J. is the fatal confrontation with Mr. Destronelli—the executioner in each of us: he sees in D. J. the grotesque reflection of his own broken image.

The heart of the matter—the heart of darkness—is revealed significantly enough in a dream that Vincent has on the night of D. J.'s eighteenth birthday. He is at a huge party with "an old man with yellow-dyed hair, powdered cheeks, kewpie-doll lips: Vincent recognizes Vincent." The old man is on Vincent's back and Vincent feels out of place until he notices that he is not alone. "He notices then that many are also saddled with malevolent semblances of themselves, outward embodiments of inner decay." The host has a headless hawk attached to his wrist drawing blood with its talons. Suddenly the host announces in a soprano voice: "Attention! The dancing will commence." Vincent finds himself dancing with a succession of old lovers.

> Again, a new partner. It is D. J., and she too has a figure barnacled to her back, an enchanting auburn-haired child; like an emblem of innocence, the child cuddles to her chest a snowball kitten. "I am heavier than I look," says the child, and the terrible voice retorts, "But I am heaviest of all." The instant their hands meet he begins to feel the weight upon him diminish; the old Vincent is fading. His feet lift off the floor, he floats upward from her embrace. The victrola grinds away loud as ever, but he is rising high, and the white receding faces gleam below like mushrooms on a dark meadow.

> The host releases his hawk, sends it soaring. Vincent thinks, no
> matter, it is a blind thing, and the wicked are safe among the blind.
> But the hawk wheels above him, swoops down, claws foremost; at
> last he knows there is to be no freedom.

The confrontation of the inner world becomes the confrontation of man's
innate guilt. The dark side of the subconscious reflects not only the death
instinct but the Christian sense of man's depravity. The burden that each carries
becomes more than the darker alter ego: it is also the sense of original sin which
each of us carries like a cross. Thus even the child is heavier than she looks; and
thus Vincent cannot transcend his wickedness, even among the blind, even
through love. Truly, there is to be no freedom from original sin.

The ingredients in all of Capote's nocturnal stories are present in their most
striking expression, "A Tree of Night." Kay, a young college girl on her way
back to her insulated environment from her uncle's funeral is intimidated by two
grotesque carnival performers: a deaf mute who plays Lazarus by being buried
alive in tank towns and his one connection with the outside world, a woman
made freakish by her huge head. Much against her will, Kay is coerced, almost
mesmerized, into buying a worthless charm which she had previously refused to
buy. Like Capote's other heroes, Kay finds herself acquiescing to an uncanny
power.

As Kay watched, the man's face seemed to change form and recede before her
like a moon-shaped rock sliding downward under a surface of water. A warm
laziness relaxed her. She was dimly conscious of it when the woman took away
her purse, and when she gently pulled the raincoat like a shroud above her head.

On the level the story may be read as a tawdry and ironic parable of
Lazarus—

> "I am Lazarus come from the dead,
> Come back to tell you all, I shall tell you all"—
> If one, settling a pillow by her head,
>   Should say: "That is not what I meant at all;
>   That is not it, at all."

—just as Carson McCullers' novel, *The Heart Is a Lonely Hunter,* can be read
as an ironic parable of Christ. But perhaps the religious significance is being
overemphasized:

> [Confronted by the afflicted mute] Kay knew of what she was afraid:
> it was a memory, a childish memory of terrors that once, long ago,
> had hovered above her like haunted limbs on a tree of night. Aunts,
> cooks, strangers—each eager to spin a tale or teach a rhyme of
> spooks and death, omens, spirits, demons. And always there had
> been the unfailing threat of the wizard man: stay close to the house,
> child, else the wizard man'll snatch and eat you alive! He lived

> everywhere, the wizard man, and everywhere was danger. At night,
> in bed, hear him tapping at the window? Listen!

Fear seems the motivating emotion in these stories just as love is the motivating force in McCullers' novels. *"All our acts are acts of fear,"* remembered Walter Ranney, the hero of "Shut a Final Door," and perhaps he was right. For the wizard men and the Master Miseries are all personifications of some form of *mana,* formalized by superstition—that primitive and perhaps honest type of religious observance. At the same time, the Master Miseries and the Destronellis are not the products of our creative imagination but the very heart of darkness, the black, destructive, guilt-ridden side of our subconscious and soul. In each of these nocturnal stories, a seemingly normal but creatively bankrupt person encounters a destructive force at once outside himself and within his depths, which is so dreadful that he is utterly vanquished by fear and surrenders his very essence—his identity. The hero is drawn towards the source of power—the primal heart of darkness—and in doing so removes himself from the public world. Like Narcissus watching his reflection, Capote's hero becomes fascinated and mesmerized by his own evil alter ego. Like Jacob wrestling with the dark angel, the hero in these stories is wrestling not only with the outside world of reality but with his own personal world, losing the former while winning the latter. For the moment of defeat, of despair, of unconditional surrender, is also the moment of revelation.

What we have discovered about the two worlds of Truman Capote's short stories is equally true in his two novels. Conveniently, one novel describes each world: *The Grass Harp* seems the daylight metaphor of *Other Voices, Other Rooms.* And yet both novels exhibit a deepening of perception, a widening of scope, and an enrichening of the dense thematic material found in the stories. On the other hand, neither novel is entirely successful, whereas some of his stories—notably "Children on Their Birthdays" and "A Tree of Night"—are striking examples of their medium. Even Capote admits he is most at home in the short story.

Still, no piece of Capote's fiction has elicited as much comment, criticism, and bewilderment as the gothic and complex first novel, *Other Voices, Other Rooms.* Indeed, the dust jacket picture of the sensitive reclining face staring out from beneath boyish bangs was perhaps as great a cause for the excited confusion as anything in the book. But the difficult and fantastic remoteness of the book has been exaggerated by the mistaken identification of the hero with his exotic and precocious creator. Basically, *Other Voices, Other Rooms* resembles Capote's twilight stories in that it concerns an adolescent's initiation into the private and inverted adult world, full of danger and evil. John Aldridge has called it essentially a search for the father and Carvel Collins has likened it to the quest for the Holy Grail: both are right. Yet Joel Knox's search for his father, which leads him from the realistic daylight of New Orleans to the fantastic twilight of Skully's Landing, can be considered as a search for identity. Joel moves from the outside world towards the personal, just as he moves from the bright afternoon heat of Noon City to the dream-like darkness of his new home—Skully's Landing.

John Aldridge has accused Capote of being metaphorical and remote, but his symbolic treatment of thematic material seems clear enough if examined in the same manner as we have examined his other stories. Like his other work, *Other Voices, Other Rooms* can be read from either a psychological or a moral, perhaps Christian, viewpoint. Basically, Joel "was trying to locate his father, that was the long and short of it," for the discovery of his father's identity would cast some light on his own essence. But when Joel discovers the horrible truth that his father is a helpless, paralyzed invalid, he must look elsewhere for help in his search for identity. Joel stands as a stranger at Skully's Landing, poised between going further into the private world with his fascinating, witty, cynical, and homosexual cousin, Randolph, and moving out into the real world with the adolescent tomboy, Idabel. Joel's initiation can be seen as a straight-line development from the outside world of Noon City through the decadent limbo of Skully's Landing to the private, dreamlike ruins of the Cloud Hotel—and back again.

In order to tell his story, Capote has expanded the technique of metaphorical use of characterization seen in "Miriam" and "The Headless Hawk." Each character in *Other Voices, Other Rooms* is a metaphor or alter ego of another. The tomboy, Idabel, has a twin sister, Florabel, because, as Florabel says, "the Lord always sends something bad with the good." Similarly, the dwarfish Miss Wisteria, "weeping because little boys must grow tall," is a grotesque reflection of Randolph's hopeless, homosexual quest for completion. Little Sunshine, the hermit who inhabits his own private world at the Cloud Hotel, mirrors the old negro servant, Jesus Fever. And, finally, Joel himself is reflected in Jesus Fever's daughter, Zoo: both must reject their fathers in an effort to escape from the Landing.

Joel's first test comes when he is not allowed to meet his father. In his mind the illusions he had built around his father are confused with the reality of his father's absence. "He couldn't believe in the way things were turning out: the difference between this happening, and what he'd expected was too great." With the confrontation of his father's impotence, Joel must look elsewhere for the key to his identity. Randolph offers him one possibility: the narcissistic immersion in the self. . . . But even in the personal world Randolph cannot escape his own guilt for "it is easy to escape daylight, but night is inevitable, and dreams are the giant cage." Like Vincent, in "The Headless Hawk," Randolph is "a victim born to be murdered, either by himself or another." He remains a broken figure hopelessly committed to, and castrated by, the destructive side of his personal vision.

Caught between a loyalty to his father and a need to escape his stultifying influence, Joel at first rejects his father for Idabel, with whom he plans to run away. But the final act of initiation—the revelation of his own guilt that smashes the tinted glasses of childhood—renders Joel powerless to escape. In leaving his father, Joel, like Zoo, is judged guilty by his father and must act as his own executioner. Both he and Zoo can never really leave the Landing; their dreams of escape from limbo are shattered. When Randolph takes Joel to the Cloud Hotel—the private world which Randolph never left—a revelation of identity comes to Joel in a flash of insight:

> (He looked into the fire, longing to see their faces as well, and the flames erupted an embryo: a veined, vacillating shape, its features formed slowly, and even when complete stayed veiled in dazzle; his eyes burned tar-hot as he brought them nearer: tell me, tell me, who are you? are you someone I know? are you dead? are you my friend? do you love me? But the painted disembodied head remained unborn beyond its mask, and gave no clue. Are you someone I am looking for? he asked, not knowing whom he meant, but certain that for him there must be such a person, just as there was for everybody else: Randolph with his almanac, Miss Wisteria and her search by flashlight, Little Sunshine remembering other voices, other rooms, all of them remembering, or never having known. And Joel drew back. If he recognized the figure in the fire, then what ever would he find to take its place? It was easier not to know, better holding heaven in your hand like a butterfly that is not there at all.)

Unable to live in either the private or the real world, Joel makes the compromise of the artist: finding his identity by walking the tenuous line between the illusory and the tangible, between the imaginative and the real:

> "I am me," Joel whooped. "I am Joel, we are the same people" . . .

And Joel realized then the truth; he saw how helpless Randolph was: more paralyzed than Mr. Sansom, more childlike than Miss Wisteria, what else could he do, once outside and alone, but describe a circle, the zero of his nothingness? Joel slipped down from the tree; he had not made the top, but it did not matter, for he knew who he was, he knew that he was strong.

Yet Joel's search for his identity contains another and perhaps more significant level of meaning. At the very beginning of the book, while riding to Skully's Landing, Joel passes a sign—a sign for him and for the reader: "The Lord Jesus is Coming! Are you ready?" But the Christ figure we meet is one we are not prepared for: the paralytic father, Mr. Sansom, who drops red tennis balls like drops of blood, an ironic, afflicted Christ similar to the deaf-mute, Singer, in Carson McCullers' *The Heart Is a Lonely Hunter*. Joel's search for his father leads to the confrontation of his innate guilt—guilt symbolized in the

desertion of his father and manifested in his sudden awareness of the disparity
between illusion and reality and his perception of the impossibility of escape
from the Landing. His situation is mirrored by Zoo, who leaves her father's
grave to escape the Landing only to find that she has taken "the wrong road" to
salvation. She is crucified by assaulters just as Joel, like Christ, is condemned
and abandoned by his father and crucified by surrendering to Randolph. But in
the act of crucifixion are the seeds of redemption: Joel is crucified a boy and
resurrected a man.

Every Capote character is scarred permanently just as Zoo bears the marks of
a razor slashing on her neck. They are all marked men, marked perhaps by
original sin. Even the artist—like Joel—is afflicted: "the feeble-minded, the
neurotic, the criminal, perhaps, also, the artist, have unpredictability and
perverted innocence in common." But Capote's nocturnal hero remains
essentially the failure. And in Randolph he has created his most fascinating and
grotesque failure, who speaks for Vincent and Sylvia, Mrs. Miller and Walter
Ranney, when he says:

> "But we are alone, darling child, terribly, isolated each from the
> other; so fierce is the world's ridicule we cannot speak or show our
> tenderness; for us, death is stronger than life, it pulls like a wind
> through the dark, all our cries burlesqued in joyless laughter; and
> with the garbage of loneliness stuffed down us until our guts burst
> bleeding green, we go screaming round the world, dying in our
> rented rooms, nightmare hotels, eternal homes of the transient heart."

In *The Grass Harp*, Capote again moves to the daylight style. Essentially, it is
the story of a group of innocents, alienated from society because of their
innocence, who move into a tree house to escape the world and discover their
true selves. The theme is again the search for *true* identity. For the tree dissolves
all of society's restrictions and replaces them with a beatific feeling of freedom;
it is a realm where wish becomes fulfillment. The tree becomes the refuge for
the outcasts from society: the saintly Dolly, the most innocent of all, who, like
J. D. Salinger's misfit hero, Seymour Glass, loves people so much she hides in
corners for fear of scaring them with her love. With Dolly is her constant
companion, Catherine, a zany mixture of Negro and Indian, harshness and
loyalty, who brings to the tree house a sense of hard-headed reality, and Collin
Fenwick, the adolescent narrator, who lives with Dolly and her brutish sister,
Verena. These three have left home after a quarrel over Dolly's home-remedy
dropsy cure: Verena wants to mass produce it and Dolly refuses to
commercialize it. They are soon joined by a retired judge, Judge Cool, whose
sons feel has outgrown his usefulness. "I sometimes imagine," he says, "all
those whom I've called guilty have passed the real guilt on to me: it's partly that
that makes me want once before I die to be right on the right side." The fifth

party is a "tense, trigger-tempered," directionless youth, Riley Henderson, who also happens to be Collin's idol.

Like Salinger's Holden Caulfield, these five stage a "quixotic" battle against hypocrisy, materialism, and anything that takes beauty away from the world. The small revolt from society forces them to move towards the inner world of the imagination. Judge Cool sums up the whole idea nicely:

> "But ah, the energy we spend hiding from one another, afraid as we are of being identified. But here we are, identified: five fools in a tree. A great piece of luck provided we know how to use it: no longer any need to worry about the picture we present—free to find out who we truly are. If we know that no one can dislodge us; it's the uncertainty concerning themselves that makes our friends conspire to deny the differences. By scrapes and bits I've in the past surrendered myself to strangers—men who disappeared down the gangplank, got off at the next station: put together, maybe they would've made the one person in the world—but there he is with a dozen different faces moving down a hundred separate streets. This is my chance to find that man—you are him, Miss Dolly, Riley, all of you."

But this leafy retreat seems hardly the place for soul-searching; Verena soon has the authorities there to demand that they return to their homes. A pitched battle occurs between the rebels and the authorities, which, with the help of the right of creative imagination and the might of an ingenious family of gypsies, is decided in favor of the rebels. However, they do leave the tree house when Verena returns broken by the swindler of her heart and money—the bogus doctor who was to bottle the dropsy cure. Dolly returns to Verena because she is needed and the magic of the "dissolving" chinaberry tree is gone.

In the story the end of innocence is twofold. For Collin, it is an elegiac remembrance of things past, a vicarious initiation at Dolly's own loss of innocence, and his real initiation at Dolly's death. But for Collin the act of initiation brings the discovery of love and the redemption of the identity. It now becomes clear that for Capote love is the redeeming element in life. Echoing the judge's words in an earlier part of the book, Dolly tells Collin just before her death:

> "Charlie said that love is a chain of love. I hope you listened and understood him. Because when you can love one thing . . . you can love another, and that is owning, that is something to live with. You can forgive everything."

Like Carson McCullers in her story, "A Tree, A Rock, A Cloud," Capote here shows "that life is a chain of love, as nature is a chain of life." Arching over the story of Dolly and Collin and the chinaberry tree is the grass harp, a symbol of the immutable moral order, an order of the good and the imaginative which always tells a story of the lives of the people, good and bad, with and without identity, who have lived and died there. And so the search for identity comes to rest in the shock of recognition—recognition of the primacy of the natural order of the creative instinct—of love and imagination over the death wish. Both Joel and his daylight brother, Collin, have learned the same thing: the search inward for identity must eventually turn outward if it is to reflect anything but the broken image of the grotesque self. . . .

From Gothic to Camp

Perhaps the best clue to Capote's talent is one line from "Shut a Final Door": *"All our acts are acts of fear."* In such early stories as "A Tree of Night," "The Headless Hawk," and "Master Misery," he presents characters who are afraid to stare at their furious shadows. Why are they afraid? What causes their exaggerated, childish reactions? We don't know. Capote refuses to analyze his characters—it is hard to call them people—he takes their fear as a psychological *axiom*, not grounding it in classic Freudian theories. In a way this is his most significant insight: he realizes that fear, never completely understood, simply lies with us—waiting, like Henry James' Beast, to spring at our throats.

Of course, we can label Capote "exotic," "infantile," or "primitive." But there is no doubt that he disturbs us. He weakens our daylight control by means of his ability to *image* fear—even to celebrate it. The high point of his Gothic art is probably "The Headless Hawk." Here is one striking passage:

> Here is a hall without exit, a tunnel without end. Overhead, chandeliers sparkle, and wind-bent candles float on currents of air. Before him is an old man rocking in a rocking chair, an old man with yellow-dyed hair, powdered cheeks, kewpie-doll lips: Vincent recognizes Vincent. Go away, screams Vincent, the young and handsome, but Vincent, the old and horrid, creeps forward on all fours and climbs spiderlike onto his back. Threats, pleas, blows, nothing will dislodge him.

This passage deliberately distorts reality; it marries the normal and the fantastic. Consider, for example, the use of "kewpie-doll lips" or the "artificial" sparkles of the chandelier. The hero—it is his dream—is as "unnatural" as his surroundings. He, too, is unstable; his identity is not fixed. Vincent is so broken,

Ramparts (November 1964): 60-61.

all his acts remain only *acts* of fear—that he becomes two creatures locked in never-ending, destructive embrace.

It is obvious that we cannot surrender to Capote's fiction unless we "suspend our disbelief." Although we have grown up, we must believe once more in goblins and witches. Such belief is "religious." Capote forces us to recognize the other world—as Vincent recognizes Vincent. We cannot remain here and now; we must go through this "hall without exit." The Gothic supernaturalism is our substitute for traditional religion—our primitive ritual to ward off fear. It has not been noticed before, but Capote deals often with archetypal situations. "A Tree of Night" has a "false" Lazarus, risen from the dead. "Master Misery" has ironic confessions to a Christ-like figure. These stories may invert Christianity—they are superstitious, pagan, and nihilistic—but they also affirm the *miraculous* danger of life.

After his first two books—*Other Voices, Other Rooms,* and *A Tree of Night*—Capote fled from his true muse. He decided to become cute and glib. (Of course, he displayed these tendencies earlier, but he did not yield to them.) Instead of dark, "headless" truths he gave us sunny reportage. It is certainly surprising that various critics—including Mark Schorer and Alfred Kazin—applauded this transformation. They actually liked *Breakfast at Tiffany's* and *The Muses Are Heard!*

When we reread these works, we realize that Capote has joined the yea-sayers. He preaches LOVE. Holly Golightly may inspire others—she is wild and pathetic—but I think she is more artificial than Vincent. She says the *oddest* things and loves funny cats. The charming cast of our *Porgy and Bess* troupe in Russia is also excessively picturesque.

Can we account for the change? If we assume that Capote once believed in fear as the "aboriginal demon"—D.H. Lawrence's phrase—we can surmise that he found he could no longer control it. He ran away, covering his tracks. In *Breakfast at Tiffany's* fear lurks in the background, but it masquerades as superficial *Angst.* The following exchange shows us how far Capote has descended:

> "You're afraid and you sweat like hell, but you don't know what you're afraid of. Except something bad is going to happen, only you don't know what it is. You've had that feeling?"
>
> "Quite often. Some people call it *angst.*"
>
> "All right. *Angst.* But what do you do about it?"
>
> "Well, a drink helps."
>
> "I've tried that. I've tried aspirin, too. . . . What I've found does the most good is just to get into a taxi and go to Tiffany's. It calms me down right away, the quietness and proud look of it; nothing very bad could happen to you there, not with those kind men in their nice suits, and that lovely smell of silver and alligator wallets."

Irving
Malin

Childish fear has become fashionable alienation. Incomplete exorcisms have become pleasure outings to Tiffany. Capote, in other words, is giving us false religion—one which soothes our souls with glittering generalities. Thus he is "popular"—he can sell this positive stuff to Hollywood.

Or he can write scintillating gossip for *Holiday* and *The New Yorker:* interviews with Marlon Brando—does *he* have a demon?—or travelogues on Ischia or Brooklyn Heights. His gift for dialogue remains; his poetic phrases still have "style." But there is little substance in these essays. Only at rare times does fear enter to save the situation, to reclaim his deep, unwilling involvement. At the end of "A House on the Heights"—even the title is annoying—Capote pictures himself walking past the "turf" of the Cobras:

> Their eyes, their asleep sick insolent eyes swerved on me as I climbed the street. I crossed to the opposite curb; then *knew*, without needing to verify it, that the Cobras had uncoiled and were sliding toward me, I heard them whistling; and the children hushed, the skip-rope ceased swishing. Someone—a pimpled purple birthmark bandit-masked the lower half of his face—said, "Hey yuh, Whitey, lemmeseeduhcamra." Quicken one's step? Pretend not to hear. But every alternative seemed explosive.

The passage presents fear again, without explaining it. (Is he courting attack in this scene?) The rhythms quicken; the style moves—perhaps too decorously. But, ironically enough, Capote ends the essay with his safe return to the pretty house. It would be good to see him outside again, pursued by ominous footsteps—like Sylvia in "Master Misery."

The narrator of *Breakfast at Tiffany's* says at one point: "the average personality reshapes frequently, every few years even our bodies undergo a complete overhaul—desirable or not, it is a natural thing that we should change." I hope that Capote returns to his Gothic muse, especially if he can, once again, worship fear in complex and courageous rituals.

NOVELS

Other Voices, Other Rooms:
Oedipus Between the Covers

MARVIN E. MENGELING

Truman Capote's first and most widely acclaimed novel, *Other Voices, Other Rooms* (1948) germinated in a mind deeply concerned with the power of darkness. Heaped with dreadful psychologies and nightmare terrors, it comes near to resembling a Gothic romance, stylistically nocturnal in the best tradition. It is a complicated work of many motifs, themes and sub-themes, a work which in the fourteen years since its publication has fallen victim to a variety of critical interpretations best described as tenuous.

John Aldridge was the first critic of *Other Voices* to exploit the theme of a boy's search for a father. Aldridge also utilizes, and within limits he is correct, the parallel subtheme of a boy's "struggle to grow out of the dreamworld of childhood and to enter the real world of manhood."[1] More recently, Ihab Hassan has exhumed and labeled the Narcissus theme as being the "central" and "unifying impulse," not only of *Other Voices, Other Rooms,* but of the whole of Capote, literary and personal. Undoubtedly Hassan has dug closest to the primal root of meaning in his detailed elaboration of Joel Harrison Knox's search for "an image which reflects darkly his own identity, his reality."[2] But even Hassan's interpretation is not complete focus. For Hassan, like Aldridge before him, has (with typical critical impatience) clutched a handy sub-theme,[3] has sincerely though mistakenly labeled it the primary theme, and been consequently led into formulating an off-center value judgment concerning the work as a whole.

It is not the intention of this writer to exercise a literary judgment in connection with *Other Voices, Other Rooms.* For the present he will gladly leave this labor to those critics with preconceived literary systems. He does wish, however, to exactly establish the propelling and predominant theme of this novel. For a correct understanding of theme must always precede a correct value

American Imago, 19 (Winter 1962): 361-74.

judgment, and it is just this understanding that has eluded such Capote critics as John Aldridge and Ihab Hassan.

The primary theme of *Other Voices, Other Rooms* is oedipal in nature. Because this is so it would be unduly difficult, if not impossible, to establish the validity of its presence without briefly touching at times upon certain Freudian theories and terms. However, it must be emphasized that the esthetic use of such a theme need not necessitate any knowledge of Freud or Freudian theory on the part of Capote, who has said in the *Paris Review*: "All I want to do is to tell a story and sometimes it is best to choose a symbol. I would not know a Freudian symbol as such if you put it to me."[4] Instead, let it be sufficient to say that Truman Capote, in writing *Other Voices, Other Rooms*, has been consciously or unconsciously interested in the aesthetic possibilities of an archetypal process,[5] and that he has exploited them in one defective way or another depending upon his dramatic purpose.

When the narrative opens Joel Harrison Knox is at the age of puberty, a time, as Freud explains, when the importance of the Oedipus complex has by no means vanished. It is at this time that the sexual instinct asserts its demands with all the strength and intensity of adolescent lust, and the parents, original objects of sexual desire, once more become the love objects of the libido. But to become a loved and loving member of a normal adult society the child must now free himself from his parents (which they help him to do) and discover a foreign object to love, one more sexually acceptable to the developing super-ego. The child must, of course, release his sexual desires from the mother. Seemingly, this break was forced upon Joel at the age of twelve when his mother died of pneumonia. Joel consequently seeks reconciliation and identification with a father he has never seen chiefly in hopes of satisfying the demands of his growing super-ego for guidance. His father, whom in absence Joel has imaginatively deified,[6] he optimistically anticipates will give him the love, guidance, and understanding that had been taken from him with his mother's death. Now it must be the father, Edward Sansom, that guides Joel from the dreamworld of childhood to the adult world of reality.[7]

But Joel's conscious efforts to grow will prove abortive, for he has, in fact, not alienated his ego from the dominance of the dead mother. Instead, he has unconsciously compensated for her loss by establishing a somewhat spurious identification with her.

Because his mother died of pneumonia in a cold, wet, New Orleans January, Joel gradually comes to project her image into the figure of a fairy tale personality, the Snow Queen.[8] Joel first hears the fairy tale "The Snow Queen" shortly after his mother's death but preceding his journey to Skully's Landing, the place where he is to meet his father. . . . Here, in effect, is what later proves to be a justifiable foreboding. For Joel is about to embark upon his own personal journey to the palace of Snow Queen, there to be entombed in a frozen state of oedipal fixation, and no one, not even his father,[9] will "brave robber barons" to effect his rescue. When, for instance, towards the end of the novel Joel dreams of the Cloud Hotel, a decaying manse equivalent in concept to the ice-palace of the Snow Queen, he decides that this "was the place folks came when they went off the face of the earth, when they died but were not dead." And as he dreams of walking through its deserted and dust-filled rooms he realizes that "even here" there is "no father" to claim him. In journeying to meet his father Joel moves away from society (Paradise Chapel) towards isolation and fixation (Skully's Landing, or as the Noon City folk call it, The "Skulls").[10] As he rides through the desolate and lonesome countryside, where "there are luminous green logs that shine under the dark marsh water like drowned corpses," certain "sickening memories" slide through his mind. . . . And even though he considers being sent for by Edward Sansom a "Godlike action" and a "wonderful piece of luck," he feels "dizzy with heat and loss and despair," not being able to keep back his tears when letting his "attention turn inward," as he does in thinking of the dead mother. Joel is approaching the point where it will be beyond his control to direct his attention outward and as the narrative progresses he increasingly seeks to discover the reality of himself in thoughts of the mother. When asked by Zoo Fever, Negro servant at the Landing, whether he had ever seen snow, Joel composes a . . . lie concerning himself, his mother, and her death by snow:

> "It was one stormy night in Canada that I saw the snow," he said, though the farthest north he'd ever set foot was Richmond, Virginia. "We were lost in the mountains, Mother and me, and snow, tons and tons of it, was piling up all around us. . . .
> "Then what happened?" said Missouri, . . .
> "Well, things got worse and worse. Mama cried, . . . and she was always cold. . . ."
> "And?"
> "And a man in a red coat, a Canadian mountie, rescued us . . . only me, really: Mama had already frozen to death."[11]

Further significance is given to this passage when Capote goes on to write: "somehow, spinning the tale, Joel had believed every word; the cave, the howling wolves, these had seemed more real than Missouri and her long neck, or Miss Amy, or the shadowy kitchen." In such wise, though at this point only momentarily, does a prophetic, snow-filled dreamworld connected with the dead mother seem more real and acceptable to Joel than the concrete environment of the Landing.

It is late one afternoon that Joel, while standing in the garden, observes a queer looking lady in one of the windows of the house. He is certain that she is no one he has ever known, though she "brought to mind his own vaporish reflection in the wavy chamber mirror." She has "marshmallow features," wears a powdered wig, and is attired in a flowing white gown. Though Joel is at this point unaware of the fact, this pale apparition is Cousin Randolph. Randolph, in one sense, is the Evil Sprite of the fairy tale, for it is through his perverted teachings that Joel by degrees comes to accept him as the concrete prototype of the Snow Queen, and therefore the image of his mother and the ego of himself. Even now he sees in this strange lady the "vaporish reflection" of his own ego.[12] When the curtain is abruptly drawn and the window is once more empty, Joel, somewhat taken aback, stumbles against a dinner bell used long before to summon slaves from the fields. "One raucous, cracked note" shatters the "hot stillness" in another prophecy of enslavement.

That evening Joel is quick to establish a definite relationship between the Snow Queen and the lady in the window: "twin to the Snow Queen, her face was pale, wintry, carved from ice. . . ."[13] And it is only a few minutes later that Randolph whispers into Joel's ear with a cooing, childlike innocence, "try to be happy here, try a little to like me." Joel, seeing his own round eyes in those of Randolph, somewhat pathetically replies, "I like you already."

Randolph, in partially winning the endorsement of Joel, begins to prepare his ego for the reacceptance of a mother-image as love object of the libido. Joel can have little inkling of the hidden meaning when Randolph says: "Have you never heard what the wise men say; all of the future exists in the past." Neither does Joel fully understand when Randolph cryptically speculates on the regressive path of love along which Joel is being led: the "true beloveds of this world are in their lover's eyes . . . remembered conversations, friends, a child's Sunday, lost voices, one's favorite suit, autumn and all seasons, memory. . . ."[14] Such an observation shows a love of things past, a dedication to the dead and the gone. Additional pertinence can be found in the fact that this observation is made in Randolph's curio-cluttered room, a chamber he refers to in "the warm blood of darkness" as being his "mother's womb."

The second of the novel's three parts opens with what is in effect a climax. Joel, in finding his father little more than a paralytic zombie,[15] a grotesque figure not possibly acceptable as a father, somewhat curbs his last feeble resistances to Randolph and all that Randolph stands for:[16] "Certainly this Mr. Sansom was not his father. This Mr. Sansom was nobody but a pair of crazy eyes." A further curb to his resistances to Randolph ensues when Joel, now without the hope of father guidance, personally experiences the inability to confirm his manhood in relation to the tomboy, Idabel Tompkins. When, for instance, on a fishing expedition he attempts to kiss Idabel, Joel finds himself not only being fought off, but actually overpowered. Another instance in which Joel fails to assert his manhood occurs as he and Idabel are treading through swamplike underbrush on way to the Cloud Hotel, a place where Joel hopes to obtain a magic and protective charm from the hermit conjureman, Little Sunshine. When in attempting to cross a millstream they are suddenly confronted by a dangerous and outsized water moccasin, it is Idabel who must slay the snake, for Joel is frozen with fear. In the eyes of the snake Joel imagines he sees the accusing eyes of his father, the father he finds it impossible to accept. It is in failing such initiation ordeals that Joel is made more eligible to the advances of Randolph.

For a time Joel's primary thought is to escape from the accusing eyes of the father, for he is sure that they know "exactly what went on inside his head." He and Idabel decide to run off. . . .

When the two runaways stop for a time at the Noon City fair Joel meets the wistful midget, Miss Wisteria. Sitting with her on top of the ferris wheel he thinks that perhaps escape is not impossible. But as an angry thunderstorm brews overhead and the crowd disappears into shelter, Joel sees in the sudden emptiness below an apparition of Randolph. Consciously unaware of Randolph's true function Joel believes him to be the "messenger for a pair of telescopic eyes," an envoy sent by the father to drag him back to the Landing. . . . [To] escape those "telescopic eyes," [Joel] seeks refuge in thoughts of the dead mother, the parent for whom Randolph is truly the envoy:

> She was cold, his mother, she passed to sleep with dew of snowflakes scenting her hair; if he could have but thawed open her eyes here now she would be to hold him and say, as he'd said to Randolph, "Everything is going to be all right."

It is at this point that the perceptive reader becomes definitely aware of Joel's fixation, for Joel, as he acknowledges, is unable to place his love in anything other than the image of the dead mother. . . . Joel is now ready to complete the transference of his affective mother fixation to the person of Cousin Randolph.

Part three of the narrative opens with Joel once more at the Landing. Ironically, he is desperately ill with a case of pneumonia. In a state of coma he experiences a prophetic dream of wish-fulfillment, a phantasy of the mother who will return from the grave to find her son and claim him in death. Joel, with a wizard-type magician named Mr. Mystery, is riding over "snowdeep fields" on his way to the palace of the Snow Queen. Suddenly, "an ice-wall rose before them . . . r-r-rip, the ice tore like cellophane, the sleigh slid through into the Landing's parlor." Gathered there, with the exception of the Snow Queen and his mother, is every figure Joel has known or thought about since coming to the Landing. As he watches transfixed, each of the black-clad figures drops an "offering" into a "gladiola-garlanded cedar chest." Joel lies inside the chest clothed in the peculiar fashion of the Snow Queen and the lady of the window. . . . In psychically identifying with the strange lady and the Snow Queen Joel has accepted Randolph as mother substitute: "He did not want any more to be responsible, he wanted to put himself in the hands of his friend, be, as here in the sickbed, dependent upon him for his very life."

Capote, however, seems determined to carry Joel beyond mere fixation to the farther point of sexual consummation. Joel, therefore, must somehow be infused with the psychological strength necessary for him to assume the position of husband, not child, in relation to Randolph, the mother image.

Having sufficiently recovered from the pneumonia Joel agrees to accompany Randolph to the Cloud Hotel, the name of which evokes the vision of "a kind of mist-white palace floating foglike through the woods." Indeed this is a journey that parallels the one of the coma-dream. The Cloud Hotel, a structure where time is frozen in the past, acts somewhat obliquely for Joel as a uniting and invigorating force. Seemingly faithful to the archetype of the descent into Hades, Joel returns to the Landing possessed of a new type of knowledge and strength.[17] He knows now "that he (is) strong," and with a "crazy elation . . . he ran, he zigzagged, he sang, he was in love." Also, for the first time he "saw how helpless Randolph was," and significantly the scene ends with Joel leading Randolph back to the Landing. Thus, during his stay at the Hotel Joel has somehow obtained the strength needed to assume the role of protector and sexual lover to Randolph.

It is in the final scene of *Other Voices, Other Rooms* that the father image, the only remaining check to sexual consummation, is recognized by Joel as symbolically and psychologically slain. Joel, standing in the twilight garden, watches the dark clouds "coming over the sun," and finally, the "meticulous setting of the sun." It is then that he realizes that "Mr. Sansom was the sun." This act of patricide opens the way for Joel's sexual consummation with the mother image, Cousin Randolph, who now appears in the window wearing a flowing white gown suggestive of the Snow Queen:

> She beckoned to him, shining and silver, and he knew he must go: unafraid, not hesitating, he paused only at the garden's edge where, as though he'd forgotten something, he stopped and looked back at the bloomless, descending blue, at the boy he had left behind.

Concerning this final scene Hassan has written: "We are not sure whether it is in triumph or defeat that Joel responds to this mute appeal. We can only sense that the traditional modes of behavior are no longer in command of life."[18] In clarification I suggest that *both* triumph and defeat are inherent in this paradoxical finale. Joel's triumph lies within the framework of the oedipal process and exists in his successful destruction of the father image which had acted as a stigma to the fulfillment of his ego desires. By denying the existence of his father Joel in effect has not only psychically slain him but has also left himself in a position to extend the oedipal process to the point of sexual consummation. But naturally defeat is inherent in, and overweighs, such "bloomless," twisted triumph. For in the process Joel's super-ego (in ironic counterpoint to Sansom's physical paralysis) has been crippled, and must now remain forever retarded and incomplete.

NOTES

1. John W. Aldridge, *After the Lost Generation* (New York: 1958): 203.

2. Ihab Hassan, "The Daydream and Nightmare of Narcissus," *Wisconsin Studies in Contemporary Literature,* I, (Spring-Summer: 1960): 5.

3. The sub-theme chosen is usually the one that will most readily force the novel either into or out of the critic's preconceived system of literary and cultural values.

4. Quoted in Hassan, 7.

5. Freud believed that each individual is born with fragments of a phylogenetic origin, or, in other words, an archaic heritage, not individual and personal, but applying to all mankind collectively. This archaic heritage includes certain dispositions, ideational contents, and memory traces of the experiences of former, primordial generations. In an abbreviated form, each individual undergoes in his psychological development a reiteration of the more meaningful events of a process so ancient that it occurred in the dawn of history. The process is Freud's scientific myth of the father-dominated, primal horde, original root of the oedipal archetype.

   Further details of this theory may be found in Sigmund Freud, *Totem and Taboo,* authorized translation with an introduction by A. A. Brill, (New York: 1918).

6. By deifying his father Joel has equated Edward Sansom with God-the-Father and all the masculine, authoritarian symbols (lightening, thunder, the sun, etc.) usually associated with such an image. In a manner of speaking, Joel is asking divine providence to guide him through the initiation rites connected with manhood, individualization, and discovery of the Self.

7. In this mode the literal theme of a boy's search for a father parallels the underlying, though primary, theme of a boy falling prey to an oedipal fixation.

8. It is for this reason that Joel, when subsequently thinking of the mother-image, invariably connects it with snow, ice, and the color white.

9. Already Joel feels that he is falling prey to some nebulous, demon-type spell because he is unable to dispel the anxiety brought to bear by the oedipal conflict. Because he is incapable of understanding the true origin and nature of this anxiety he ascribes its most painful aspects to external, non-human types (e.g., demons, wizards, his deified father, a malevolent God) that for some inexplicable reason have the will to do him harm. The fact that he includes Edward Sansom and God-the-Father within this group of external types is evidence of the fact that his attitude toward the father is ambivalent, and can be seen in such statements as the following: "Joel didn't much like God, for He had betrayed him too many times." Or: "He believed there was conspiracy abroad, even his father had a grudge against him, even God. Somewhere along the line he's been played a mean trick. Only he didn't know who or what to blame."

10. To show this shift Capote also utilizes the transitional metaphor of daylight into darkness. This same metaphor, to give another example, is used in the final scene of the narrative.

11. In passing, it is interesting to note that the female genitals are often symbolically represented in dreams (though Joel is not in this instance dreaming) as being a cave. The male genitals, on the other hand, are often represented by mountains. On a less unconscious level, the "ice-cold cave" in which Joel is for a time imaginatively

imprisoned acts as a poorly disguised version of the Snow Queen's ice palace. The tacked on reference to the "Canadian mountie" obviously acts as the idealized father-image whom Joel desires to effect his rescue and give him guidance.

12. It is in this way that the Narcissus sub-theme, as outlined by Ihab Hassan, parallels the primary theme.

13. This passage is interesting not only because of the Randolph-Snow Queen relationship, but because of the "wedding cake" image which foreshadows the symbolic marriage of Joel and Randolph at the end of the novel.

14. Once again it is interesting to note that such things as lilacs, ships, bells, and landscapes are primary dream symbols that represent the female genitals.

15. By a simple inversion of the letters n and m in the name Sansom we arrive at the name Samson, a biblical hero shorn of his strength by the hands of a woman. The ineffective Edward Sansom was shorn of his strength to act as a true father by the hands of the effeminate, homoerotic, Randolph.

16. Among other things, Randolph stands for homosexuality, though this is on the most literal level of the book's meaning. It is because Randolph must assume the role of mother-wife to Joel that Capote finds it of dramatic necessity for Randolph to be of the effeminate variety.

17. It is during this stay at the Cloud Hotel that the mule John Brown (acting here as a symbolic and sterile counterpart to the father, Edward Sansom) accidentally hangs itself.

18. The John Brown of historical fame had tried unsuccessfully to free the slaves and was hung for his efforts.

19. Hassan, 12.

A Blizzard of Butterflies

H. P. LAZARUS

The imitation of the real thing is always more popular than the real thing, and Mr. Capote's new novel exhibits once again how the imitator becomes the imitation. This particular form of purveyance to popular taste occurs when the real thing no longer exists. Here it is the small town, the characters that are characters, the folksy humor, and the tall story made to order for a class of readers who can well afford such sophisticated luxuries. Since Mr. Capote is aware that recreation of the small town is now largely a matter of sentimental archaeology, he exploits even its deadness by serving it up as a dream. *The Grass Harp* is the end of a long and sturdier line. From Main Street to a tree house the descent is upward, and the dream is the greater luxury.

The tree dwellers are a sixteen-year-old orphan boy, Collin, through whose older but still innocent "I" the story is told, an old lady cousin, Dolly, "whose presence is a delicate happening," and Catherine Creek, an old Negro who thinks she is an Indian and calls Dolly, Dollyheart. They are in the tree house to escape from Dollyheart's masculated sister Verena, whom Catherine calls That One and who is mean, although she doesn't mean to be mean, because, with a little help, she too finally climbs up. The three are joined by Judge Cool, a transcendentalist papa whose "chain of love" embraces Dolly, and by Riley Henderson, a wild boy who doesn't want to be wild and succeeds. Under the tree stalks authority, represented by the two bad men, Reverend Buster and the Sheriff, who are given a slapstick beating. In addition there is a goodly assortment of homespun types like Sister Ida, a revivalist with fifteen illegitimate children and a story, the Katydid bakery woman, a cute little fairy barber, and Dr. Morris Ritz, a city slicker. Except for the Sheriff and the Reverend, all these folks—and others with only walk-on parts—have good hearts.

The Nation, 173 (1 December 1951): 482.

In the old days such wretched or eccentric characters were not endowed with the local color of a good heart. Now Dolly is *civilized* by her own private world, and this really astounding process of civilization is nullified by the every now and then impinging cruel world. The patriarchal Judge's "No matter what passions compose them, all private worlds are good, they are never vulgar places," is where, presumably, we have arrived. A very public statement, it is addressed to those who, seeing the tree from their own superior point of view, can indulge in the private world and the good heart as the refreshments of good society. Of course the credo need not be taken seriously even in its own terms. The isolation of the tree dwellers is made palatable by being pitched in a dreamlike key. Like the precious "deepdown ownself part of you," it has only a sentimental currency.

Mr. Capote's reading includes Huck Finn and Carson McCullers, and he is knowing enough about the American themes of innocence and the good heart to exploit them. But the ingredients are stale even if they are more than ever pre-digested, dished up with cuteness and a fine artificial flavor equal to the exactions of the most up-to-date reader of women's magazines, spiced with delicate indelicacies, and served with sensibility. He is best in the creation of moods of suspended animation during the progression of which the tree dwellers are united in a hazy undetermined state which dissolves them into a twittering oblivion—"a blizzard of butterflies." And the relationship between the boys is convincing because he lets it alone.

Certainly Mr. Capote has abused what talent he has—and, perhaps, his own fans—in the crassest manner. No one knows better than he that he has come a long way from the tree house.

Birth of a Heroine

IHAB H. HASSAN

For ten or fifteen years now some critics of the novel have been going around, like Diogenes, with a lamp in their hand looking for a good novelist in the broad light of day, and some, like John the Baptist, have been crying aloud in the wilderness. This is well: death and taxes take their toll, the Cold War is still on, critics quarrel with themselves, and who does not yet know that ours is an age of organized conformity? But there is a "new" type of hero born to American fiction, and whether we call him saint or criminal, rebel or victim, rogue or picaro, his heart, though not entirely pure, is in its place. The moment, it seems, has found the character to embody its absurdities and crazy yearnings.

All of which brings us to Holly Golightly, the heroine of Capote's latest novella, *Breakfast at Tiffany's*. Holly may remind some people of Salinger's Holden Caulfield, Bellow's Augie March, or even Kerouac's ragged collection of holy bums. But we had better let Holly remind us of Joel Knox, the protagonist of Capote's first novel, *Other Voices, Other Rooms*, or of no one at all. For in a real sense the story of Capote—and, incidentally, of a good part of contemporary fiction—can be told by following the transformation of one type of personage into the other. It is a story, of course, that requires a preamble.

Capote has two styles, two moods, which he uses within the ambit of romance, that form so ably defined by Richard Chase as possessing "a formal abstractness," véering more freely towards "the mythic, allegorical, and symbolistic" modes, and rather prone to "ignore the spectacle of man in society." Of the two styles one may be called "nocturnal," the other "daylight." The nocturnal style makes the greater use of dream imagery, uncanny trappings, supernatural motifs; it is shot through with the sense of underlying dreadfulness, and reveals to characters the disintegration of their psyche in "the instant of petrified violence." In "Miriam," "Shut a Final Door," "A Tree of Night," "The Headless Hawk," and *Other Voices, Other Rooms* what the characters seek, like

Prairie Schooner, 34 (Spring 1960): 78-83.

a dark Narcissus, is the most secret knowledge of their *identity*. But if the supernatural defines the nocturnal mode of Capote, humor defines his daylight style. The style, evident in "My Side of the Matter," "Jug of Silver," "Children on Their Birthdays," and *The Grass Harp*, assumes the chatty, first-person informality of anecdotes. It specifies character and admits the busy-ness of social relations more than its darker counterpart. And the scene which it lights upon is usually the small Southern town, not the big city which witnesses in abstract horror the so-called alienation of man from his environment. In the daylight mood, the characters break through the circle of autism and introspection in a broad gesture of *love*—compare Joel's moment of hallucinatory self-revelation at the Cloud Hotel with Collin's humorous, nostalgic, and loving recognition as he remembers Sister Ida and her thirteen children cavorting in a sunny stream. Capote's latest creation, however, goes still farther than the retrospective Collin, who confesses that his life seems more like "a series of closed circles, rings that do not evolve with the freedom of the spiral. . . ."

With *Breakfast at Tiffany's*, the closed rings begin to evolve into a spiral, some open and continuous motion of the heroine's spirit, Miss Holiday Golightly, Traveling, as her Tiffany cards insist. But whether the driving motion of a spiral, so endless and implacable, possesses more freedom than a circle affords is a conundrum only Euclid may solve.

Holly, like Capote's other protagonists, is not yet out of her teens: "It was a face beyond childhood, yet this side of belonging to a woman." But her initiation began long ago, before she becomes the child-bride, at fourteen, of Doc Golightly, a horse doctor in Tulip, Texas; begun, probably, when she lost father and mother and was dumped with her brother Fred, half starved, on "various mean people." The process of that initiation remains secret—there are intimations of outrage and misery beyond a child's endurance—for Holly behaves as if past and future were no more substantial than the air she breathes; but its results are none the less permanent: a wild and homeless love of freedom. When we see her during the war years in that New York brownstone of the East Seventies, she is fully nineteen, and she strikes us as an improbable combination of the *picaro*, the courtesan, and the *poète maudit*.

Improbability is indeed the quality she uses to criticize a dreary and truthless round of existence, and artifice—she is an inspired liar—to transform it. "I'll never get used to anything. Anybody who does, they might as well be dead," she cries at one point, and we realize that her rebellion against the *given* in life, the useful and prudential, is one of the sources of her vitality. It is as her dwarfish friend and Hollywood agent puts it, the "kid" is a "*real* phony," and her specialty is presenting "horseshit on a platter." Screwball, phony, or saint— some will find it more convenient simply to say "sick, sick, sick"—it does not take us very long to recognize Holly's hold on experience. Her "philosophy" is quite elementary—and hopelessly at odds with the times. "I don't mean I'd mind being rich and famous," she tells the narrator. "That's very much on my schedule, and some day I'll try to get around to it; but if it happens, I'd like to have my ego tagging along. I want to still be me when I wake up one fine morning and have breakfast at Tiffany's." When Holly's dream comes true—the vision symbolized by the "*ordre, luxe, et volupté*" of Tiffany's which she employs to cure her spells of "the mean reds"—she wants to be no other than herself. Implied here is no revulsion against one's identity, no holy surrender or unattachment. Holly is in fact very much attached to this world, and therefore to herself. In this respect, she seems the opposite of Salinger's Holden Caulfied with whom she shares the quixotic gift of truth, and shares the ability to gamble everything on a wayward love for, say, Man O'War—Holden's ducks in Central Park—or her brother Fred—Holden's sister, Phoebe. But also unlike Holden, whose stringent idealism limits the scope of his *joy,* Holly's truth refers to no self-transcending ideal. As she candidly admits:

> Good? Honest is more what I mean. Not law-type honest—I'd rob a grave, I'd steal two-bits off a dead man's eyes if I thought it would contribute to the days enjoyment—but unto-thyself-type honest. Be anything but a coward, a pretender, an emotional crook, a whore: I'd rather have cancer than a dishonest heart.

Her loyalty to others—the inmate Sally Tomato, for instance—is a loyalty to her own feelings for which she is willing to risk all.

Morality, we see, is defined in the privacy of the passing moment. But as the phantasmal vision of young Knox was followed, in Capote's novels, by the elegiac insight of a more mature Fenwick, so does the latter give way to Holly's sustaining faith in the honesty of the heart. The last allows Capote's heroine to implicate herself in a wider range of experience than her predecessors could encompass; it permits her to check her code against the play of reality in a manner Knox and Fenwick would have been powerless to command. But the crazy valor of Holly does not prevent her from carrying the customary burden of pain; the price of unorthodoxy, the intensity of her involvement with life, is fully paid. In this she is not unlike the hipster whose badge, the dark glasses, she constantly wears. Holly has no possessions other than the moment requires—she is "camping out" in New York. Like the ugly tomcat she picks up by the river one day, her existence is thoroughly improvised: "I don't want to own anything until I know I've found the place where me and things belong together." And like a wild thing she lives in the open sky; but she knows, too, that "it's better to look at the sky than live there. Such an empty place; so vague. Just a country where the thunder goes and things disappear." When her beloved brother, Fred, dies in the war—her brave soul goes berserk, the jaunty dark glasses are shattered, and her true piteous human nakedness is revealed—when her Brazilian lover abandons her pregnant, when she becomes involved in a narcotics scandal and the friends who fed on her emotional bounty desert her, when she jumps bail and takes off for Latin America, and thence to darkest Africa, the defiant spiral of her life, swirling into the unknown, leaves us breathless and afraid that so much light can diffuse itself into darkness, that such brave exuberance could be the product of greater desperation. And indeed Holly herself becomes afraid. On her way to the airport she stops in Spanish Harlem to let "her" cat off, admonishing it in a scene frankly sentimental to find a proper home for itself. Then she breaks down: "I'm very scared, Buster. Yes, at last. Because it could go on forever. Not knowing what's yours until you've thrown it away."

Holly Golightly may be what we should all like to become if we could put away comfort and respectability in an insured bank account; and her breezy excesses of fancy as of intuition may be, again, just what our stuffy age most requires. In her case the misfit hero certainly shows a fitting genius for *living*— rebellion here is secondary, spontaneous. But Capote himself is not entirely taken in by Holly's verve and piercing glitter. His tale, though lovingly told, has wit and sharp precision. As Holly sweeps through her zany adventures, one becomes conscious of a groundswell of gentle criticism. Mildred Grossman, the grind whom the narrator recalls from his schooldays, may be a "top-heavy realist," but Holly by the same token must be considered a "lop-sided romantic"; and antithetical as the two girls seem, both "walk through life and out of it with the same determined step that took small notice of those cliffs at the left." Even Holly's incorrigible tomcat finds at last a home with potted palms and lace curtains, a home and a name; but for Holly the narrator can only pray that she may be granted, sometime, somewhere, the grace of knowledge and repose. Narcissus found both in a reflected image; Holly, whimsical child of old Faust, looks for them beyond a vanishing horizon. For Holly—sooner or later we must say it—is a child too. She is premature in ways both delightful and regressive. (The latest avatar of Capote's Wizard Man is the "fat woman" who haunts Holly's "red nightmares," threatening to inflict punishment, withhold love, or destroy everything high and rare). But does not childhood itself, to which adults wend back in such tortuous ways, present a criticism of maturity for which we seldom have a ready answer?

Criticism, the interplay of views, is sustained by right form. The form of *Breakfast at Tiffany's* approaches perfection. It has pace, narrative excitement, a firm and subtle hold on the sequence of events from the first backward glance to the final salutation. A novelette in scope, it still manages to treat a subject usually accorded the fuller scope of the picaresque novel with marvelous selectivity. The point of view, the tone, the style herald no technical discoveries in the field of fiction: they simply blend to make the subject spring to life. Capote allows the story to be told in the first person by a struggling young writer whose vantage of perception, now in the shadow, now in the light, captures the elusive figure of Holly with the aid of such minor figures as Joe Bell and O. J. Berman. The device is both revealing and discreet, for there is, no doubt, something about Holly's complexion that cannot bear too sharp a light. By establishing the right relation between his narrator and subject, Capote also strikes the right tone. For though the whole story is unfolded backwards in one sweeping flashback, the tone is not, like *The Grass Harp's*, elegiac. Elegy, where so much hope is called to question, is out of place. The tone comes closer to that of an invocation, a blessing: hail, Holly, and farewell. Criticism, as we have noted, is implied, patronage never. What keeps the tone from becoming patronizing—look at that wonderful spoiled child!—is the style. The style matches the exotic quality of the subject with its clear-headedness, matches whimsy with wit, though here and there, as in the description of the cat, Capote indulges himself in a superfluous flourish of imagery. Holly's lack of self-criticism is balanced by the searching temper of the narrator. Tension and control are maintained. This is evident in the most casual bit of description. Here is one of Holly:

> She was still on the stairs, now she reached the landing, and the ragbag colors of her boy's hair, tawny streaks, strands of albino-blond and yellow, caught the hall light. It was a warm evening, nearly summer, and she wore a slim cool black dress, black sandals, a pearl choker. For all her chic thinness, she had an almost breakfast-cereal air of health, a soap and lemon cleanness, a rough pink darkening in the cheeks. Her mouth was large, her nose upturned. A pair of dark glasses blotted out her eyes.

Holly Golightly will remind a good many readers of Isherwood's Sally Bowles, and remind the greater community of movie-goers of Julie Harris's fine rendition of that role. But it is not chauvinism, we hope, that compels us to recognize her peculiarly American quality: her quixotic ideas of hope, sincerity, truth. (Sally may or may not have stood up for the gangster Tomato, while Holly could not have done otherwise.) Though Holly's life is completely open-ended, and her "initiation," once again, brings with it no confirmation or knowledge— neither does it bring nostalgia—it is a life, like Verena's, that leaves behind it a trail of love and affection. Secret doors, which might have remained forever closed, are unlocked where she passes, and even savages commemorate her presence in carved images. She is in this, we see, like other heroes of contemporary fiction, scapegoats and liberators all, and if we refuse to emulate them or accept their painful destiny, noting in our wisdom their shortcomings, we cannot in good conscience ignore the truth their proud fate so urgently implies.

Breakfast at Tiffany's happens also to include three short stories earlier published in magazines. The best one can say of them is that they have great charm and that they represent a livelier awareness of interpersonal relations, a more open concern with people, than some of Capote's earlier, and perhaps better, stories showed. Some will feel that "A Diamond Guitar" owes much to

Carson McCullers—the tense style and the doctrine of love are hers—and others that "House of Flowers," which sustained the frills and trills of a Broadway musical, discovers no new aspect of Capote's imagination, an imagination that the fairly autobiographical sketch, "A Christmas Memory," helps us understand.

It is the novelette itself that gives new shape to the emergent pattern of Capote's work, a pattern, as we said, that reflects the central concerns of contemporary fiction. For as Joel, Collin, and Holly stand for knowledge through dream, love, and free action, they also represent typical attitudes struck in the post-war novel. Joel embodies the current feeling that our world is now discovered, our life organized, our vision confined to some lost room of childhood. The only freedom we still possess is the freedom to dream, and as reality becomes more intractable our dreams become compulsive. Collin Fenwick, in his nostalgic and backward glance, expresses the need to redeem the present, to redeem reality through love, a need to which the contemporary novel is intensely dedicated. As for Holly, she approaches the ideal of the new picaresque, the free-wheeling hero who insists on the freedom to experience and to denounce precisely because that freedom is no longer tolerated by society. In all cases, the American hero, equally so much more innocent *and* experienced than of yore, remains an outsider, a fugitive from the dominant concerns of American life, hiding in secret rooms or up a chinaberry tree, or still "lighting out for the territory ahead," which is now situated in Africa.

A Final Door

TERRENCE RAFFERTY

Truman Capote's *Answered Prayers: The Unfinished Novel* (Random House; $16.95) is an enigma and a ruin. Like the mysterious house at Skully's Landing in Capote's first novel, *Other Voices, Other Rooms*, this shattered, forlorn thing teases the imagination by suggesting that there's more—much more—in it than we've been allowed to see. The unfinished novel, no less than the haunted house, invites us to give body to the dispersed, unfulfilled spirits we sense there. "Answered Prayers" had achieved its spectral aura long before the author's death, in 1984, doomed it to eternal formlessness. In what was, as far as we can tell, its original conception, the novel was to illuminate the shadowy world of what were once called "the beautiful people" in a style that would re-create, in a heightened, poetic way, the texture of gossip—that art of secrets, half-truths, and rumors by which these fabulous creatures narrate themselves. And almost from the moment he signed the contract, in 1966, Capote started spinning that feathery stuff around his own work, mystifying it thoroughly, as if the mystification were the art itself. In a way, it was.

In interviews and essays Capote gossiped about his book—before even a word of it had been written—in hushed, solemn tones: it would be Proustian, immense ("triple the length of all my other books combined," he wrote in 1972), the work he meant to be remembered by. After briefly exposing the work in progress, publishing four tantalizing chapters in *Esquire* in 1975 and 1976, he returned to whispering about it, embellishing the myth of a masterpiece struggling into being. He wrote of a "creative crisis" following the appearance of the *Esquire* excerpts, a spasm of doubt which "altered my entire comprehension of writing, my attitude toward art and life and the balance between the two, and my understanding of the difference between what is true and what is *really* true," and which, he claimed, prompted him to rewrite two chapters of "Answered Prayers" and drop another ("Mojave," the first of the *Esquire* chapters); he

The New Yorker (21 September 1987): 113-119.

presented his next book, *Music for Chameleons*, which was a ragged miscellany of semi-factual pieces, as the result of and a preview of the breakthrough that would be "Answered Prayers." Throughout, he kept dropping hints about chapters and passages completed, and a master plan that would justify everything: he'd show us where the treasure was when he was good and ready, and we would know that he'd had the map all along.

But there's no more to "Answered Prayers" now than there was in 1976—no new chapters, no revisions, just three fragments about which nothing has changed in eleven years except the form of their publication. Like the creepy Southern mansion in Capote's first novel, this final project, for all its air of mystery, seems merely to have got stuck in time, arrested at a shockingly early stage of development. There were never any more rooms in Capote's house of gossip, and its voices, though they all have different tales to tell, are curiously identical—conspiratorial but desperately weary, like the Landing's effete Cousin Randolph, whose great secret is that he doesn't really exist: "Faceted as a fly's eye, being neither man nor woman, and one whose every identity canceled the other, a grab-bag of disguises, who, what was Randolph? X, an outline in which with crayon you color in the character, the ideal hero: whatever his role, it is pitched by you into existence. Indeed, try to conceive of him alone, unseen, unheard, and he becomes invisible, he is not to be imagined." The Capote of "Answered Prayers" is that vaporous: trying to produce a true self-portrait, he seems terribly alone, unable to imagine himself. Maybe that's why he expended so much energy in babbling provocative nonsense about the book: the lies and feints and teases were his grab bag of poltergeist tricks, ways of pricking our imaginations so that we might, somehow, pitch him back into existence.

"Answered Prayers" was, after all, the one book of Capote's long and varied career which required genuine self-knowledge, not only because it was intended to be "*really* true"—it was based on the author's personal letters, diaries, and journals from more than twenty years of his life—but also because, formally, the material was too scattered and ephemeral to survive without a fully articulated identity at its center. Capote, who always had a sure sense of structure, clearly knew this. (He once described the book as "like a wheel with a dozen spokes.") It's also clear that he was looking, against all his instincts as an artist, for ways to get around it. The first section he published in *Esquire*, "Mojave" (which ultimately appeared as part of *Music for Chameleons*), was a bleak little anecdote, written in the third person, about an affluent bad marriage. The author claimed that "Mojave" had been intended to appear in "Answered Prayers" as a short story written by the book's narrator, but there's no good reason to believe that; it's more likely that the story is a remnant of an early, discarded approach to the novel. The second excerpt, "La Côte Basque," reads like another failed stab at finding the novel's form and voice—a better try, though still tentative, guarded. There's a narrator now, who has a name, Jonesy, but no personality: the character is purely a listener, a recorder of gossip. Without a strong central consciousness, this section—the one that got Capote into trouble with his society friends—is weightless, insubstantial, at best a tour de force of bitchy remarks, name-dropping, and scurrilous tales overheard in the course of a long lunch at a fashionable Manhattan restaurant. It's entirely a technical exercise, enlivened only (and mildly) by the author's evident delight in being naughty, and Capote must have sensed that something was missing—that the spirit was somehow wrong, and that the artful orchestration of gossip would never, in itself, amount to much in the ambitious aesthetic terms he'd set for himself. Lunch at La Côte Basque in 1965 is a meaner-spirited affair than *Breakfast at Tiffany's* in the innocent fifties; middle-aged ladies, crusted with jewels and spite, referring to each other as "bull dykes" and "tramps," just don't lend themselves to the sort of graceful, delicate literary effects that Capote brought off so effortlessly in his novella about the buoyant young gold-digger Holly Golightly.

The gorgons and icy mannequins who munch and dish their way through "La Côte Basque" may represent the kind of people Capote hung around with. They aren't, however, the kind his fiction was usually about. The subjects of his early work were typically outcasts, losers, children, and the childlike old—rarely safe, settled adults who knew their place in society (much less Society). Capote, with a defensive, belligerent sense of his own freakishness, seems to have believed always that the only identity lies in the imagination and that only those outside society could develop their imaginative powers freely. That's an awfully romantic view—most baldly expressed in Capote's fablelike second novel, *The Grass Harp*, in which a motley handful of dreamers and eccentrics gather in a tree house to escape the pressures of conforming to their small town's respectable life—and a particularly useful one for someone who defined himself as a writer of fiction, an imaginative artist, from early childhood, as Capote apparently did. By all accounts, his adolescent dedication to mastering literary technique was intense, and it was certainly successful. His earliest stories, published when he was just twenty-one, are almost oppressively perfect: they glitter with the vanity of a fully achieved identity, a vindicated self, and have no content. What he had, really, was an identity that was based on his skill at manipulating forms and was, in a sense, itself purely formal: he was the very image of the craftsman-like writer, forties style.

Capote's investment in technique, in the varieties of literary play, was so great that he didn't even notice when bits of another, more essential self started creeping in, haunting his work. Twenty years after *Other Voices, Other Rooms,* he wrote of the novel, "I was not aware, except for a few incidents and descriptions, of its being in any serious degree autobiographical. Re-reading it now, I find such self-deception unpardonable." He may not have been aware, either, that the stories he was writing in this period revealed him, too. The protagonists of the unsettling horror stories "The Headless Hawk," "Shut a Final

Door," and "Master Misery" are all adults, with homes, acquaintances, and jobs, who are routed from their normal lives by the recognition of a void in themselves. A woman sells her dreams and, unable to get them back, wanders the streets like a displaced person, with "nothing left to steal"; an advertising executive, forced into introspection by a callous blunder and a series of ghostly anonymous phone calls that always say "You know me," discovers that "he did not know where to begin thinking about himself, did not know where to find the center." And they're all, like Cousin Randolph, nightmare images of selves whose forms have been eroded by time, whose spirits have scattered like pieces of broken dolls because they had no core, nothing inside strong enough to bind them.

This core is precisely what "La Côte Basque" lacks; it might have been written by the vacant, aimless adman of "Shut a Final Door." Perhaps Capote recognized at this point that he'd better find the center fast—at least for aesthetic reasons—and that it had better be himself. In the next section to appear, "Unspoiled Monsters" (intended as the first chapter, and printed that way in the current volume), the narrator Jonesy has become P. B. Jones, and this time he's a real presence: the character is mercilessly, even masochistically, detailed—pinned down like a laboratory frog. Jones is a minor writer who slept and groveled his way to a small early success—the publication of a book of stories called "Answered Prayers"—and has since descended, in the absence of either the inspiration or the acclaim to sustain his writing, into a restless life of hobnobbing with the rich and, when the need arises, selling them whatever services they imagine he can provide. Living at the Y, trying to write a novel (also to be called "Answered Prayers") that will give his wasted life the justifying form of art, and venturing out only to peddle his body through an escort service presided over by a woman named Miss Self, Jones indulges in some pretty fancy self-loathing. He admits immediately to having a "numbed, opportunistic nature" and, from then on, seizes every opportunity to elaborate: "I was a kind of Hershey Bar whore—there wasn't much I wouldn't do for a nickel's worth of chocolate"; "I thought of myself as a serious young man seriously gifted, not an opportunistic layabout, an emotional crook who had drilled Miss Langman till she geysered Guggenheims. I knew I was a bastard but forgave myself because, after all, I was a *born* bastard—a talented one whose sole obligation was to his talent"; "I am cowardly—in the frivolous sense and also the most serious; I can never be more than moderately truthful about my feelings toward another person, and I will say yes when I mean no"; "You're a loser, an asshole dumb drunk loser, P.B. Jones"; "I am a whore and always have been." This is *some* center: Jones's self-disgusted voice gathers the ephemeral, unrelated anecdotes and nasty one-liners of a lifetime into a tight package of hopelessness, a gossip column in the form of a lament.

"Unspoiled Monsters" and the next chapter, "Kate McCloud," which is in the same style, are probably the clearest indication of what a full "Answered

Prayers" would have been like: it would have been unbearable, even at a lot less than triple the length of all Capote's works. Its stillborn state is a mercy, both to its author and to us. By the time he got to "Unspoiled Monsters," he had obviously exhausted most of his literary tricks, had abandoned the subterfuge of journalistic objectivity (perhaps because, with *In Cold Blood,* he had produced a piece of third-person reportage of unsurpassable formal perfection), had shut all the doors that might have allowed him to escape himself and his (to him) only true identity, as a writer of fiction. This was, after all, a man who insisted that *In Cold Blood* was a "nonfiction novel"; who wrote of "The Muses Are Heard," his 1956 account of an American company performing "Porgy and Bess" in Russia, "I imagined it as a brief comic novel"; who even called the casual nonfiction doodles in *Music for Chameleons* "short stories." Most of his readers undoubtedly didn't care; but Capote often seemed obsessed with giving everything he wrote the holy name of fiction, as if he needed to justify himself. We can feel his panic in the pages that remain of "Answered Prayers," the only serious fiction he addressed himself to in the last two decades of his life, as he searches for an identity distinct from his previous ones as pristine romantic stylist and cold, dead-accurate reporter, because neither of them would serve. The style he found in "Unspoiled Monsters" is raw, self-pitying, and typically hyperbolic. In "creative crisis," he O.D.s on the vanity of human wishes. He's telling us that he has always been a whore, that *everyone's* a whore; that his works are dust, transitory as gossip; that the self is fiction, of the meanest, emptiest, most trivial kind; and that the glorious, redemptive fiction he once staked his life on is heartbreakingly unapproachable, a mythical form, a monster like the chimera.

There is no more depressing portrait of an artist struggling with his limitations than this. It's too extreme to be convincing, but it seems to have convinced the artist himself—probably because, in an eerie way, the writing of "Answered Prayers" was a fulfillment of his early fiction's prophecies of the terrifying emptiness of maturity. It must have seemed to him that his work and his life had described a circle whose center he'd never seen. In a sense, this is true. "Answered Prayers" provides ample evidence of diminished skills and coarsened spirit—nothing left to steal, even from himself. But there's something rather brave in this nightmare self-imagining, even if part of its intent is to spur us to argument, to make us tell him that it isn't so. He always claimed that he had written the final chapter of "Answered Prayers" first (though no one ever saw it), and that it was "a genuinely happy ending": he had at least imagined the redemption of all the pain and waste and ignorance and despair in this book of his life, some ultimate vindication. In an introductory note to this volume, Joseph M. Fox, who was Capote's editor at Random House, speculates, not very productively, about whether Capote had ever written the last chapter (along with others he'd spoken of) or had written and then destroyed it. All that matters is that he didn't leave it in this world—as if, with the peculiar integrity of despair, he could not finally utter what the experience of writing "Answered Prayers" had caused him no longer to believe. It's terrifying that a writer so gifted could suffer such a failure, but oddly heartening that Capote, at the end, refused to fake it, as he surely could have—as he *would* have—in his confident youth. In what he omitted from "Answered Prayers" Capote, for once, stayed true to his spirit—bleak and bitter as it had become—and shut the final door on his easy mastery of technique. He just turned into Cousin Randolph and disappeared, and "Answered Prayers," broken, with cold winds howling through its deserted rooms, achieved its inevitable, its perfect form.

III

FACT INTO FICTION

Capote's Crime and Punishment

DIANA TRILLING

One can dispose quickly enough of the issue Truman Capote has himself made salient in discussion of his book—*In Cold Blood* is not a novel, as Mr. Capote would have us think; it is "only" a book, a work of journalism of an exceptionally compelling kind. Whatever else it may or may not be, the novel is a literary form in which the writer is free to make any use he wishes of material drawn from real life. It was Mr. Capote's decision to stay wholly with the facts of the Clutter murders; in their presentation he employs various strategies learned in his practice of fiction. This does not mean he has discovered a new fiction form nor—for that matter—a new form of nonfiction. Works of autobiography such as Isak Dinesen's *Out of Africa,* works of history such as Cecil Woodham Smith's *The Reason Why,* works of journalism like James Agee's *Let Us Now Praise Famous Men* are all at least as close to, or far from, proposing a new nonfiction form as Mr. Capote's *In Cold Blood.*

Indeed, a comparison of Truman Capote's report on the Clutter murders with James Agee's report on the condition of the sharecroppers during the Depression is useful in demonstrating some of the accomplishments, but more of the shortcomings, of *In Cold Blood* even as a work of nonfiction. That Mr. Capote's prose is flaccid, often downright inept, and that his narrative is overmanipulated in order to keep things at a constant high pitch of suspense: these are defects apparent without reference to Agee's uncommon talent. But it is in the difference in their approaches to the journalistic enterprise that comparison makes its sharp—but not simple—point.

Let Us Now Praise Famous Men was conceived not in loyalty to fact but in its author's loyalty to himself as an artist; which is to say, in the interplay between the actuality on which Agee had undertaken to report and his own sensibility. Just as Mr. Capote went West for *The New Yorker,* Agee had gone South on commission from *Fortune* magazine. But Agee's "assignment" had at once

Partisan Review, 33 (Spring 1966): 252-59.

yielded in importance (perhaps perversely, but this is of only tangential, chiefly biographical, interest) before the imaginative possibilities of the material which presented itself to him. He comprehended only subjectively the world he had set out to describe—in splendid lyrical bursts, he castigated, and eventually celebrated, himself for being a well-fed man, a middle-class man, a writer (of all improbable human apparitions!) daring to spy upon lives this remote from his own. It turned out that this subjectivity was so intense that it largely dominated the object under investigation; *Let Us Now Praise Famous Men* implicates us much more with its author than with the sharecroppers. Its bias also distorted the social actuality on which Agee was supposed to be reporting—surely people are not, as *Let Us Now Praise Famous Men* would have it, innocent in proportion as they are miserable and poor, nor can one readily suppose that sharecroppers are the superlative instance of humankind that Agee, in his impulse to self-abasement before suffering, makes them out to be. Nevertheless, by licensing his consciousness to prevail over external fact, Agee was able to create an artistic reality, that of his own felt experience. His book intensified our capacity to feel acutely about something, if not about sharecroppers.

Truman Capote's method is exactly the opposite. It was Mr. Capote's decision to report the Clutter case wholly objectively, in as much as possible of its manifest social and personal complication, and to give us both the Clutter family and their murderers without permitting himself any partisanship to either of the extreme oppositions embodied in the two sets of characters. Now on first glance this seems an acceptable enough intention. But, not too surprisingly, it develops that in his submission to actuality, or factuality, and his abrogation of the artist's right to emphasize or even to suppress or distort reality for his own purposes, Mr. Capote prepared for himself an almost inevitable artistic defeat. The neutrality of his posture announces itself even in his prose, whose indistinctiveness is of a sort with which we are familiar in popular writing, where communication is believed to be impeded rather than created by an author's presence on his page. The social object of Mr. Capote's investigation remains intact. And the dramatic impact of his story is not diminished by the impersonality of his approach. On the contrary, it is reinforced, but this only makes for a sensationalism proportionate to the horror of the actual events which are being described. The overtones of *In Cold Blood*—if, in a book so lacking in literary resonance, we can call them that—are those of a socially, well-documented story of crime and detection, not of a work of the imagination.

Still, even as we admit the inadequacy of *In Cold Blood* as a work of literary art, it is hard for us to suppose that this alone would account for the large, odd, often unformulable, reservations which so many different kinds of readers have about it. These seem to me to be reservations of a moral, or "human," more than of an esthetic nature, and they derive, I think, from Mr. Capote's stance as the wholly neutral reporter of facts-from-life which, while themselves so highly charged, are presented to us by a mind which refuses to be adequate to their tortuous meanings or appropriate to their terror. By his unwillingness to be implicated in his story, whether by the way he disposes his emotions between the murderers and their victims or by the way he invests his narrative with the intensity and anxiety proper to an unresolvable moral dilemma, Mr. Capote is employing objectivity as a shield for evasion. This is what is resented.

Certain of Mr. Capote's readers would wish he had thrown his weight to the Smith-Hickock side of the moral equation; these, of course, are the readers who believe that psychopaths and criminals, because they live outside the social order, have a special call on our tenderness. There are other readers who, though immune to the particular appeal of psychopaths and criminals, feel that in his unquestioning acceptance of Kansas farmers, members of 4-H Clubs, even KBI agents, Mr. Capote by strong implication gives his assent to American society in terms long outmoded in serious writing. Still others accuse Mr. Capote of having been seduced by personal acquaintance with Smith and Hickock, of having let himself forget the hideousness of their crime and of portraying them *too* sympathetically. If this diversity of negative response requires some common denominator of disappointment, it must be found in the sense shared in some dim way by virtually all of Mr. Capote's audience of having been unfairly used in being made to take on the burden of personal involvement pridefully put aside by Mr. Capote himself. An unpleasant critical charge leveled against *In Cold Blood* is that it is itself written in cold blood, exploiting tragedy for personal gain. One does not have to concur in this harsh opinion (I do not); one can even recognize that if anyone is misused by Mr. Capote it is not the Clutters or their murderers but we, the public, and still understand what inspires the charge of exploitation and, however imprecisely, warrants it.

And yet Mr. Capote's book has virtues which are perhaps not to be detached from the objectivity of his method. It is full of well-reported social detail; here at least Mr. Capote handsomely takes over what was once, in a less subjective day, an important function of the novelist. And his book speaks to us with disquieting force on psychiatry and the law—Mr. Capote may not tell us to what end he delved so deep into the Clutter killings, but he thoroughly impresses upon us the small progress our society has made in solving the legal problems posed by criminals like Smith and Hickock. And certainly *In Cold Blood* has a healthily unsettling effect on some of our easier assumptions about social and human causality.

What—Mr. Capote asks us—are we to do about our psychopathic murderers: kill them; put them in prison; put them in hospitals? Although little approval is now given to capital punishment for any class of criminal, it still exists in the majority of American states. But let us suppose—hopefully—that soon this form of punishment will everywhere be abolished (and the movement for its abolition can only be forwarded by Mr. Capote's harrowing description of a hanging: it took twenty minutes for Hickock to be legally strangled), what then do we do with our Smiths and Hickocks? Obviously they cannot be let free in society.

Shall it then be prison or hospitalization? If prison, rehabilitation is hopeless. But so too, in the case of murderers like Smith and Hickock, is psychiatric cure virtually hopeless in our present state of therapeutic knowledge. What distinguishes these cold-blooded killers, Smith, Hickock, the young Andrews who was with them in the death row, from at least some persons who commit crimes of passion is their incapacity to feel remorse for their crimes. Where there is no guilt for a murder, there is nothing to stop further killings— psychiatry as yet knows no way to inculcate the capacity for remorse, of sufficient strength to be counted on as a restraint of action, in someone lacking this human dimension. It may scarcely seem practical to commit incurable criminals to hospitals for the rest of their lives; but this is what we do with incurable noncriminals who cannot live in society, and to make a distinction between the two categories, criminal and noncriminal, could only mean that it is punishment and not protection of others which guides our conduct.

But there are even knottier problems than this which Mr. Capote's book brings out of the professional parish where they usually stay hidden from general view. Not only has the law not discovered a proper disposition of the incurable criminal, it has not yet devised a reliable method for separating out the offender who is susceptible of cure from incurables like Smith and Hickock. The legal sanity of these two men was tested by the M'Naghten Rule which still obtains in most states, not only in Kansas. In accordance with this Rule, which asks but a single question, whether the defendant was able to distinguish right from wrong at the time of the crime, Smith and Hickock were clearly able to stand trial for the Clutter murders. True, they had been "driven" to commit these terrible killings by forces beyond their control, and they had none of the emotions appropriate to wrongdoing. Under psychiatric examination they exhibited a wide range of symptoms of severe mental disorder. But there is no doubt that they were intellectually capable of telling right from wrong, and knew they had done wrong in killing the Clutter family; the awareness of wrongdoing may in fact have given added zest to their criminal acts. None of this complicated pathology could of course be introduced into a court which abides by the M'Naghten Rule, or certainly not without clinical evasion or imprecision.

Nor is the Bazelon Rule, which substitutes for the M'Naghten Rule in the District of Columbia, a useful advance on the older test for criminal insanity. According to the Bazelon Rule, a criminal need not stand trial if he can be proved to be mentally ill. But at least one wing of psychiatric opinion holds it as self-evident that the mere commission of a crime is indicative of mental illness. The Bazelon Rule, no less than the M'Naghten Rule, fails adequately to meet the central question of criminal responsibility—to trace, that is, if only for legal purposes, the chain of causality in the life of the individual in order to discover in what sense he can be said to be responsible for the way he is and acts.

By his equal emphasis upon the life stores of Smith and Hickock and of the family they killed, so that it is in the glaring immediate light of the *outcome* of the pathologies of the two murderers that we examine their personal histories, Mr. Capote gives an unusual stringency to the enterprise of socio-psychological understanding. The presence of the Clutters within the same pages as the men who so vagrantly murdered them denies us, or should, recourse to sentimentality; it restrains us, or should, from sliding too smoothly into the grooves prepared for us by our present-day preference for the deterministic view of society. Perry Smith, to be sure, has a life story so casebook as to be a cliché of the environmental explanation of mental disease and crime. So awful were the circumstances of his early life—a brutish incompetent father, a raging alcoholic promiscuous Cherokee mother, a vicious Catholic orphanage, ignorance, poverty, degradation—that the question in our minds is not how did this man come to be as he was but, rather, how did his sister manage to salvage herself, if we can think it salvation, for her life of tortured respectability? But the Hickock story is different; Hickock is not at all the social victim, or at least not in the sense of being a product of gross want, mistreatment and neglect. While he was disadvantaged economically, it was in circumstances which according to old-time fable are supposed to make for the peculiar American heroism of success. His parents were industrious, honest, clean-living, loyal and loving. Even after their son had been caught in his crime, they never deserted him. A picture like this controverts our readiest notions about the genesis of the psychopathic criminal—until we look more closely and see that, shamed and anguished though they were by what their son had done, Hickock's parents felt no more actual revulsion (however mitigated by love) from their son's crime than the son did himself. The peculiarly awful nature of the Clutter killings reached them only as an idea—a social idea, so to speak—without an emotional affect appropriate to the act itself. One is led to conclude that well before Hickock had arrived on the family scene, the tragic outcome of his life had already been made emotionally possible for him.

Nor is this the only element in the Smith-Hickock story to upset our too-mechanical psychological assumptions. If the two men were unable to experience guilt for taking human life, this does not mean, as we might expect, that they were simply lacking in conscience, any kind of conscience. What someone else might feel about committing murder, Smith and Hickock would seem to have felt about being physically dirty: washing, shaving, showering, caring for their nails was a major occupation of their nonviolent hours. Even more demanding was their concern with language. For Smith, the more literate of the pair, it constituted a measurable and well-exercised superiority to Hickock that he could correct his friend's errors or infelicities of speech, and offer so many more and better words for communicating the complex life of feeling. Everywhere on his travels, as far as his last jail, Smith took with him lists of "beautiful" and "useful" words, obscure bits of information, poems and literary quotations he had anthologized in substitute for the education he had missed. He thought of himself as someone who might have been, who should have been, an artist, and it was from his sense of himself as an artist that he plumbed the depths of his "sensitivity" and nourished his spirit in self-pity. This was met, on Hickock's side, by a highly ambivalent respect for so gifted a friend, an envious admiration which could not but encourage at least his half of their (concealed) homosexual attachment. If we are to say of Smith and Hickock that they were emotionally incapable of our usual old-established moral valuations, we must in accuracy add that they were not without other valuations of a sort to which we are accustomed to give moral weight.

But it is not alone Smith and Hickock but the Clutters too, who, especially as we are shown them confronting their murderers, reveal a far more complicated personal and social principle than we are in the habit of ascribing to virtuous, substantial, Republican, churchgoing, civicminded citizens of the Middle West. At the head of the family stands Mr. Clutter—and was anyone ever more the head of his family, more the whole source and apex of its authority? Certainly there was never such a man of policy, in formulated control of every minute and act of his life, even—or so he would have hoped—of every secret terror. He not only took no stimulants himself, not even tea or coffee, but contracted his employees to total abstinence. He disbursed money only by check, so that every penny could be accounted for to whatever still higher authority might probe his affairs. He permitted himself no rage, even kept a dog that was gun-shy. He was a pillar of his community, himself so fashioned for respect that he could even depend upon it for his "nervous" wife, who, after the birth of each of her children, had wandered always further into sadness and uncertainty. But this pillar of strength was a murderee—or so at least I read the story.

From Mr. Capote's detailed reconstruction of the night of the murders, Mr. Clutter was not only himself unable to meet the aggression directed against him by this invasion of his home, he would seem to have incapacitated his grown son and daughter for any self-defense, even by effective guile. Smith and Hickock were of course armed. But it was an hour between the time they arrived in the Clutter farmhouse and the killings. In this period, which included an interval when the family was locked, untied, in a bathroom and several intervals when the two intruders were separated from each other in different parts of the house, no one screamed, no one fought, no one tried to drop out of the bathroom window to run for help. It was apparently inconceivable to Mr. Clutter, and therefore to his obedient son and daughter, that the two men might do worse than rob them, harm them. Only the poor neurotic Mrs. Clutter was available to this kind of imagination. Her "fantasy" was quickly countered by Mr. Clutter's "realism"—it would, one can suppose, have been a familiar situation as between this husband and wife.

Indeed, for me, by far the most interesting aspect of Mr. Capote's book as an American story lies not in the gratuitous violence of the crime it describes—this

is not an American invention, though it is as ready to hand for us as if it were—
nor in the dreary circumstances of the lives of Smith and Hickock—of this we
already have some knowledge—but in the curiously ambiguous personality of
Mr. Clutter. If Mr. Capote is at all a novelist in this book, it is, paradoxically
enough, as an accident of his entirely literal reporting of this highly "masculine"
character undone by his passivity and by—if you will—his lack of actual
identity. One is reluctant (it seems like chic) to draw so exemplary a citizen, a
successful teetotaling Republican devout progressive farmer, into the circle of
self-alienated Americans. Yet manifestly this was a man without connection
with his inner self, living by forced intention, by conscious design,
programmatically, rather than by any happy disposition of natural impulse. His
response to anger could not have been more contemporary in its "enlightened"
propitiatoriness and in its lack of instinctual manliness. Otherwise, would it not
have allowed for something other than the guilt-ridden reaction—if these people
less fortunate than himself wanted his money, he must give it to them—which
was his only reaction to an invasion of his home? Mr. Clutter was a towering
figure in his community. One of the last things said to him on the day of his
death was said by a neighbor: "Can't imagine you afraid. No matter what
happened, you'd talk your way out of it." This sounds like a compliment to
courage. But then one thinks of what is actually implied in the idea that we now
can define fearlessness as the ability "to talk your way out of" danger: is there
nothing beyond the reach of reasonable persuasion? Certainly Mr. Clutter was a
talker—not a conversationalist—and this is an American and contemporary
thing to be. But according to most folk wisdom, it is also not a very masculine
thing to be; it is not supposed to go along with power, force or any other older
principle of manliness. In men who had come to his home "to splatter hair on
the walls," Mr. Clutter confronted a spirit which he was unprepared to meet and
before which he was fatally disarmed.

The Kansas Farm Murders

KENNETH TYNAN

One Saturday in November 1959, two young men drove 400 miles across the State of Kansas to an imposing white house in the lonely village of Holcomb. There they killed—at pointblank range, with a shotgun—four people whom, until that day, they had never seen. The victims were a prosperous farmer named Herbert Clutter, his wife, Bonnie, and their teenage children Nancy and Kenyon. The murderers (though this was not known until weeks later) were Dick Hickock and Perry Smith, former cell-mates in the Kansas State Penitentiary.

Hickock, aged 28 at the time of the crime, was a petty thief of bright cruel intelligence. Since 1950, when his head was battered in a car accident, he had shown increasing evidence of what a psychiatrist was later to call "severe character disorder." Perry Smith, 31 years old had a record of arrests that began when he was eight, shortly after his vagabond Irish father parted from his mother, an alcoholic Cherokee Indian. He had been confined in many institutions, among them a Catholic orphanage where the nuns thrashed him for bed-wetting. It was here, for the first of many times, that he dreamed of a giant yellow parrot that would swoop down, destroy his persecutors and lift him up to paradise.

His brother and one of his two sisters had committed suicide. He had amorphous artistic yearnings, and hotly resented his lack of schooling. Like his partner, Dick, he had suffered on the public highway: his legs were dwarfish, the aftermath of a motorcycle crash in which they had been broken in five places. It was this classic paranoid who fired the shots that obliterated a family.

Dick (who planned the expedition to Holcomb) had been told by a fellow-prisoner, once employed on the Clutter farm, that Mr. Clutter kept thousands of dollars at home in a safe. But there was no safe; in spite of which the two intruders proceeded to kill, and departed the richer by less than 50 dollars. They

The Observer (13 March 1966): 21.

took a trip to Mexico, where (though not queer themselves) they briefly accepted the hospitality of a rich German homosexual in Acapulco. Having hitchhiked back to the States, they were arrested in January 1960, seven weeks after the crime.

Trial, conviction, and sentence to death followed in April. George Docking, Governor of Kansas from 1957 to 1961, opposed capital punishment throughout his term of office; but his successors were less liberally inclined, and after a series of appeals and postponements lasting five years in all, Smith and Hickock were hanged in April 1965.

What took place in Holcomb was a nightmare collision of two incompatible Americas: the land of heart loving, God-fearing families and the land of vengeful, anarchic outcasts. In the end, they annihilated each other.

Truman Capote arrived in Kansas towards the end of November 1959 to cover the case for the *New Yorker*. When Smith and Hickock were brought back in custody, they refused at first to see him; by offering them 50 dollars each for an interview he managed to change their minds. Before long all three were on first-name terms, and by the time Perry and Dick reached the scaffold, Capote had spent hundreds of hours in their company. He had also consulted everyone living, traceable, and willing to talk who had ever been closely acquainted with them or their victims.

In all this prodigious research, spread over five years, he neither took notes on the spot nor employed a tape recorder. Instead, he relied on his memory, which he had sedulously trained until it could retain 95 percent (or 92 percent or 97 percent: his interviewers differ) of total recall.

SENTIMENTAL

In Cold Blood, the result of these unique and protracted exertions, is certainly the most detailed and atmospheric account ever written of a contemporary crime. Sometimes, you suspect that Capote's vision of Kansas is over-sentimental (too many phrases like "the well-loved piece of prairie where he had always hoped to build a house"); often, that he bowdlerizes out of deference to the *New Yorker*'s well-known primness. At one point (p. 240) Perry says "shit" this is the only four-letter word used by any of the characters, criminal or law-abiding, and it was omitted from the *New Yorker* serialization.

Again, how can we verify events and statements that only the hanged men could corroborate? Driving towards Mexico, Dick deliberately swerves to run over a dog and says: "Boy! We sure splattered him!" Capote adds that "it was what he always said after running down a dog." But did he get that from Dick, or is it Perry trying to make Dick look bad? We are given no clue here or in many similar dilemmas.

Even so, the book is by any standards a monumental job of editing and most seductive piece of writing: the first section, cutting back and forth between the unsuspecting Clutters and the approaching killers, is agonizingly well constructed. That said, we must pose the two central questions: is it art? And is it morally defensible?

The first is easier to answer. Capote calls the book a "nonfiction novel," by which he means a documentary tale handled with the psychological insight of a novelist. He believes that much of modern fiction is merely a device to evade the libel laws: thus, a breezy, adipose Londoner absurdly appears in print as a tight-lipped, skeletal Scot. If I remember him correctly (my median percentage of recall is in the high sixties). Capote feels that unless you are a Joyce or a Kafka, able to create a world of your own, you are likely to find your richest artistic opportunities in the world of fact. This will be news only to those who (perhaps like Capote himself) were brought up to despise journalism; or who never heard John Grierson's famous definition of documentary—"the creative treatment of actuality." Like any other art, of course, creative journalism can be abused: witness *Time* magazine, that weekly anthology of nonfiction short stories.

DAZZLING

The question of morality is tougher and (for me) more personal. Early in 1960, when I was in New York, upper-Bohemian dinner guests were already full of "Truman and his marvelous bit about Perry and Dick." I attended one such party, which Capote regaled with a dazzling account of the crime and his friendship with the criminals. I said they seemed obviously insane, and agreed they were "nuts." And what would happen to them? "They'll swing, I guess," he said.

When I asked whether he thought insane people should be hanged, he said I couldn't understand unless I had read Nancy Clutter's diary: Perry and Dick had destroyed "such a lovely, intelligent girl." "You mean it would have mattered less if she'd been ugly and stupid?" I said.

I don't recall his answer to that, but I do remember several subsequent disputes—one in which I failed to persuade him that he (or the *New Yorker*) ought to provide Perry and Dick with the best available psychiatric testimony: and another in which I convinced him, much against his will, that if he was writing a book about death in cold blood he owed it to his readers to be present at a really cold-blooded killing—the legal strangulation of his friends.

Capote's references in the book to the mental state of the murderers are confused and ambiguous. Early on, we learn that, in Dick's opinion, Perry was "that rarity, 'a natural killer'—absolutely sane but conscienceless . . ." (my underlining.) Later, Capote cites the belief of Dr. Joseph Sattan, a veteran psychiatrist working at the Menninger Clinic in Kansas, that when Perry killed Mr. Clutter "the first and hence the crucial murder, since the other three had the rational purpose of eliminating witnesses), he was "under a mental eclipse, deep inside a schizophrenic darkness." The phrase is Capote's and it has the same fanciful vagueness as something he afterwards said to an interviewer: "Perry never meant to kill the Clutters at all. He had a brain explosion."

In essence, the only explanation Capote offers for the gratuitous slaughter of Mr. Clutter—the raison d'etre, after all, of his book—is a single remark of Perry's: "It wasn't because of anything the Clutters did. They never hurt me . . . like people have all my life. Maybe it's just that the Clutters were the ones who had to pay for it." And maybe not: the woolliness is contagious. Nowhere does Capote commit himself to stating that the killers were technically insane, and therefore ought not to have been executed. Indeed, he goes out of his way to stress that Dick was a supporter of capital punishment: "I'm not against it. Revenge is all it is, but what's wrong with revenge?" "Essentially," Capote told *Life* magazine, "I'm on the side of the victim, not the murderer."

The accused men received only the most perfunctory psychiatric examination: so much is brutally obvious. The day before the trial began, a young psychiatrist named Mitchell Jones volunteered to interview them without payment. He asked them to write out autobiographical statements, which they did in the courtroom while the jury was being selected. And that was all.

In Dr. Jones's view, Dick might have been suffering from "organic brain damage," and Perry showed "definite signs of severe mental illness." But he was not allowed to say this in court. Kansas follows the ancient McNaughten Rules, whereby a man is held to be sane and legally responsible for his actions if he knows that what he is doing is wrong. Dr. Jones testified that Dick did know, and when asked about Perry, said he had no opinion. He was dismissed at once from the stand. Had he been a psychiatrist of national repute, more skilled in courtroom niceties, would his evidence have been heard? We shall never know.

FIVE YEARS

What we do know, however, is that when the verdict was appealed, three federal judges declared: "There was no substantial evidence then, and none has been produced since, to substantiate a defense of insanity" (my underlining.) And they were right, none was produced: although Capote, who investigated so much else had five years in which he might have unearthed it. He could surely have faced the expense. In cold cash it has been estimated that "In Cold Blood" is likely to earn him between two and three million dollars. Had Perry and Dick been reprieved, the book might have been rather different. George Plimpton, in an interview for the *New York Times Book Review*, asked Capote whether his "artistry" would have suffered if clemency had been granted: he hedged, and changed the subject. He also told Plimpton that neither Perry nor Dick saw the manuscript in toto; that Perry's "greatest objection" was to the title; that Dick wanted changes made ("to serve his purposes legally") and expressed the opinion that "what I had written wasn't exactly true."

In the same interview Capote says that someone suggested the breakup of a marriage as a possible theme for a future "nonfiction novel": he rejected the idea because "you'd have to find two people . . . who'd sign a release." Perry and Dick did sign a release after reading "three-quarters of the book." (Capote's words.) This shows a remarkable degree of tolerance in them, since in the course of the book Capote alleges (a) that Dick frequently tried to rape pubescent girls, (b) that he intended (but failed) to kill a fellow prisoner in a Kansas jail, and (c) that he and Perry were prevented only by chance from carrying out the premeditated murder of a traveling salesman who gave them a lift. (In his chat with Plimpton, Capote adds: "They had two other murders planned that aren't mentioned in the book.") There is no evidence to substantiate these charges outside the killers' graves to which Capote contributed the cost of the headstones.

RESPONSIBILITY

A prominent Manhattan lawyer has given me the following opinion: "I would doubt whether the book would have been released prior to the decease of the accused."

We are talking, in the long run, about responsibility; the debt that a writer arguably owes to those who provide him—down to the last autobiographical parenthesis—with his subject matter and his livelihood. And we are not discussing a third-rate crime reporter or professional ghoul; one does not waste space on condemning trash. For the first time an influential writer of the front rank has been placed in a position of privileged intimacy with criminals about to die, and—in my view—done less than he might have to save them.

The focus narrows sharply down on priorities: does the work come first, or does life? An attempt to help (by supplying new psychiatric testimony) might easily have failed: what one misses is any sign that it was even contemplated. It is irrelevant to say that Capote writes with genuine pity of his dead friends, and gives them a fraternal quatrain from Villon by way of epigraph. Compassion is the least we expect of an obituarist.

In a recent letter to a former colleague, Dr. Satten of the Menninger Clinic agrees that Capote didn't try to help the condemned men, but sees nothing wrong in this. "In the conversations I have had with Mr. Capote over the years I think he saw his task as that of an observer and recorder rather than that of an active participant." By this reasoning, a writer who befriended Timothy Evans at the time of his conviction would have been under no obligation to tell society that it was executing a probably innocent half-wit. Where lives are threatened, observers and recorders who shrink from participation may be said to betray their species: no piece of prose, however deathless, is worth a human life.

The colleague to whom Dr. Satten addressed his letter (and who showed it to me) is a woman psychiatrist who knows the Clutter case well. For professional reasons I will not divulge her name. She worked in Kansas, mainly with criminal patients, in 1963-64, and has no doubt that if the Clutter murderers could have been shown to be paranoid schizophrenics, they would have won their appeal. On their relationship with Capote she takes a firm and original line. In her view, he set himself up—consciously or not—as their analyst and confessor; not, however, to bring them comfort but to gain their trust and obtain information.

In a letter to me she reconstructs the situation. She writes: "The same dependence and fascination that Dick once evoked in Perry is now expanded in both of them towards Capote. In a sense they are telling him what Perry told Dick: 'I'm going to put myself in your power. I'm going to tell you something I never told anybody.' We know what Dick did with this confidence: he used Perry to kill the people he had in mind. And what did Capote do with their trust?"

CONTENTED

Perry, she hazards, came to identify Capote with his father, with whom he had spent many of his few contented days. And at the same time, Capote may have begun to see aspects of himself in Perry: the diminutive stature, perhaps, and the voice that Capote describes as "both gentle and prim—a voice that, though soft, manufactured each word exactly, ejected it like a smoke ring issuing from a parson's mouth."

She continues: "The situation now becomes chaotic. Who's who? Who is the criminal? Who is the interviewer? . . . Is it possible that Capote was gaining satisfaction out of acting as 'confessor' to the criminals because of an intense identification with them? At some time or other all of us feel like killing; but now Capote can avoid the real situation since someone with whom he strongly identifies has done the killing instead."

Whether Capote identified or not, it seems to me that the blood in which his book is written is as cold as any in recent literature.

The "Non-Fiction" Novel

WILLIAM WIEGAND

By the time Truman Capote's book, *In Cold Blood*, gets waxed into paperback and moving pictures ("the crime that shocked a million readers by the author of *Breakfast at Tiffany's*"), what remains of the integrity of the original work will probably be forgotten. Also forgotten may be Capote's notion that he had created something new in writing this book. *In Cold Blood* was not like a "documentary novel," or a "historical novel," Capote said. Least of all did it need a crime to make it work; its nature could only be described as a "nonfiction novel."

A "non-fiction novel" was a term the purists were not ready for, but rather than disturb the sleeping issue of the difference between literature and journalism, which Hemingway had pretty well settled for this generation, Capote's claim was left as simple vanity. Surely this sort of thing had been done before even if, as most were ready to allow, seldom so well.

Still, if the book is good, one wants to know why, and Capote's term, ungainly as it is, serves to call attention to the high standards against which the book wants to be measured. "Non-fiction" implies a willingness to be held responsible for the data included as literally factual. The story actually happened. Newspapermen could "cover" it, and in the Clutter murder case newspapermen, of course, did.

Being covered though need not imply that the primary aim of the book is the same as journalism's aim. Ordinarily, journalism seeks to inform the reader about a particular event, or to "discuss" it. But the purpose of *In Cold Blood* is closer to that of the "novel," the chief aim with other art forms. What is therefore important in defining the novel, Capote would say, is not the imagined, or fictional, character of the material (compare the factual fidelity of many historical novels); but it is rather the suggesting and extending capacity all art forms share.

New Mexico Quarterly, 37 (Autumn 1967): 243-57

In a novel, the particular formal techniques employed will be those generally associated with fiction. Now, some of these techniques have long been used by journalists. At an elementary level the newspaper columnist may include the dialogue of a public figure for something more than the information it contains. The feature writer who writes about Kennedy's "vigah" or Johnson's "you-all" is reflecting an intention to characterize a public figure's personality. If he goes further and "imagines" satiric episodes (as Russell Baker and Art Hoppe do), he is "discussing" public issues entertainingly. But some of the better comic strips, such as *Pogo* and *L'il Abner*, do the same thing, and comic strips (maybe with the exception of *Peanuts*) are not "art."

In the somewhat longer forms, magazine writers have also used techniques of fiction: "scene" for its immediate evocative quality; dramatic development instead of rhetorical development; occasional distortion of chronology for emotive effect; even attempts at "depth" psychology. With certain techniques, it is not always easy to say whether they belong inherently to journalism or to fiction. The elaborate use of detail, for instance, has marked the development of at least one kind of novel, but when Defoe and others first used it, they were essentially copying the fact-oriented journalist or the popular autobiographer. Since then, "formal realism" has become so intimately associated with the business of fiction that a writer of a magazine article who uses it will probably write not with the blunter rhythms of a journalistic Defoe but with the more sophisticated overtones of subsequent fiction. But rarely—except in occasional pieces like E. B. White's "The Door"—is there a full formal control such as fiction has.

Full-length books of nonfiction have used these techniques and probably a few others. Any book which totally avoids them—unless it is the Warren Commission Report on the Kennedy assassination—will probably go unread, since the hunger for "objective truth" is hardly ever so great that the laboratory report is considered a proper model. The natural and social scientists learned from the novelist. Oscar Lewis's book, *The Children of Sanchez,* proceeds from a series of tape-recorded accounts of the experiences of a lower-class family in Mexico City as Lewis, a sociologist, recorded them. But Lewis edits out the conventional questions of the interviewer, and after his introduction does not interrupt the dramatic flow of each of his narrators. He imposes order on the accounts by omitting the "extraneous." Moreover, he juxtaposes the various narratives in such a way that one narrator can comment on events that another has just described, thus increasing the ironic significance of the counterpoint. This device is completely familiar in American fiction, at least since Faulkner's *As I Lay Dying* and *The Sound and the Fury.*

Scientists notwithstanding, as a general rule the newsworthy public event, like the inconspicuous private one, is nearly always altered and re-imagined when the suggesting and extending power of the novelist is sought for. Few writers with this object want to stick to *all* the facts. Thus, when Thornton Wilder writes about the collapse of that footbridge in South America, to treat it as he wants to treat it, he felt he had to fictionalize. When Stephen Crane writes of the sinking of the Cuban gunrunner, which he actually experienced as a correspondent, the most he can risk in his newspaper account to suggest the emotive effect of the disaster is a metaphor or two. It is only later when he distills the meaning of the experience and its impact in the short story, "The Open Boat," that the irresistible conventions of journalism can be unloaded for the sake of a rendering in which many of the facts are changed and the local metaphors effective in the newspaper account do not even appear.

With experienced novelists, cross-fertilization between fiction and journalism produces some paradoxes. When, for example, John Hersey chooses as subject for a novel the uprising of the Warsaw ghetto in World War II, he elects to invent "documentation" for the story by employing journals, notebooks, and other records from the inhabitants of the ghetto, as though to imply that the best insurance for the novelist is to convince the reader that it actually happened.

But when Hersey decides in writing about Hiroshima not to fictionalize it, he now chooses fictional techniques in order to maximize the emotive impact of the dropping of the bomb. He preserves the dramatic fluency of each subject's account of the experience. Further, he multiplies the force of it by making the reader undergo five times the violence of the event. The effect of the extended intensity of a single point of view is exploited in a way that was unknown before certain developments in the technique of the novel took place. But for all that, *Hiroshima* is not a novel, and Hersey would be the last to claim that it was.

It is only with Capote that the growing obliteration of the lines that demark journalism from fiction seems virtually complete. He wages total war with journalism and its conventions by his conscious intention to keep the instinct to inform and discuss subordinated to the novelistic objective throughout. With this perspective the new form he seeks can evolve (and perhaps it is the way all forms evolve) because the intentions are no longer mixed.

Some of this can be seen by comparing Capote with the kind of writer who on the surface does the same sort of thing. Stanley Kauffman chooses John Bartlow Martin, a veteran true-crime man, whose work Kauffman finds sufficiently like Capote's to make him feel that *In Cold Blood* is no particular innovation. The apparent logic is that both Martin and Capote treat a criminal case at considerable length, with drama and with "depth" psychology, and both publish originally in installments in the most well-paying periodicals.

Beyond this, their assumptions are really quite different. Martin writes in the old *Police Gazette, American Weekly* tradition as it was sophisticated by the slick magazines in the Thirties and Forties. This sophistication was achieved chiefly by the infusion of sociological and psychiatric method into a narrative which still basically depended on the old Gothic evocation of the scene of the crime. Martin's one full-length, true-crime book, the story of an Ann Arbor, Michigan, murder committed by three teenagers, depends on these habits.

Martin begins with the "shadow-lined" streets on which the crime occurs and proceeds from there through the newsman's catalogue of names and places to a series of interviews with people who knew the principals in the case. He emphasizes the class levels of the three defendants in these interviews. The attitude of the community toward the principals is also examined. At last, he answers his question, *Why Did They Kill?*, which serves as the title of the book, almost entirely by means of the psychiatrist's reports, here a labeling process which discerns after the fact that criminals had criminal tendencies. Martin's narrative specialty is the observation of incongruities, and again this reflects *Police Gazette* technique—"Revered Clergyman Slain," "Illiterate Pig Woman Key Witness," and so forth. For Martin, it is the guise of innocence, the handsome teenager, the shocked parent, which supplies the paradoxes that keep the reader interested.

In crime writing, the case history technique is naturally even more particularly emphasized by those who have their credentials along with their professional title. Frederic Wertham and Robert Lindner are two successful examples. Generally their approach relies on the convention of a scientific age that the best way crime can be treated is one which cools the phenomenon into a safely clinical aberration. The aberration is testified to by the medical authority who may accidentally deliver us a prurient glimpse into the haunted secrets of the criminal, but who at the same time will relieve us of the burden of much real empathy for the culprit by casting that gulf between health and disease into the issue. As a convention, the sick-well dichotomy may not be much different from the old elect-damned dichotomy that was the basis of the pleasant stimulation of *American Weekly* true-crime.

It is odd that Capote has been criticized for "cold-bloodedness" on the grounds that he is acting "scientific" without the proper diploma. The business of crime-reporting would appear to Kenneth Tynan and Dwight MacDonald and some others properly to belong to the pro. The police reporter and the psychiatrist can dispose of the matter with what are evidently the only answers it is decent for us to have.

Actually, Capote handles the clinical matters almost with diffidence. Although the psychiatrist's report is included in the data pertinent to the case file on Smith and Hickock, by the time the reader reaches this report in the book, the medical diagnosis does not seem to mean very much. Its conclusions are intelligible in terms of the evidence Capote had previously presented. But the conclusions as such seem no more than a professional label fixed on a pair of consciousnesses that have been rendered more justly and more emphatically in the material that has preceded. The subject Capote chose has already been realized, and such realization transcends the functionalism of a clinical analysis. For by this point he has also realized the Clutter family, the small-town life of western Kansas, and the spirit of a certain time and place. None of the victims are made to seem mere integers, created for the purpose of being acted upon.

They hold their space in existence for the short hour of their time; and what they stood for, unsentimentally, endures side by side with what is represented by their aimless and pathetic antagonists. Nor are the impulses of the Smiths and the Hickoks vanquished by an execution, even though the period is placed with stubborn impassivity at the end of this particular case.

The real strength of the Capote book is achieved by the way he exploits a whole battery of novelistic techniques which enforce the structure and hence the meaning of the Clutter case. First, in the opening section he builds the emphatic involvement of the reader by the familiar technique of cross-cutting. Scenes taking place in the Clutter home are alternated with scenes between Smith and Hickok preparing for their trip and en route to their destination. At first the two stories are made to seem completely independent. They take place hundreds of miles apart; the respective principals are strangers to the opposite party. In a machine age, antagonisms are impersonal; what you don't know is more likely to hurt you than what you do. The Clutters don't know, and neither do Smith and Hickok. They don't know the pot of gold at the end of the rainbow is nonexistent, but such uncertainty is of the order of things.

Within this section of the book, Capote also keys the identity of the two forces before they collide. Smith and Hickok are identified with the road and the automobile. They are introduced in a garage, subsequently they are seen in quick-stop cafes. The Clutters, on the other hand, are rigidly established on their homestead. Where they have settled seems not only the heart of their family, but the heart of the community. In the scenes recorded on the final day of their lives, friends visit them at their home, and even though the family is shown as tremendously interested and active in events occurring outside their home, the core of existence is first settled and stable before it can eddy outward to become productive. The home is sustenance and health; it is defined by apple pies and the Four-H Club. Remote places are "sickness"; the mother in the family was once in a Wichita sanitarium ill, but now she is returned and is well.

At the end of the first section of the book, with the last guest of the Clutters departing into the darkness of the night, the terrible collision between the two forces is about to take place. But Capote tells nothing about it here. On one hand, he is delaying the impact of it until later in the book where weight will be required and where its more immediate relevance to Smith and Hickok as independent psychologies can be apprehended. On the other hand, to dramatize it directly, as all the early sections of the book have been dramatized, will be too much for the reader. The crime needs the cushion of an interpolater; it needs to be recounted secondhand, as violence was on the Greek stage.

Also, more important to Capote at this early point is the shattering effect of the crime on the community. He takes up the story from its first felt moment within the house the following morning when the Clutters are discovered by friends who would pick them up on the way to church. The interdependence of the Clutters and the community has already been demonstrated in the first section. Now, as the news whirls into the larger vortex, Capote shows how self-doubt, and even doubt of the Clutters, produces a cacophony of discordant opinion. Various dialects and idioms are registered in separate interviews as the organism that is the town reacts to the cancer it thinks it detects within. Capote selects the postmistress, nominally the agent of interpersonal communication, as the chief and most articulate spokesman of the new feeling of subversion and isolation.

Thus, it is not shock as much as it is a more dangerous force—disunity—which must be coped with in Holcomb and Garden City. At this point, Capote introduces his folk hero, Police Captain Dewey, who must restore the town to health. A thoroughly inconspicuous and unprepossessing man, Dewey must be carefully and subtly developed. He must be given space in the book where he is by himself occupied not so much in thought as in solemn meditation. Accordingly, there are paragraphs in which Dewey contemplates nothing, except perhaps the land. For there is nothing to contemplate. The clue-hunting methods which might succeed in a rational universe are almost useless here. Dewey goes though the motions, but Capote never tempts us to feel that the little grey cells, as the detective story would have it, offer very much hope. Dewey is cast as the conscience of the community, a moral force. Untroubled by the winds of mistrust, he does what decency can do. If he is to catch the biggest fish that anybody in port ever saw, he will have to be lucky but he is not too proud to keep trying for that luck.

In the meantime, the antagonists, Hickok and Smith, are shown like hurled pebbles still skipping across the water after their refracting impact on that half-yielding, half-impenetrable surface. Their flight is not presented as panicky. Instead, it is more like the dissipation of momentum. They are "on the road," reflexively, as they have always been. They experience neither hope nor fear. Their stops whether long or short afford encounters with other transients, and it is only their fantasies perhaps that give them any appearance of having a will, a plan.

In this part of the book Capote distinguishes Smith from Hickok. While earlier the spectacle of their combined force has received the emphasis, now the components of their individual mediocrities are separated out. Smith and Hickok derive from different native heritages. Hickok belongs to an exhausted bourgeois line of clock-watchers; his father is dying, his mother whines and clings, and refuses to believe. Smith, on the other hand, comes from an older frontier tradition, of medicine shows and Indian rodeo riders, of prospectors and extravagant aspiration. In a way, both of them are distorted shadows of their forbears, both of them are reflected as if in funhouse mirrors. But it is important to understand, or to try to understand, that an incompetent father or a clumsy mother is only part of the story, that that father had a father too. If it is fair to say that Hickok wanted too little in life and Smith wanted too much, it is worth knowing what contributed to the different aspirations.

Distinguishing them as Capote does during this section prepares the reader for an acceptance of the dramatic climax of the book, the account of the murders by Smith after the arrest. In order that the morbid and sensational aspects of the account may be softened, the question of "who?" has been allowed to become more central than "how?" The gory details of the crime, while they are not denied, are thus sublimated in the rather more pertinent psychological, and social, question as to which of these two forces—that represented by Smith or that represented by Hickok—is the more violent, the more ruthless, the more unstable. Wanting to know who pulled the trigger each of the four times may be beneath the law's notice (Smith and Hickok were both guilty "ten times over"); but Capote creates the curiosity in the reader. It is of more than passing interest to know who presses the button—the glib, initiating Hickok or the Christ-painting, guilt-ridden Smith. Capote says that, four times over, it is Smith.

The last quarter of the book, a longer proportion than most writers would allot to this part of the case, shows Smith and Hickok in the community of the condemned, ironically the only community in which they have existed with such lingering permanence. Capote takes the trouble of describing the personalities and the crimes of some of the other inhabitants of death row in order to give definition to the community in which they spend their final years. The temper of this place gets contrasted, in alternate sections, with the temper of Garden City, which is seen in the last part of the book both during the murder trial and in the appeal. While Garden City, that solid reality earlier in the book, drifts off in the mists of the ephemeral words of some undistinguished attorneys, the drier reality of the prison and the inevitable execution scene replaces it. Capote includes the "last words": Hickok, like Willy Loman appreciating the good turnout at a funeral, and Smith, not unlike Raskolnikov, "apologizing."

There is a brief coda, a cemetery scene between Dewey and one of Nancy Clutter's girl friends. The scene restores consideration of the Clutters to the proper importance for the reader. Further, it turns again to the landscape, the concealing earth, and to Dewey, the hero of the narrative, who endures, untriumphant, with decency and luck.

Real Toads in Real Gardens: Reflections on the Art of Non-Fiction Fiction and the Legacy of Truman Capote

DAVID GALLOWAY

Two decades have passed since Truman Capote electrified *New Yorker* readers in the fall of 1965 with his account of the brutal and senseless murder of a Kansas farm family. Even before its official release the following spring, the hardcover version of *In Cold Blood* had soared to the top of bestseller lists, and translation rights were being auctioned off to the highest bidder. The writer himself, never shy of the media, became a familiar face on late-night talk-shows, together with his contentious contemporaries Norman Mailer and Gore Vidal. The author as pop-culture commodity was a new phenomenon for Americans; even Scott and Zelda Fitzgerald, at the peak of their photogenic zaniness, could not have winterdreamed of such celebrity. The much-publicized loss of Capote's private address book sent a seismic tremor through the upper social registers on both sides of the Atlantic. The self-proclaimed "nonfiction novelist," furthermore, was as likely to provide headlines for literary quarterlies and high-brow newspapers as for gossip-columns and decorating magazines.

For many critics schooled in the Great Tradition, stardom and seriousness were an incompatible combination. In a pragmatic, materialistic society, the true artist's fate was callous rejection (as in Hawthorne's "The Artist of the Beautiful"), posthumous acclaim (Melville and Poe), the dissipation of creative energies (Fitzgerald, Hemingway, Miller), self-destruction (Poe, Fitzgerald, Wolfe, Hemingway, Kerouac). In time, of course, Capote would richly fulfill the latter two criteria, but in 1966 he rode the crest of an improbable wave. Unlike the narrative junk-food of Grace Metalious or Jacqueline Susann, his writings had been praised as "minor classics." Recognition came early, with the publication of *Other Voices, Other Rooms* in 1948, though the image it projected of a Wilde-Huysmans decadent owed as much to the Cecil Beaton

---

In *Gattungsprobleme in der Anglo-Amerikanischen Literatur*, ed. Raimund Borgmeier. Tübingen: Niemeyer, 1986.

portrait on the cover as it did to the novel's sultry and sensuous tone. Another short novel, a play, a short-story collection and the novella *Breakfast at Tiffany's* (1958) consolidated the image, and critics waited impatiently for the major work that would confirm the promise of a decade's graceful achievements.

When that work appeared, many academic critics expressed outrage over the author's presumptuousness in describing *In Cold Blood* as a "Nonfiction Novel" and subtitling it "A True Account of a Multiple Murder." The blatant contradictions of the title-page provoked Kenneth Tynan to vent his rage week after week and across page after page of the London *Observer*. He disputed the "truth" of Capote's account, the hybrid genre in which it was composed, and the author's own moral cowardice in not fighting for the reprieve of the convicted murderers. By implication, the novelist required their execution for a dramatic climax to his story of crime and punishment. Capote was not, in principle, opposed to capital punishment, and he had no doubt of the guilt of Perry Smith and Eugene Hickock. The only hope for commuting their sentence from the death penalty to life in prison rested entirely on psychiatric testimony which the novelist—however great his insights into the troubled minds of the killers—was not qualified to give. He might, of course, have used his influence to organize an additional defense fund, to press for re-trial, to raise the larger question of whether a society has the right to destroy "monsters" of its own creation or an obligation to rehabilitate them. (Fellow nonfiction novelist Norman Mailer would later initiate such a campaign, with tragic results.)

Capote chose, instead, to adapt the classic novelistic stance of observing consciousness; unlike Norman Mailer in *The Armies of the Night* or *Of a Fire on the Moon* he does not even appear as a narrative persona in his own work. However we read the moral implications of the author's detachment, *In Cold Blood* plainly contributed to a shift in public opinion that led to the temporary abolishment of the death penalty in the United States. Kenneth Tynan's charge that Capote exploited the anti-heroes of his book is best settled by the novelist's future biographers. The assertion that he consciously tampered with truth to add color and suspense to the story has already been verified,[1] though the discrepancies might be described as peripheral rather than substantive. Fine-combing the text for "falsehoods" is a variation on Tynan's more general (and more serious) question of artistic ethics. The formal controversy, which stirred tempests in so many fragile academic teacups, is another matter entirely, for it presupposed that fiction and fact were congenitally antagonistic. How, traditional readers asked, could a work be simultaneously "true" (as the author claimed) and novelistic? Yet those same readers had accepted without so much as an intellectual gulp the traditional disclaimer that libel-wary publishers once automatically included behind the title page of a novel. The familiar formula appears, even, in James Jones's *Go to the Widowmaker*, published like *In Cold Blood* in 1966: "This novel is a work of fiction, and any resemblance to real people, living or dead, is completely coincidental, and totally outside the author's intention."[2]

Regardless of the writer's avowals or disavowals, one of the greatest and most frequent compliments that the average reader of fiction pays to a work is that its characters "seem so real"—i.e., so much like living, breathing, flesh-and-bone mortals. Negatively formulated, the response becomes "I couldn't identify with X or Y" or "I didn't believe in the character." Whatever else it attempts, the sense of a felt reality remains one of the novel's greatest strengths—whether the reality of a desert island, a whaling ship, a battlefield, a dinner-party, or a voyage to the heart of darkness. Even the later works of Samuel Beckett cannot entirely banish the note of "resemblance." One can, of course, tamper with it— ghoulishly, fantastically, absurdly and metafictionally, but without the sense of a "real" counterpart, the variation itself—whether hissing Hydra or glaring Cyclops—is meaningless. For James Jones himself, verisimilitude was always a novelistic prerequisite, and his professed "intention" thus seems far more preposterous than Capote's insistence on dubbing his own work a "nonfiction novel." The latter term, however, had to contend with a Puritan inheritance that equated fiction with lying, together with genre classifications firmly ratified by George Orwell's "Geneva conventions of the mind."

For five years Capote researched the apparently motiveless murders of four members of the Clutter family on a farm near Holcomb, Kansas. Observing that a tape-recorder often inhibited interview subjects, he trained himself to recall lengthy passages from books read aloud to him by a friend. As the facts emerged, they assumed metaphorical patterns of their own: the scene of the crime, near a suburb of Garden City, was situated at the geographical center of the United States; the Clutters seemed, at first glance, an apple-pie embodiment of the American Dream; the killers were the classic victims of a success-oriented society. Underprivileged, dispossessed, resentful of those who had achieved their dreams, Perry Smith and Eugene Hickock struck out at a world from which they felt unjustly excluded—like the sensation-hungry mob in Nathaniel West's *The Day of the Locust*, originally entitled *The Cheated*. The details and implications and insinuations that gathered about this frame-story were often of the sort popularly described as "beggaring the imagination." Capote saw no necessity to invent or to disguise—no necessity, that is, to "fictionalize" his findings.[3]

The author had long toyed with the idea of a nonfiction novel, and first practiced its techniques in *The Muses Are Heard* (1956), an account of his journey through Russia with the all-Negro cast of *Porgy and Bess*. A violent crime, however, seemed to him the ideal subject of such a work,[4] and he gave detailed advice to his friend and childhood neighbor Harper Lee, whose Pulitzer Prize-winning novel *To Kill a Mockingbird* (1960) focused on the sensational trial of a Negro charged with raping a white woman. (Harper Lee, in turn, accompanied Capote on his first visit to Holcomb, only three days after the murders were committed, and when there seemed little hope of apprehending the culprits.) For his own purposes, a sensational murder case seemed most likely to deliver the basic ingredients of a "found" narration, and he would have been aware of his literary antecedents—Poe's "The Mystery of Marie Rogêt," Dostojevsky's *The Possessed,* Dreiser's *An American Tragedy.* All were based on actual murder cases, which the authors had transformed not merely with the banal intention of "protecting the innocent," but in the interest of art. As Alfred Kazin has observed, Capote wanted to go a step further: while remaining literally true to the record, he was "not content to make a work of record. He wanted, wholly and exclusively, to make a work of art. . . . He wanted, ultimately, not the specificity of fiction, which must be content to be itself alone, but to make an emblematic human situation for our time that would relieve it of mere factuality."[5]

Why, then, should he stir the critical hornets' nest by evoking the word fiction? If a subtitle was necessary at all to establish the authenticity of persons, places, and events, "A Documentary Novel" would surely have sufficed. The term works admirably well for a book like John Hersey's *The Algiers Motel Incident*, which offers a chronological reconstruction of the killing of three Negroes during the bloody Detroit riots of 1967. It is written in a functional, reportorial style complete with maps, coroners' reports, confessions, lengthy swatches of official transcripts, and interviews conducted by the author himself. Hersey's work is passionately committed to what he sees as one of the most shocking episodes in American race relations, but the very rigor of its documentary method—its zeal to record the specific facts of a specific incident, together with all possible variants—precludes its achieving the larger metaphoric dimension of *In Cold Blood.*

In one of the rare passages in which he gives rein to a modest poetic license, Hersey describes the setting of Detroit's sniper battle:

> The Algiers Motel was one of many transients' hostelries on Woodward Avenue, a rod-straight street, the city's spine, that divides eastern Detroit from western Detroit. A couple of miles north of the cluster of massive buildings called "downtown," and only a few blocks from the section of Twelfth Street where the black uprising of those July days and nights had started, the Algiers stood at the corner of Woodward and Virginia Park, an elm-lined street elegantly brick-paved in the old days but pot-holed now and patched with asphalt, a street of once prosperous wooden and brick houses with boastful porches and backyard carriage houses recently declined into rooming houses and fraternity houses and blind pigs, as Detroit calls its illegal after-hours drinking spots.[6]

Beyond a "rod-straight street" and "boastful porches," Hersey is even here, where he might have sought to generalize or elaborate the theme of urban decay, making a conscious effort to restrict himself to photographically verifiable details: "elm-lined," "brick-paved," "pot-holed," "patched." Even the faint evocation of "the old days," when this was a peaceful, elegant neighborhood, is substantiated by visible remnants of that earlier time—trees, brick paving, porches, carriages, houses.

It is instructive to compare this restrained and calculatedly objective style with Capote's own *mise-en-scène:*

> The village of Holcomb stands on the high wheat plains of western Kansas, a lonesome area that other Kansans call "out there." Some seventy miles east of the Colorado border, the countryside, with its hard blue skies and desert-clear air, has an atmosphere that is rather more Far West than Middle West. The local accent is barbed with a prairie twang, a ranch-hand nasalness, and the men, many of them, wear narrow frontier trousers, Stetsons, and high-heeled boots with pointed toes. The land is flat, and the views are awesomely extensive; horses, herds of cattle, a white cluster of grain elevators rising as gracefully as Greek temples are visible long before a traveler reaches them.[7]

A comparison of Hersey's "cluster of massive buildings called 'downtown'" with Capote's "cluster of grain elevators rising as gracefully as Greek temples" offers a compact demonstration of the authors' divergent methods. It is not simply that the latter indulges in poetic simile. Nor is it a question of his being a more gifted and original writer (though the argument would not be difficult to substantiate), but of being a different kind of writer composing a very different kind of book that required the application of techniques more commonly associated with fiction.

Throughout the opening paragraph of *In Cold Blood* the author is systematically and artfully shaping our initial vision of the scene; observations are made—narrow trousers and high-heeled boots, for example—that go beyond documentary necessity to create an explicit sense of place. The reader becomes a "traveler," approaching across the wide plains; unlike the objective camera-eye, however, his also registers emotions and insinuations: "lonesome," "awesomely," "gracefully." Every physical detail contributes to the overall realism of the passage, yet each slots into a larger scheme of inference if not, literally, of symbolism. From this point individual images begin to cluster into leitmotifs—birds wedged into the grills of pick-up trucks, dead animals beside the highway, a beaten dog, a slaughtered pig, the corpses of the Clutters. Perry Smith's technicolor fantasy-world finds unexpected parallel in Mrs. Clutter's retreat into a realm of glittering baubles; the cabin-building adventure of his childhood is an ironic echo of the myth of the self-made farmer which Mr. Clutter embodies.

Structurally, too, *In Cold Blood* departs from the linear mode of documentary reporting; Capote has rearranged chronology and introduced flash-backs to lend narrative drama and thematic richness to the story. He has, furthermore, reconstructed long, vividly detailed conversations that he could not possibly have overheard. Such intrusions and overt manipulations of point-of-view are hostile to the documentary. In describing his own method, John Hersey piously insisted "that the events could not be described as if witnessed from above by an all-seeing eye opening on an all-knowing novelistic mind; the merest suspicion that anything had been altered, or made up, for art's sake, or for the sake of effect, would be absolutely disastrous. There could be no 'creative reconstruction.'"[8] There can be no doubt that Hersey wrote this passage with the Capote controversy in mind, and consciously sought to distance himself from the two-headed beast known as "the nonfiction novel." Others, including new-journalist Tom Wolfe, saw Capote's novel as confirmation of their own efforts to break down the barriers between so-called fiction and so-called fact, high-brow and low-brow, art and journalism, and ultimately between art and life.

With twenty years of hindsight to focus the critical faculties, one can now see that Capote's experiment was neither unique nor unprecedented. Far more, it was symptomatic of a richly fertile period in the cultural life of the United States—the most creative eruption of talent since that early nineteenth-century flowering which F. O. Matthiessen dubbed "The New England Renaissance." The once-impervious Geneva conventions of the mind were assailed from all sides. While novelists like Truman Capote and Norman Mailer coopted the techniques of journalism, journalists like Tom Wolfe and Gay Talese raided the camp of the novelist. Andy Warhol took soup cans from the supermarket and displayed them in galleries and museums; he proclaimed the Coca-Cola bottle to be as worthy of aesthetic contemplation as the wine-bottle; and he transformed the jerky, out-of-focus home-movie into an underground art form. Choreographer Merce Cunningham, composer John Cage, and painter Robert Rauschenberg collaborated on improvised "happenings"—multimedia events that mingled conventional disciplines with an indiscriminate zest and contagious irreverence for traditions.

In the new, anything-goes aesthetic, nothing was quite where one expected it to be. Accustomed to films based on novels (and generally convinced of the "superiority" of the book both in time and in quality), moviegoers were confronted with bestsellers based on films: *Love Story, Last Tango in Paris, Deep Throat, 2001.* Where music fans had once awaited recordings of popular performances, they now attended performances based, like *Jesus Christ Superstar* or *Tommy,* on recordings. Such apparent displacements of the technological or "synthetic" event offer an important key to the revolutionary spirit of the times. Roy Lichtenstein, James Rosenquist, and Andy Warhol did not merely take commercial icons as their subjects; they also put aside traditional painterly tools in favor of commercial mass-reproduction techniques—stencils, spray-guns, photo-offset screens. Warhol referred to his studio as "The Factory," and developed assembly-line methods for producing and signing his canvases. In *The Philosophy of Andy Warhol from A to Z and Back Again,* the prince of pop (who had illustrated a volume of Capote short stories in 1952) recalled his youthful affair with a television set, "which has continued to the present, when I play around in my bedroom with as many as four at a time. But I didn't get married," he confesses, "until 1964 when I got my first tape recorder."[9]

By the mid-1960's, an estimated 95 percent of American households had at least one television set; before the end of the decade, a third of those were two-TV households.[10] Establishment guardians direly predicted that the resulting image-bombardment would deprive the arts (both literary and visual) of one of their most time-honored components, for the image itself was rapidly becoming a throw-away commodity, no more precious or cherished than the beer-can or disposable diaper. (The introduction of a mass-produced photocopier in 1960 further aggravated the problem; and since the first Xerox machines were too heavy for salesmen to carry about, they were marketed primarily through television.) Narrative also seemed bankrupted by the new fad—not just through serials, televised plays, and movie reruns, but by the medium's overall preference for organizing information into instantly digestible mini-narratives with recognizable beginnings, middles, and ends. Even the ubiquitous commercial followed suit: from the disgrace of dingy laundry to the wind-flapping penants of cleanliness, godliness, motherhood; from bad-breath ostracism to Pepsodent romance; from a tyrannizing Excedrin-headache to the serene control of hearth and home, office and classroom—from Mr. Hyde to Dr. Jekyll within minutes. Many writers, to be sure, reacted to this overkill by retreating into fabulism or intellectual riddles; others consciously stripped the novel and short story of contaminating traces of plot, scene, and character. Non-objective painting had already become the fine-arts dogma, and serious composers strove for increasing "abstraction." Such artists demanded aesthetic results that were not accessible to the hyperliteral modes of film and television or the banalities of popular culture. Others, however, began to experiment with such media, producing results through the underground cinema or video art that have, in turn, exercised a measurable influence on their commercial counterparts. It was, after all, a time-honored American principle: "If you can't beat 'em, join 'em."

Though he assailed the documentary as "the bleeding heart of television land," Mailer adapted several of its devices to his own ends in *The Armies of the Night.* That idiosyncratic venture into the realms of nonfiction marked the beginning of a vital stage of experimentation in Mailer's art. Whereas Capote intentionally excluded himself from the structure of *In Cold Blood,* Mailer placed himself at the vital center of his work—a metaphysical and political commitment too often dismissed by hostile readers as simple narcissism. But if fiction, like history, is always the distinct and biased hypothesis of an individual intelligence, then the intelligencer must be prepared to submit to such scrutiny. In the oft-quoted metaphor that introduces Part II of *The Armies of the Night,* the author compares both historian and novelist to an astronomer working with faulty tools. "Of course," he argues,

> the tower is crooked, and the telescopes warped, but the instruments
> of all sciences—history so much as physics—are always constructed
> in small or large error; what supports the use of them now is that our
> intimacy with the master builder of the tower, and the lens grinder of
> the telescopes (yes, even the machinist of the barrels) has given some
> advantage for correcting the error of the instruments and the
> imbalance of his tower.[11]

Capote systemically denies us this advantage. What we can never know about his view of Holcomb, Kansas, and its citizens is the degree to which their responses to him as a lisping Easterner/intellectual/homosexual colored their response to his tireless questionings. We see too little of him to make such corrections. In *The Armies of the Night* as in *Of a Fire on the Moon* Mailer stands before us with his psyche bared, loudly proclaiming his faults and fears, his broken marriages, his drinking habits, his political prejudices. The book opens with a brief article from *Time* magazine describing the author's drunken misbehavior at the Ambassador Theater rally preceding the march on the Pentagon in October 1967; it is followed by Mailer's own confessional account of that episode and the events surrounding it. Then, in the book's concluding section, he adopts the sober and objective voice of the historian to comment on the Pentagon march. Which of these versions of reality can one trust? On the basis of its tone, the historical treatment would seem more reliable than the subjective one, but the author of "History as a Novel" presumably shares the same flaws revealed by the author of "The Novel as History." It is, after all, the same man; he has merely donned a different hat.

Mailer's projection of himself as imperfect spokesman for his time continues in *Miami and the Siege of Chicago* (1968), but finds its richest expression in *Of a Fire on the Moon* (1970). In the narrative persona of Aquarius, the author reflects on the Apollo launch as a human undertaking deeply resonant with meaning, and therefore despairs that it has been reduced for much of the world to a second-rate television spectacular. The horror of our time, he suggests, is "the size of each new event, and the paucity of its reverberation."[12] In an inversion of Nick Carraway's romantic contemplation of the moon hanging over Gatsby's house, he refers to America as an "empty country filled with wonders."[13] Yet through the sheer generative power of his own language, he restores the wonder, guides us into unplumbed, metaphysical depths, launches us on a fantastic voyage into the unknown, transforms NASA's nuts-and-bolts technologies into soaring poetry. The immense satellite is a grain elevator, a chalice, a cathedral, a white whale, Icarus and Madonna, ghost, angel, and devil. Mailer has done his journalistic homework, but it is the allusive, self-doubting, probing mind of the novelist that produces the following description of lift-off:

> Flames flew in cataract against the cusp of the flame shield, and then sluiced along the paved ground down two opposite channels in the concrete, two underground rivers of flame which poured into the air on either side a hundred feet away, then flew a hundred feet further. Two mighty torches of flame like the wings of a yellow bird of fire flew over a field, covered a field with brilliant yellow bloomings of flame, and in the midst of it, white as a ghost, white as the white of Melville's Moby Dick, white as the shrine of the Madonna in half the churches of the world, this slim angelic mysterious ship of stages rose without sound out of its incarnation of flame and began to ascend slowly into the sky, slow as Melville's Leviathan might swim, slowly as we might swim upward in a dream looking for the air.[14]

The Apollo-Saturn moon launch also plays a central role in Tom Wolfe's *The Right Stuff* (1979), but the later book never achieves the demonic energy that animates Mailer's account. (Furthermore, having so brilliantly recapitulated a "media event" that his readers have all witnessed for themselves, Mailer has the audacity to relate it a second time within the same volume.) Though his more recent anatomies of the art and architecture establishments are at best extended essay-harangues, Tom Wolfe remains a central figure in the emergence of the nonfiction novel. Like Gay Talese and Hunter Thompson he began his career as a journalist, but was uncomfortable with the formal hegemonies of his craft. He entered the arena of nonfiction fiction in 1963 with an article in *Esquire* magazine entitled "There Goes (Varoom! Varoom!) That Kandy-Kolored (thphhhhhh!) Tangerine-Flake Streamline Baby (Raghhh!) Around the Bend (Brummmmmmmmmmmmmmmmmmmm) . . ." The first of a series of remarkable pieces on pop-culture fads and personalities, it was allegedly composed as a memorandum, which the *Esquire* editors chose to publish in the "unfinished" form.

The discovery that Wolfe and a number of his colleagues were making was that "it just might be possible to write journalism that would . . . read like a novel."[15] With his first, serendipitous venture into "parajournalism," the young reporter discovered a heady sense of liberation. As he later recalled,

> What interested me was not simply the discovery that it was possible to write accurate nonfiction with techniques usually associated with novels and short stories. It was that—plus. It was the discovery that it was possible in nonfiction, in journalism, to use any literary device, from the traditional dialogisms of the essay to stream-of-consciousness, and to use many different kinds simultaneously, or within a relatively short space . . . to excite the reader both

> intellectually and emotionally. I am not laying all those gladiolas on
> that rather curious first article of mine, you understand. I'm only
> talking about what it suggested to me.[16]

The suggestions were to flower into *The Electric Kool-Aid Acid Test* (1968)—a psychedelic picaresque, a wistful reminder of the paradoxical need for heroes in a faceless society, and a comment on technological clutter. Wolfe's protagonist, the novelist Ken Kesey, is a charismatic leader of tremendous energy and frenetic drive who acts as the compelling center for a new family of man. On the darker side, his career suggests parallels to that of Charles Manson: both "families" travel across the country in busses; both experiment heavily in drugs; both are so intimately linked to technology that individuals themselves often seem no more than cyborgs. The American Dream in its spatial, spiritual, and economic dimensions is once more turned to nightmare—as in *The Great Gatsby* or *In Cold Blood*. And the long-sought earthly paradise that inspired countless pioneers has now been wired for sound.

Stylistically, Wolfe's work helps focus some of the most tantalizing questions concerning the nature and responsibilities of art in a technological society. He himself creates a style directly dependent on the technical variables of the printed page. "I found," he says, "a great many pieces of punctuation and typography lying around dormant when I came along—and I must say I had a good time using them [. . .]. I found that things like exclamation points, italics, and abrupt shifts (dashes) and syncopations (dots) helped to give the illusion not only of a person talking but of a person thinking."[17] Together with the use of the historical present, such devices lend *The Electric Kool-Aid Acid Test* an electrifying feeling of immediacy. The language of the book spits and curls and drips and turns in upon itself; it races ahead, slows to a near stand-still, or chirps and whines and drones like the machines compulsively manipulated by Kesey's Merry Pranksters. Ken Kesey himself emerges here as a seminal figure for his generation—not merely as the creator of two distinguished novels, but more significantly as the champion of a lifestyle intensely dependent on technology and the drugs of technology; as initiator, too, of such technological phenomena as the multimedia show and acid rock.

Kesey is, in short, not merely an individual but a commodity, a phenomenon, an event—for the culture of the West what Warhol was for the East; and Wolfe's style provided uniquely suited to explore such a personality, suggesting the various forces, fads, compulsions, illusions, and needs that spiral round him. The figure is a compelling one, to both author and reader, but only a frail line separates the ego of a Kesey from the psychopathology of a Manson, and Wolfe clearly sees the threat, reflecting it in the very disintegration that attacks his prose in the concluding chapter. Plugged into their instruments, Kesey and one of his lieutenants sit alone in The Barn, communicating through variable-lag microphones, and the very images of their dissociative dialogue are significant—soldiers, fleas, latrines, suicide, Hitler, psychedelics, heroin, trading stamps. Like the book itself, this final duet is a study of creative frenzy as it verges on madness; the grandfather of this particular acid test is Edgar Allan Poe. Such are the themes that Mailer reiterates two years later in *Of a Fire on the Moon*—the aching need for heroes, the journey as a search for human definition, the obsession with technology, the fear of technology. Phrased in more traditional terms, Capote and Wolfe and Mailer are all obsessed by the loss of innocence; their protagonists, whether bound for a farm, a barn, or the caverns of the moon, are all picaresque voyagers. But unlike the resourceful Huckleberry Finn, who makes a charade of murder, Capote's vagabonds are ruthless killers. Mailer, too, would focus his own most compelling nonfiction novel on a vicious murderer—Gary Gilmore of the *Executioner's Song* (1979).

Mailer referred to his gargantuan book on Gilmore as "a true life story,"[18] perhaps consciously echoing a popular-fiction formula that has recurred since Defoe's *Moll Flanders*. Indeed, the nonfiction novel, however directly it responded to contemporary realities, was also a return to an older narrative idiom that freely mixed observed fact with imaginative elaboration—as in Defoe's *Journal of the Plague Year* or Sterne's *Sentimental Journey*. Audiences were once blissfully untroubled by such liberties, as the early Norse sagas, Greek epics, or Shakespeare's history plays richly confirm. Tom Wolfe cites, as more immediate antecedents, DeQuincey's *Confessions of an English Opium Eater*, Dickens's *Sketches of Boz*, Twain's *Innocents Abroad*, and Orwell's *Down and Out in Paris and London*. But he repeatedly suggests that, for his generation—for novelizing journalists and journalizing novelists alike—*In Cold Blood* was the catalyzing experience.

Its author never again found the "true life" materials from which he could mold a major work of fiction. Significantly, the rambling and self-indulgent *magnum opus* with which he wrestled in the final years of his life was hopefully entitled *Answered Prayers*. The few chapters to appear in print reveal a progressive blurring of critical faculties—a fundamental confusion between social history and tittering gossip that would suffice to set the ghost of Samuel Pepys on chain-rattling midnight rambles. Sporadically, Capote published shorter works—essays, interviews, and short stories—that recalled the virtuoso performances of the 1950's; in addition to composing television and film scripts, the aging *Wunderkind* of American letters made his own shrill film debut. The best of his later writings were collected in 1980 as *Music for Chameleons*. The lyric title story is a bravura performance, but the book's real strength lies in the gothically grim novella *Handcarved Coffins*, subtitled "A Nonfiction Account of an American Crime." That the author found an entirely new voice for this second exploration of the theme is a final tribute to the genius pathetically dissipated in drugs and alcohol. And it was a reminder that *In Cold Blood*, more than any other single work of the postwar period, had helped to redraw the map of American fiction.

NOTES

1. See, for example, William L. Nance, *The Worlds of Truman Capote* (New York, 1970), 179-180.

2. James Jones, *Go to the Widowmaker* (New York, 1966), unnumbered page with a "Special Note" by the author.

3. The "instant metaphors" of the case are discussed in detail in my own article, "Why the Chickens Came Home to Roost in Holcomb, Kansas." See Truman Capote's *In Cold Blood: A Critical Handbook,* ed. Irving Malin (Belmont/Cal., 1968), 154-163.

4. In an interview with George Plimpton, Capote recalled reading the first, brief article on the Kansas murders: "[. . . .] it suddenly struck me that a crime, the study of one such, might provide the broad scope I needed to write the kind of book I wanted to write. Moreover, the human heart being what it is, murder was a theme not likely to darken and yellow with time." See George Plimpton, "The Story Behind a Nonfiction Novel," *New York Times Book Review* (January 16, 1966), 3.

5. Alfred Kazin, "The World as a Novel: From Capote to Mailer," *The New York Review of Books* (April 8, 1971), 26.

6. John Hersey, *The Algiers Motel Incident,* Bantam (New York, 1968), 10.

7. Truman Capote, *In Cold Blood* (New York, 1966), 3.

8. Hersey, 27.

9. Andy Warhol, *The Philosophy of Andy Warhol* (From A to B & Back Again) (New York, 1975), 26.

10. The statistics are taken from Daniel J. Boorstin, *The Americans: The Democratic Experience* (New York, 1973), 393-394.

11. Norman Mailer, *The Armies of the Night,* Signet (New York, 1968), 245.

12. Norman Mailer, *Of a Fire on the Moon* (Boston, 1970), 40.

13. *Ibid.,* 98.

14. *Ibid.,* 95-96.

15. Tom Wolfe, *The New Journalism, With an Anthology* Edited by Tom Wolfe and E. W. Johnson (New York, 1973), 9.

16. *Ibid.,* 15.

17. Tom Wolfe, "The Birth of 'The New Journalism,'" New York, 5 (February 14, 1972), 37.

18. Norman Mailer, *The Executioner's Song* (Boston, 1979), 1053. The context in which the phrase appears, with Mailer's own italics, is the following: "Let it be said then that without the cooperation of Nicole Baker, there would not have been a way to do this factual account—this, dare I say it, *true life story,* with its real names and real lives—as if it were a novel."

Religion and Style in _The Dogs Bark_ and _Music for Chameleons_

JOHN C. WALDMEIR

There are several reasons to compare Truman Capote's two works, _The Dogs Bark_ and _Music for Chameleons_.[1] In both Capote has collected previously published prose that varies in length and subject matter. He has structured the pieces carefully that together they might convey certain themes and intentions. In the course of organizing them he also has tended to place similar works in parallel places. Both books, for example, begin with prefaces that discuss his experiences as a writer, end with creative dialogues in which Capote converses with himself, and contain, in their respective middles, long works that Capote valued for what they contributed to his development as a writer.

In addition to these similarities, both books also treat a topic that few critics have examined in Capote's writing: religion.[2] _The Dogs Bark_ introduces the topic in a number of selections, including the piece that opens the volume, "A Voice from a Cloud," Capote's early travelogue, _Local Color_, and his much publicized (and somewhat controversial) interview with Marlon Brando, "The Duke and his Domain." _Music for Chameleons_ refers to the topic consistently throughout the text; all fourteen works employ a terminology that is either recognized or best interpreted as "religious."

Though long neglected, religion in fact holds a prominent place in Capote's writing. His first novel, _Other Voices, Other Rooms_ opens with a quote from the prophet Jeremiah. _Answered Prayers_, his final, unfinished work, takes its title from a quote by St. Theresa. In between there are Gothic tales with religious overtones, such as "A Tree of Night," "Master Misery," and "The Headless Hawk"; extended treatments of holidays with religious significance, like _The Thanksgiving Visitor_ and _One Christmas_; and an array of nonfiction prose that repeatedly describes the significance of people and events in religious terms.

If religion offers readers a basis for comparing works within Capote's corpus, it also provides them with a reason for contrasting certain texts. Despite their similarities, _The Dogs Bark_ and _Music for Chameleons_, for example, assume very different positions toward the topic. The first uses words associated with traditional religious vocabularies to describe a sense of sacred "otherness." From its opening pages "God" is objective, like the statue in a New Orleans courtyard with "stark glass angel eyes" that "stare upward" (*Dogs*, 21). No narrative voice in this work experiences the deity as "close." By contrast, *Music for Chameleons* speaks of the divine as a source of "help." The confession Capote utters at the close of this collection suggests his faith: "I began to believe in God again, and understood that Sook was right: that everything was His design, the old moon and the new moon, the hard rain falling, and if only I would ask Him to help me, He would." Here the "other" is not only omnipotent but also intimate, he heals the fractured voice of the "drug addict," "homosexual," "genius" who speaks (*Music*, 264).

As a direct result of such theological assumptions about the ways of God to man, Capote's collections differ in significant ways. They are organized, for instance, toward different ends. In keeping with the emphasis upon objectivity and "otherness" in *The Dogs Bark*, that work builds toward selections anthologized from a book Capote published with photographer Richard Avedon, *Observations*. From their text Capote selects an assortment of reflections on a cast of characters, including Mae West, Louis Armstrong, Humphrey Bogart, and Marilyn Monroe. All of the selections examine the public side of these figures, Mae West speaking in a "sassy drawl" or Armstrong as a "grinning Buddha" stomping and shouting "his way into the sunny side of the street" (*Dogs*, 366, 368). *Music for Chameleons*, by contrast, ends with a section that is suited to its dialogic approach to matters of ultimate meaning, "Conversational Portraits." Here Capote talks and interacts with his cleaning lady, Mary Sanchez, the proprietor of a New Orleans waterfront bar, Big Junebug Johnson, convicted murderer Robert Beausoleil, and with himself. "Conversational Portraits" also contains a piece on Marilyn Monroe. But unlike the essay in *The Dogs Bark*, which celebrates the ripe sensuality that was so essential to her on-screen persona, "A Beautiful Child" in *Music* seeks to understand this quality and to connect it with that side of Monroe that resembles "thin fleecy clouds fragile as lace" (*Music*, 243).

To support their theological assumptions, both *The Dogs Bark* and *Music for Chameleons* refer to traditional, organized forms of religion. But they use those references in different ways. In *The Dogs Bark* Capote cites religious practices from a variety of traditions, but he does so in ways that are almost incidental to the action. In "Tangier" he writes of the Islamic holy month of *Ramadan*, in "The Duke and His Domain" he refers to "Zen meditation" and "Yogi breathing," and in "Haiti" he offers interesting insights into Voodou. Despite possibilities raised by each reference, however, Capote rarely develops his thoughts or integrates them into the worlds he depicts. In "Haiti," for example, he never connects his final claim that "in Voodou . . . there is no boundary between the countries of the living and the dead" with his earlier depiction of

Hyppolite, the country's "most popular . . . primitive painter" whose eight-month old daughter has just died as the piece opens (*Dogs,* 67, 58-59). As a result, "Haiti" remains disjointed and similar to the type of "film" Capote claims he would like to make of that country: ". . . soundless, nothing but a camera brilliantly framing architecture, objects" (*Dogs,* 60).

In *Music for Chameleons* Capote uses words and images associated with traditional forms of religion in ways that seem to offer critical commentaries on its social role. Capote's visit to the magical Mrs. Ferguson in "Dazzle" takes place amid a "Sabbath stillness"; Pearl Bailey's arrival at Los Angeles International Airport to save him from being arrested is called a "miracle" in "Derring-do"; Mary Sanchez's day of cleaning New York apartments and smoking pot ends with a visit to church to pray the "rosary."

In addition to these references, though, there are others in *Music* that seem incidental but in fact are extremely important to the stories in which they appear. Both "A Lamp in a Window" and "Hospitality," for example, use their references to establish sustained reflections on a religious theme: hospitality. Mrs. Kelly's admission in "A Lamp in the Window"—"I was raised a Catholic, but now, I'm almost sorry to say I have an open mind. Too much reading, perhaps"—seems at first to be a humorous aside. A better interpretation, however, recognizes that the comment describes the dynamics of the entire tale. This story begins with the narrator as a passenger in a car driven by the drunken Mr. and Mrs. Roberts, a hostile, argumentative environment that he claims resembles a scene from *Who's Afraid of Virginia Woolf.* It moves from there to the cozy fireside hearth of Mrs. Kelly, which calls to mind the worlds of "Jane Austen . . . Thoreau, and Willa Cather," to name but three. It is Mrs. Kelly who facilitates this transition, and she succeeds because she expresses a hospitality that we should recognize as not only "religious" but decidedly "Christian." "With hazel eyes like the small lamp shining on the table beside her," she embodies the Gospel charge to be "the light of the world (*Music,* 18)." She is the "lamp . . . on a stand" that "gives light to all in the house" (Matthew 5:15). That text from the Sermon on the Mount informs the entire story as it asks readers to ponder the religious meaning of hospitality. "Too much reading" may have diminished Mrs. Kelly's "Catholic" faith, but it has not dimmed her "religious" character.

Capote continues to call our attention to the religious dimension of the host/guest relationship in "Hospitality." Like "A Lamp in the Window" this story uses an incidental reference to organized religion, this time in the form of a visiting Presbyterian missionary to the depression-weary farm of Jennings and Mary Ida Carter, to emphasize religiously-motivated acts of kindness. The fact that the visitor is a Presbyterian minister seems to be of little importance until the reader realizes that Capote contrasts him and his position with two subsequent visitors, one an escaped convict named Bancroft and the other a young unmarried mother named Zilla. Through both contrasts the religious qualifications of the missionary begin to look suspect. Bancroft may be a criminal, but at least he offers to work for a meal. Of the preacher, who devours food "with both hands," the narrator says he "never saw a greedier fellow" (*Music*, 45). Zilla comes with nothing more than a "broken-down suitcase" and a little boy named Jed. But the love between mother and child is evident in a powerful fashion as Zilla bathes him naked in a nearby creek, the two of them "laughing" during this symbolic baptism. By contrast the preacher baptizes nothing and speaks not of love but of horror and hate. His element is not water but fire, and he terrifies his listeners with tales of "cannibals" who have assured him that "the best eatin' is roasted newborn baby" because it "tastes just like lamb" (*Music*, 46).

References to religion in these and other tales suggest a great deal about the value of interpreting in religious terms the pieces that comprise *Music for Chameleons*. But the value extends far beyond a commentary on organized expressions of faith. These works introduce religion as a topic or issue that informs and shapes other literary conventions such as theme and style. The theme of hospitality, for example, assumes religious characteristics in part because Capote employs a recognizable religious vocabulary. Without the dichotomy in "A Lamp" between Catholicism and reading literature, for instance, the reader would have a more difficult time identifying the Sermon on the Mount as the subtext that moves both the narrator and us from a scene that is as fragmented as an Edward Albee play to another that is as seamless as a novel by Jane Austen.

Capote believed that *Music for Chameleons* differed from his previous works principally through its innovative style. "I eventually developed a style," he wrote, "into which I could assimilate everything I knew about writing" (*Music*, xviii). As Jack Hicks points out, the result is an eclectic combination of literary conventions that are "parenthetical" and "reduced." "The frequent use of interrupting commas, ellipses, and dashes," writes Hicks, "illustrates [Capote's] diversionary technique: these all highlight disjointed thought rhythms undercutting plain language."[3] In *Music for Chameleons* the style reflects a polyphony of genres and texts that includes essays, diaries, stage directions, asides to the audience, and numerous other innovations. The tendency toward control that manifests itself in Capote's earlier works gives way here to unpredictability. And if one source of these changes, as Hicks maintains, is that "the role of the narrator" has been expanded "considerably," the reason that such an expanded role should lead to change is that Capote, as narrator, is far less certain of himself.[4] His authority over his text reflects nothing less than a new understanding of God's authority over creation and the ability of sacred language to undercut its "plain" counterpart. Capote illustrates the perils of that relationship as early as the second paragraph in the book. "When God hands you a gift he also hands you a whip," he writes; "and the whip is intended solely for self-flagellation" (*Music*, xi).

In a review of *The Dogs Bark* Willie Morris writes that Capote's "attention to style, to the extraordinary pull of places," is what "gives this volume . . . durability far beyond the perfunctory compendia of [its] pieces."[5] Interestingly, however, he makes this observation while reading a passage from "To Europe," are one that describes Capote's inability to feel "part of" a place. "I was not part of Europe, I never would be," he writes. "Safe, I could leave when I wanted to. . . ."[6] Because Capote uses literary style in *The Dogs Bark* to distance himself from his reader and from the drama he depicts, style in this work is treated as an element of the prose that is distinct from the experiences of writing or reading. Capote describes this model of stylistic excellence in a brief essay from the collection entitled "Style: and the Japanese." There he writes of Mr. Frederick Mariko, a Japanese florist who ran a shop in New Orleans when Capote was a boy. Mr. Mariko's creations, which extend beyond floral arrangements to a series of toys that he fashioned for Capote, provided the future writer with nothing less than "my original aesthetic experience."

Significantly, the wire fish, paper dancers and ornate flowers that Mr. Mariko fashions are experienced by Capote as creations set apart: they are "much too exquisite to be **played** with" (*Dogs*, 354-55). As such they are emblems of a style Capote prefers and tries to imitate in his prose. Like Mr. Mariko's carefully-shaped toys, Capote's essays in *The Dogs Bark* participate in a "ceremony of style, a phenomenon that seems to rotate, in a manner quite separate from emotional content" (*Dogs*, 355). These essays are in many respects dispassionate "silhouettes and souvenirs of persons and places" that constitute, according to Capote, "a prose map, a written geography of my life over the last three decades" (*Dogs*, xvi). Capote's metaphor emphasizes distance. Essays in *The Dogs Bark* form an objective map that delineates not only a specific geographical region but also a particular historical period, 1942-1972. Capote offers them to his audience as objects of study that, like their prototypes, are too exquisite to be "played with."

Capote interprets them this way as well. He announces his attitude in the initial essay when he describes the experience of re-reading his first published novel, *Other Voices, Other Rooms*: "I stood there and looked back at the boy I had left behind" (*Dogs*, 4). Compiled and presented in this format, these pieces are set apart from one another and from Capote. They seem to fit the category of "static writing" that Capote refers to in his preface. "I am not a keen reader of my own books," he writes, "what's done is done" (*Dogs*, 10). Because they do not engage him, Capote can speak only of "controlling" them, of enacting through them the "artist's principle task: to tame and shape the raw creative vision" (*Dogs*, 7). Once it is tamed and shaped, Capote understands its product as entirely "other." In these essays "**history**," as Warner Watson says at the end of the central piece, *The Muses Are Heard*, "is fenced in" (*Dogs*, 307).

Capote dramatizes this sense of otherness through his frequent use of enclosed spaces. *The Dogs Bark* opens with references to the bedrooms in Alabama and

Louisiana where he wrote *Other Voices, Other Rooms*; it closes with his efforts to answer the question: "if you had to live in just one place—without ever leaving—where would it be?" (*Dogs*, 405) In between there is the New Orleans courtyard that begins *Local Color* and the train compartment that ends that collection. There is the old house, Fontana Vecchia, Brooklyn's "House on the Heights," Marlon Brando's hotel room in Kyote, Isaac Dinesen's parlor at tea-time, and the courthouse in Western Kansas that stimulates thoughts about filming *In Cold Blood*. In each case Capote crafts spaces that "contain" action, character, mood, tone. If the writing generates a sense of energy from conflict, it does so in part because of pressure from depicted environments. Like the image of Ezra Pound (in the essay that bears his name), striding back and forth on the deck of a ship bound to carry him to Italy, each one of these pieces serves as "a cage that . . . becomes life itself."

To make the "cage" seem like "life itself"—to create what he describes in his "observation" of Marilyn Monroe as a "verbal imprisonment"—requires a style that calls attention to itself by emphasizing, even celebrating, objectivity as a source of power and authority (*Dogs*, 380). One example in *The Dogs Bark* of such a style is the piece "A House on the Heights," which Capote admired for the fact that "all the movement depends on the writing itself," on "how the sentences sound, suspend, balance, and tumble" (*Dogs*, xviii). This rather long, highly stylized reflection on Brooklyn Heights contains the following description of a group of sailors Capote sees tanning themselves on a small stretch of beach along the river.

> But the bare-footed sailors on the beach, the three I saw reclining there, profiles against the sundown, seemed mythical as mermen: more exactly, mermaids—for their hair, striped with albino streaks, was lady-length, a savage fiber falling to their shoulders; and in their ears gold rings glinted. Whether plenipotentiaries from the pearl-floored palace of Poseidon or mariners merely, Viking-tressed sea-men out of the Gothic North languishing after a long and barberless voyage, they are included permanently in my memory's curio cabinet: an object to be revolved in the light that way and this, like those crystal lozenges with secretive carvings inside. (*Dogs*, 147)

The passage is typical of much writing in this and other essays from *The Dogs Bark*, because it turns on several characteristic elements of Capote's style. For example, alliteration runs throughout the passage, most obviously in the repetition of words beginning with the letter "m" in the first sentence—mythical, mermen, more, mermaids—and the use of words that begin with "p" in sentence two: plenipotentiaries, pearl-floored palace of Poseidon, permanently. One effect of such repetition is humor, and clearly Capote intends to make light of numerous circumstances in this text. A second effect, related to the first but more basic, is that the passage calls attention to itself.

The reader notices Capote's writing here, the way his sentences sound and the way his words tumble. To notice the writing is to recognize the presence of a writer. Such a presence, however, does not imply that the author is involved in his work in ways that reflect a deep interest or passion. On the contrary, the style suggests a craftsman who shapes his prose in a very objective way. As though to reinforce that sense of stylistic objectivity, Capote deliberately describes an object here. His sailors exist in his "memory's curio cabinet," each one "an object . . . sealed inside."

In this passage Capote's style is consonant also with the way he treats religion in the book. The "distance" Capote establishes between himself and his memories invites him to depict the sailors as possessing what he calls "mythical" qualities. Androgynous figures, these sailors are both "mermen" and "mermaids." They seem to have come "Viking-tressed" from the "Gothic North," and they shall return to a sea that is described as nothing less than "the palace of Poseidon." They are portrayed humorously as gods in language that follows naturally from the highly objective style that Capote adopts. Distant from Capote, they are like the house on the Bay of Lindos that Capote writes about in "Greek Paragraphs": "all I will ever do," Capote acknowledges, "is remember it."

This particular nexus of style and religious subject matter is no accident. *The Dogs Bark* opens with a piece that establishes a theological paradigm for the style of all subsequent essays in the collection, and its assumptions parallel the guiding assumptions of much Biblical prose. "It is unusual," Capote writes in this opening piece, "but occasionally it happens to almost every writer that the writing of some particular story seems outer-willed and effortless; it is as though one were a secretary transcribing the words of a voice from a cloud." (*Dogs*, 7). The words provide the essay with a title and the book with perhaps its most succinct statement of Capote's tendency to treat his creation as something decidedly "other." A vehicle of God's word, he creates as if he were that word, one who spoke "another language" and embodied "a secret spiritual geography" (*Dogs*, 6).

Such a "secret" implies privileges and indicates that this text addresses questions about power in a style that enacts a very traditional theology. In it God is sovereign and necessary to human life and character, and theology serves to translate that sovereign otherness in ways that respect its essential difference from secular realms of experience. The controlling metaphor describes God as "Lord," the fundamental text is Exodus, and the subsequent theological approach is neo-orthodox, a tradition that reaches its zenith in the twentieth-century with the writings of Karl Barth.

By the time Capote publishes *Music for Chameleons*, this religious paradigm changes in significant ways for him, and because of these changes readers encounter a very different religious style. Central to this later collection is Capote's "nonfiction account of an American crime," *Handcarved Coffins*, and in the middle of that tale is a scene that illustrates the fundamental theological change that underwrites Capote's style. In that scene Capote and detective Jake Pepper are visiting Bob Quinn, the rancher whom Pepper suspects is responsible for a string of murders. Quinn knows that Pepper suspects him but that he has no substantial evidence; Capote is meeting Quinn for the first time and has agreed to play him in a game of chess. While Pepper and Quinn trade barbs about whether Quinn could have taken and developed photographs of his victims before their deaths, Capote ponders moves on the chessboard. "Look here, Jake," Quinn exclaims at one point. "Your friend almost has me checkmated. **Almost** . . . ." Capote then goes on to write:

> It was true; with a skill subconsciously resurrected, I had been marching my ebony army with considerable, though unwitting, competence, and had indeed managed to maneuver Quinn's king into a perilous position. In one sense I regretted my success, for Quinn was using it to divert the angle of Jake's inquiry, to revert from the suddenly sensitive topic of photography back to chess; on the other hand, I was elated—by playing flawlessly, I might now very well win. Quinn scratched his chin, his grey eyes dedicated to the religious task of rescuing his king. (*Music*, 116)

The passage compares in interesting ways with the earlier one quoted from *The Dogs Bark*. Here too Capote uses alliteration to help the passage flow. However, with one notable exception the sounds come in pairs: "skill subconsciously," "ebony army," "managed . . . maneuver," "Quinn's king," "perilous position," "suddenly sensitive," "well win," "Quinn . . . chin," "chessboard . . . blurred." The pairings make alliteration (and therefore the passage) far less noticeable than its predecessor in *The Dogs Bark*. Readers pay less attention to the writing as an object in and of itself and more attention to the drama, which depicts a series of divisions between Pepper and Quinn, Quinn and Capote, and, as we soon learn, between Capote and Pepper as well. The pairings therefore emphasize the importance of cohesion over sound and rhythm or melody. As Quinn, for example, seeks to reclaim his king and all it symbolizes in this struggle between innocence and guilt, alliteration heightens the drama associated with that goal.

The exception to these pairings is the alliteration between words beginning with the prefix "re" that run like a thematic string throughout the paragraph. "Resurrected," "revert," "religious," "rescuing" all appear in the paragraph and together they suggest that cohesion, which should result from some resolution to the various dramatic conflicts, involves a re-turn to another time, place, or individual. This return is "religious" because it requires that Capote "re-ligare" or "bind-back" together what he had considered dead or forgotten. This sense of the term is very different from the one that informs *The Dogs Bark*, and Capote's two styles clarify the difference. In that earlier work Capote seemed bound to nothing, and his distance from his subjects allowed him to describe them as both mythical creatures and figures in a curio cabinet. Although the discussion of photography and the game of chess that frame the setting in *Music* offer Capote an ideal opportunity to once again style a very objective scene, he chooses instead to use them to begin a most personal revelation. Suddenly he is five years old and spending his summer with relatives in a small Alabama town.

> There was a river attached to this town, too; a sluggish muddy river that repelled me, for it was full of water moccasins and whiskered catfish. However, much as I disliked their ferocious snouts, I was fond of captured catfish, fried and dripping with ketchup; we had a cook who served them often. Her name was Lucy Joy, though I've seldom known a less joyous human. She was a hefty black woman, reserved, very serious; she seemed to live from Sunday to Sunday, when she sang in the choir of some pineywoods church. (*Music*, 116-17)

The flashback continues important features of the style that precedes it. There is some pairing of words through alliteration: "river . . . repelled," "water . . . whiskered," "captured . . . ketchup." The more significant pairing, however, occurs within entire sentences. Each sentence in the passage joins two separate statements; three of them denote this union with a semicolon. None of these statements seem particularly congruent when examined closely. The river he refers to in the first part of the second sentence, the Blue River that is central to *Handcarved Coffins*, is clear and rapid (it has at least one waterfall where Addie swims); as such it is the opposite of the "sluggish muddy" and dangerous water Capote describes in the second half of the same sentence. The third sentence describes both Capote's like and dislike for catfish (as well as a basic structuralist dichotomy between the raw and the cooked). The fourth contrasts Lucy Joy's demeanor with her name while the fifth points out that she is both "reserved, very serious" and someone who is not afraid to sing out in the choir of her Pentecostal church. Only Capote's style binds these sentences together and allows readers to move easily from one to the next.

Capote describes that style in his Preface to *Music* in ways that help readers understand how it enacts religious ideas, themes, even language in the book. In writing *Music*, he states that he set himself "center stage, and reconstructed, in a severe, minimal manner, commonplace conversations with everyday people. . . ." After he writes page after page of this "simpleminded" prose, he develops "a style," what he calls a "framework into which I could assimilate everything I knew about writing." According to this passage, one way to read the alliterative pairing of words that appear, for example, in *Handcarved Coffins*, is as an expression of the pairings Capote sought as he developed his minimalist style: relationships between himself and others. Capote challenges himself to cultivate a literary style that is true to the experience of relationship.

"Commonplace" and "simpleminded," the style is also, Capote goes on to say, "underwritten" and "clear as a country creek" (*Music*, xvi-xvii).

The "severity" of the pairings help to keep the style "simple," and one could equate this simplicity with naive faith in a God to whom Capote calls at the end of "Nocturnal Turnings" with the traditional bedtime prayer for children: "Now I lay me down to sleep . . ." (*Music*, 264). However, the pairing is deceptively simple. Stylistically, passages from *Music* tend to bring words, clauses, sentences together only to highlight the tension that threatens to force them apart. This situation applies not only to those selections from *Handcarved Coffins* discussed above, but also to other texts. Consider the following from the title story.

> Raising my eyes from the mirror's demonic shine, I notice my hostess has momentarily retreated from the terrace into her shadowy salon. A piano chord echoes, and another. Madame is toying with the same tune. Soon the music lovers assemble, chameleons scarlet, green, lavender, an audience that, lined out on the floor of the terra-cotta terrace, resembles written arrangement of musical notes. A Mozartean mosaic. (*Music*, 12)

The passage describes a group of chameleons coming together to hear piano music. Notice, however, how fragile is their bond. Not only are the creatures likely to "scatter like sparks from an exploding star" (*Music*, 4), every element of the text threatens to do the same because of the duplicity or "doubleness" that defines its references. In the first sentence, for example, Capote raises two eyes from his image or second self in the mirror, which is both demonic (dark) and shiny (light), in order to notice that his hostess, the Martinique aristocrat who entertains him during the afternoon, has moved from the light of the terrace to the shadows of the salon. From the salon she plays two chords on her piano, which gives the narrator the sense that she is "toying with" or doubling "the same tune." As a result of her music, chameleons gather ("they are very fond of music," she points out earlier) on the terra-cotta floor of the terrace. They come as an "audience" but resemble in their arrangement the music itself. They are, therefore, both a "mosaic" of listeners and the music they hear.

For a writer who has traded throughout his career in themes of doubleness—light and dark, child and adult, good and evil—the duplicity of this passage is not entirely novel. What is new in this story and this collection is precisely what Capote calls our attention to in his Preface: his attempt to embed those traditional themes, and the corresponding tensions they create, into the style of the prose. Style now provides a "framework," he writes, to contain all facets of his prose; it becomes; he says, the palette onto which he places "all his colors" (*Music*, xvii).

Conceived of in this way, style enriches content. Within this framework, the "colors" of religion—its themes, images, vocabularies—suggest certain theological premises about the relationship between God and human life, the sacred and profane. The tension between coming together and coming apart that is evident within Capote's style both reflects the pairings he dramatizes and enacts the tensions created by that drama. Through this stylistic doubling, features of the text that readers traditionally associate with religion become theologically-rich symbols.

One example of such a symbol is Blue River, which weaves throughout *Handcarved Coffins*. Jack Hicks's analysis of this river helps link that symbol to Capote's writing, thereby indicating its "double" quality. "The Blue River is a metaphor for the author's desire for historical/mythic continuity," writes Hicks, "his hope for a revivified narrative flow." Initially it is a "source of life," Hicks says, but soon it assumes qualities that are "demonic and death-dealing" as it becomes more closely associated with the demise of several characters. When it undergoes this transformation as a symbol, it helps to transform Capote's writing. Like the river, "the narrative," Hicks points out, "churns itself into broken forms, subsumes other genres, seeks power in the conflation of screenplay, confession, diary." In a simultaneous fashion, both symbol and narrative are found doubling in their textual function and meaning.[7]

Read in the light of all the. religious meaning Capote invests in Blue River—the fact that it stimulates a series of flashbacks to his own forced baptism forty years earlier, performed against his will by Lucy Joy and the reverend Bobby Joe Snow, a double of Bob Quinn—the symbol begins to illuminate the theological complexity of Capote's writing in *Music*. In addition to dramatizing all that is at stake in the ritual of baptism, the complex and dangerous exchange between life and death that Saint Paul described a "dying to Christ," this central symbol in *Handcarved Coffins* suggests the doubleness of all language about God. Through narrative and symbol, and in the style he employs to join both, Capote explicates the relation of human life to "God," that word that Paul Ricouer asserts holds a "double power to gather all the significations that issue from partial discourses [uttered by humans] and to open up a horizon that escapes from the closure of discourse."[8] Moving between these two options, and therefore following a very different trajectory than the one initiated by *The Dogs Bark*, Capote seemed prepared to embrace the leper he refers to at the conclusion of "Nocturnal Turnings," the one whom St. Julien kissed and discovered to be God. *Answered Prayers* is the result of that embrace, and no critical study of it has yet been written to determine if in fact Capote continued to dramatize the tension between the joy of the gift and the lash of the whip that was his—and is our—lot.

NOTES

1. Truman Capote, *The Dogs Bark: Public People and Private Places,* (New York: Random House, 1973); *Music for Chameleons*, (New York: Random House, 1980). All references in the text will be to these editions.

2. Throughout this essay I use "religion" as a concept that organizes an extensive vocabulary or "lexical field." "Religion" gives us a vocabulary for describing, analyzing, and asserting the meaning of certain traditions, texts, practices, images, etc.

3. Jack Hicks, "'Fire, Fire, Fire Flowing Like a River, River, River': History and Postmodernism in Truman Capote's *Handcarved Coffins*." In *History and Post-War Writing*, Theo D'haen and Hans Bertens, eds. (Amsterdam: Rodopi, 1990), 182.

4. Ibid., 182.

5. Willie Morris, "Capote's Muse Is Heard: *The Dogs Bark*," *New Republic* (13 November 1973): 22.

6. Ibid.

7. Hicks, "'Fire, Fire, Fire Flowing Like a River, River, River,'" 179.

8. Paul Ricoeur, "Philosophy and Religious Language," *Journal of Religion* 54 (1974): 71-85. Reprinted in and quoted from Ricoeur, *Figuring the Sacred: Religion, Narrative and Imagination*, ed. Mark Wallace, (Minneapolis: Fortress Press), 46.

"Fire, Fire, Fire Flowing Like a River, River, River": History and Postmodernism in Truman Capote's *Handcarved Coffins*

JACK HICKS

The waters of history have long made a nurturing mother for us, as they play down to us traditionally through prose in tides of genre, rivers of continuous narrative, deep mimetic lakes of character. But for many postmodern American writers of fiction and nonfiction, this mother has become a diabolical matriarch—comic, deceptive, murderous. As an informing matrix for human life, she ceases to exist.

Turn first to fiction. For prose postmoderns disparate as John Barth, Kurt Vonnegut, Jr., Jerzy Kosinski and Thomas Pynchon, history is a deceiving agent, and the fictive tropes and texts giving her voice must be self-consciously exposed and undone. Barth burlesques the founding nostalgias of the New World, limning, instead, a bawdy new *ur*-myth, at the heart of which is an America opened as a fresh market for the international opium trade. His "historical" Captain John Smith is a mythic counteragent, and the tools of his founding trade are not beads and trinkets, blunderbusses, or the healing modern sciences, but texts: a trunkful of pornography to woo the New World "salvages," and a secret diary, in which lurks an eggplant recipe guaranteeing the eternal, conquering priapus.

For Vonnegut in *Slaughterhouse-5*, the urge to history, encased in martial fiction, is a vicious comic ruse, and even the anti-war novel, which rejects warfare, valorizes the individual warrior of conscience, and is thus complicit in extending a history of senseless brutality. The form and its inevitable awakening protagonist, from Henry Fleming to Yossarian, make warfare morally palatable. Earth people are *easy*, the Tralfamadoreans tell us—they already know our accidental and absurd end—and they posit a planet and literature in which everything happens at once and leads finally nowhere. In Vonnegut's hand, they expose the petty human urge to cloak self-destruction in self-deluding myth.

In *History and Post-War Writing*, Theo D'haen and Hans Bertens, eds. Amsterdam/ Atlanta: Rodopi, 1990, 171-84·

In his postmodern fable *The Painted Bird*, Jerzy Kosinski also takes the historic World War II as his canvas. The will to yoke such grand terror in continuous narrative, and the need to create a young warrior who awakens in battle are both shown as annihilating impulses. The child protagonist blunders from village to village and realizes finally that the social cord itself is diseased. To be fully free, he must reject society and all its institutions, from language to history to the life narratives of others, all of which promise his extermination.

Similarly, for Thomas Pynchon in *V*, the urge to historicize is rooted in psychological paranoia, and it leads to omnivorous narratives of conspiracy that devour all of existence in quest of pattern and accounting. What once suckled us is an infernal machine here, ratcheting through phenomenal life as surely as the letter V yawns up and open, yearning forever at the acme of its own shape.

I cite Barth, Vonnegut, Kosinski, and Pynchon because they are internationally known, and show in the mainstream radical doubts and revolutionary techniques deemed threatening and destructive two decades ago. In brief, while some of their postmodern peers are far more innovative and/or *avant garde*, this quartet illustrates the power of *influence*, the extent to which postmodernism has pervaded. And influence, I suggest, is one true test of any *avant garde*. The truly revolutionary can never content itself with remaining marginal or peripheral, and however violently it resists assimilation, it is most prominent—at least in literature—in how it refigures the core.

American literary postmodernism, then, brings strong counter-pressures into the mainstream, seen nowhere more vividly than in the reexamination of the will to historicize, and of the philosophical validity and implications of history herself. Note that I write of both fiction and nonfiction, and nowhere to this point have spoken of the term "novel" or of companion genres. Radical doubt now denies us the comfort of using such categories with ease. Indeed, writing free of history and thus beyond genre is a literary dream of some postmodern artists, and with the rise of serious literary nonfiction (the nonfiction novel to the new journalism, including work by Joan Didion, Norman Mailer, Tom Wolfe, Truman Capote, Edward Abbey, Hunter S. Thompson, Frederick Exley, and others), the full blurring of the lines between fiction and fact is real.

-2-

Recent research takes me into the realm of American literary nonfiction since 1960, a profound and abundant surge of work calling for serious scrutiny. Many of our finest writers—including Didion, Mailer, Wolfe, Capote, and Peter Matthiessen—have turned away from fiction, either because they sense elsewhere dramatic new, uncharted potential (Mailer's *Armies of the Night* and *The Executioner's Song* are results), or feel that conventional narrative forms (fed by myth and history) cannot perceive or contain recent strangenesses in the United States. Didion's *The White Album*, Wolfe's *The Electric Kool-Aid Acid Test* and Capote's *In Cold Blood* are varying issues of such convictions. And some writers work with a special passion to amplify/diagnose symptoms of the national heart, seeking new instruments for deep work. In Matthiessen's case, *The Snow Leopard* constitutes the former, *In the Spirit of Crazy Horse* the latter urge.

Hidden in this tide has been the assumption, as well, that the familiar categories within this genre (auto/biography, confession and memoir, long nature or wilderness meditation, the narrative of national achievement or catastrophe, the diary, the character study, the travel narrative, and the occasional essay)—ill-defined as they are—now impede our vision and are no longer reflexive literary modes. Thus unfamiliar, perplexing hybrids appear, many of which question the assumption that nonfiction functions to record history and the real and the forms it takes: Is Joan Didion's "The White Album" simply an intimate account of the profound social crises of the Manson Era? Or can it be more than the psychic historical diary it pretends to offer, a "confession" that draws power from fiction to create the certainty of intimate fact that it mimics? Is the "I" of the narrative, certified by her doctor's psychiatric evaluation, truly congruent with the "real" Joan Didion?

Against this backdrop, I will examine Truman Capote's *Handcarved Coffins*, for several purposes. First, recent American literary nonfiction is now a field of serious art requiring close attention, and Capote's *corpus* is a major mark. Second, the "fire, fire, fire flowing like a river, river, river" of *Handcarved Coffins* enacts, in the process of the text, the intrusion of the postmodern sensibility, in both a very unlikely author and in markedly atypical narrative and stylistic aspects.[1]

-3-

In contrast to that of Mailer and Didion, Capote's work is an unlikely candidate for the irruption of the postmodern, for as a literary heir to William Faulkner, he draws in fiction and nonfiction upon his Southernness. He writes with a poet's eye for exotic landscape and eccentric character in both his early fiction (*Other Voices, Other Rooms* [1948] and *A Tree of Night* [1949]) and nonfiction (*Local Color* [1950]).[2] But however misty or gothic the surfaces, he writes from a received assumption that history and myth—often tragic—are reliable informants, restless and alive. Even in the environment itself, be it New Orleans, New York, Haiti or the wild rocks of Greece. As Faulkner's, his work is implicitly traditional, even conservative, in its acceptance of home and hearth and nurturing place, all held in a dense mythic/historic matrix.

Capote is far more conventional in technique, for there are few Faulknerian soundings of point of view, chronology, plotting, or interiority. Conventional, as well, in his acceptance of genre: elegant as the prose and mystic the places of *Local Color* may be, it is a collection of travel pieces, each written on commission from magazines catering to mass audiences.

Similarly, *The Muses Are Heard* (1956) is a direct nonfiction novella of a rare 1955 tour of the USSR by a wide-eyed *Porgy and Bess* troupe. "The Duke in His Domain," his celebrated bitchy profile of actor Marlon Brando, brings artistry to a hitherto journalistic form—much as Lillian Ross did earlier in her *New Yorker* portraits—but it remains a character study, a genre piece.[3]

Even *In Cold Blood,* which Capote proclaimed wholecloth a new genre—"the nonfiction novel"—is decidedly realistic in philosophy and form.[4] The work remains riveting, a contemporary masterpiece, and while it is structurally informed by montage, the double narrative is continuous and unfaltering, driving the reader through with cinematic immediacy. The rich store of Midwestern detail, the lives of the Clutters, Smith, Hickock blended in a history of the newer West, offers Capote a metaphoric bank, and both victims and murderers are rendered with alarming mimetic credibility.

The arc of the plot—from random mass murder as wound to the body politic, to the purgation of evil and the restoration of communal harmony in a graveyard close—employs history and myth as organizing and nourishing modes. Indeed, the protagonist is Detective Alvin Dewey, an embodiment of the need for moral right, and his quest traces ancient mythic forms. Like many recent fictional quests (both popular and serious), his pattern has sources in an ancient literary river, with antecedents in classic Greek and Shakespearean tragedies of violation and redemption.

The power of the work issues also in auctorial repression. The point of view is omniscient, author, and/or narrator rigorously excluded from narrative episodes. We know Capote was no mere after the fact recorder in *In Cold Blood,* and found himself painfully involved with his subjects, especially Smith and Hickock, but he permits himself no appearance as character, save a ghostly reference or two as "a journalist."[5] There is, as well, no hint of postmodern narrative self-consciousness or textual self-reference.

"I wanted to produce a journalistic novel," he writes of *In Cold Blood,* in the Preface to *Music for Chameleons,* his last collection of nonfiction, "something on a large scale that would have the credibility of fact, the immediacy of film, the depth and freedom of prose, and the precision of poetry."[6] He achieved that height, but almost immediately questioned its value, finding himself in deep depression. By 1975, he was central in the rise of literary nonfiction to art, but he doubted the validity of the pattern of both his life and craft. When he undertook *Handcarved Coffins* on a tip from Alvin Dewey, he quickly realized that the impulse to twin *In Cold Blood* was a decade too late and a lifetime away: a nostalgic wish, doomed.

Capote, who found himself "suffering a creative crisis and a personal one at the same time," claimed to have reread every line he ever wrote. He sensed his work had come to a dead end:

> I felt my writing was becoming too dense . . . by restricting myself to the techniques of whatever form I was working in, I was not using everything I knew about writing—all I'd learned from film scripts, plays, reportage, poetry, the short story, novellas, the novel. A writer ought to have all his colors available on the same palette for

mingling (and, in suitable instances, simultaneous application). But how?[7]

The writer's crisis was personal—he was, by 1975, sorely impaired by drugs, drink, failing physical/mental health—but profoundly philosophic and artistic as well. The answer to his quandary lived in tapping the deepest sources of his disease, his doubts of personal power, the social fabric, the continuing reliability of the historical impulse. And all fourteen of the pieces collected in *Music for Chameleons* reflect this decision.

Handcarved Coffins was undertaken in the sanguine hope that it would revive the time and achievement of *In Cold Blood*, that the mythic Blue River flowing through an even grislier plain than the earlier Kansas, would power another model of narrative continuity and social balance. But the dream dies, the source slows down and dries up, revealing a loss of faith in history and myth as viable patterns for life and art and in the narrative techniques that create such patterns. But this drying of old sources yields a variety of postmodern traits, at once destructive and creative: the deflection of the tide of single form into generic conflation; the disruption of mimesis once held in rushing narrative, pools of credible character. What emerges are techniques such as Capote's pastiche of diary extracts and dramatic scaffoldings, and an insistent, interrupting parenthetical style. Such devices jar the plates of social realism, bare the artifice of the narrative scape, insist on the textuality and intertextuality of setting, character, and plot.

Prior to working (c. 1970-1980) on the posthumously published *Answered Prayers* and *Music for Chameleons*, he admits, "I had tried to keep myself as invisible as possible." It is wise to be chary of writerly attribution of purpose and design well after the art has emerged; creation rarely stops at the border of the typed page. But Capote is accurate, continuing, "Now, however, I set myself at center stage . . . ," and correctly describes his new style as "a severe, minimal manner."[8]

Thus we find a highly self-conscious and self-referential narrator, with an urgent swerve from the masterly omniscience that served *In Cold Blood* so well, toward text as free assertion of personality, as a projection of the inner life: of hope, frustration, and most, fear.

-4-

The force of *In Cold Blood* flows from the dense social and psychological vision of victims and murderers, two mingled versions of the American myth of success. The Clutters make a doomed Eden in River Valley Farm, "a patch of paradise," and their prize apple orchard is not far from the county seat, Garden City. (23) Patriarch Herb Clutter embodies our dream of success by sweaty work and ingenuity, his spread won from the Kansas Depression dustbowl of the 1930s. Psychopathic killers Perry Smith and Dick Hickock are rootless, wandering, compelled by perverse democratic fantasies of utter mobility and windfall fortune. Every man a king at any moment, they tell themselves; life is a gamble each instant, as they realize ironically on their capture in Las Vegas.

The surface of *In Cold Blood* is sectioned into four books, eighty-five episodes, and it moves back and forth in time by flashback and flashforward. But it plays seamlessly as an accurately (as far as we can tell) imagined history of murder and social retribution. Under the orderly historical surface run multiple patterns that first bind us uncomfortably, then set us uncertainly free, healed for a time. Victims and murderers—two versions of our founding myths—there are elements of each in the Other, they will not remain comfortably apart. This is a source of anxiety for the careful reader, right from the opening excerpt of Francois Villon's *"Ballade des Pendus,"* in which the condemned and the watching crowd are linked at the gallows.

The four Clutter killings, for example, are committed during the Thanksgiving season, an occasion with pagan, Christian, and national mythic dimensions. The restoring protagonist, Detective Alvin Dewey, is an Anyman, and it is his lot to imagine the crime from clues, pursue the guilty, and set the trial in motion. On his course, he is ordained to take on the suffering (and wrath) of the community—in body and spirit—and heal himself and society in the final ritual purgation of Smith and Hickock.

Against this narrative of rich metaphor, informed by mythic and historical patterns, runs the deracinated text of *Handcarved Coffins*. The nonfiction novella is an account of multiple murder "in a small Western state" Capote fearfully elects not to name (67), and the apparent murderer a wealthy rancher he calls Bob Quinn. When a citizens' committee votes to change the course of the local Blue River, spreading water rights among his neighbours, Quinn plots and undertakes the murders of all eight members. Shortly before a grotesque death, each receives an intricately handcarved tiny balsam-wood coffin, on the pillow of which rests a candid photograph, a portent.

What originates as sequel is very quickly truncated. Bob Quinn is the murderer to Detective Jake Pepper and author Capote, but while the burden of proof is weighty, it is all circumstantial. Thus what the author hoped to find a second ritual of social violation and restoration refuses to assume that shape. The detective quest that structures *In Cold Blood* is denied certainty here. Nine victims fall, and the suspected killer's fortunes go unchanged, actually improve. The text reflects first Capote's increasing frustration with, then rejection of, history and myth as organizing and just forces, and this is most evident in the disruption of the narrative itself.

The Blue River is a metaphor for the author's desire for historical/mythic continuity, his hope for a revivified narrative flow. It is first a source of life, gathering from the snow of distant mountains, nourishing the many ranches and lives in the valley. But it is soon treacherous (an accomplice in the drowning of Pepper's fiancée, Addie Mason), and finally demonic and death-dealing, a mirror in which to see his own forced, infernal baptism forty hears earlier. To be born ritually into this world, Capote implies, is to be dragged in unwillingly, to be ceremonially drowned, inundated first beneath the waters of a hell-on-earth.

The waters no longer nourishing, the narrative churns itself into broken forms, subsumes other genres, seeks power in a conflation of screenplay, confession, diary. By the end of the second page, Capote has rigorously restricted his setting to that of a stage, with dialogue set off as lines for his actors, stage directions appended in parenthetical glosses. But this artifice flags, and as the Blue River surges and people continue to die, Capote moves almost chess-like through reduced narrative modes, inscribing his growing rage at Jake Pepper's impotence (and his own), and a rising awareness that his anger is funded by fear of social collapse and a very private demonology.

First screenplay, then the text is conflated to appropriate the apparent confession, as Capote mimes the structure of admission, seeks forgiveness for his own failings and those of the world in which he now finds himself. Errant lover to questioning mate: penitent to priest: patient to therapist: political criminal to torturer: murderer to interrogator: putative autobiographer to engrossed reader: These are all confessional structures by which truth may be revealed, redemption begun in apparent admission and purgation. But as in Joan Didion's "The White Album," they may also be powerful artistic ploys by which the illusion of self-scouring candour yields a highly effective mode of deceiving narration. And this, I suggest, is what Capote is up to.

Jake Pepper is powerless, doubted even by his superiors in the State Bureau. Denied effective solution to the horror continuing around him, Capote plumbs the cause for his own terror of Quinn and the Blue River. He finds it in the flow of nightmare images the two release, as they force repressed memory to the surface in dream and flashback. Beyond personal empathy for the victims and social indignation, the narrator reimagines his own forced, hellish river baptism by Reverend Bobby Joe Snow forty years earlier. Thus the narrative is further conflated, to absorb the stream of nightmare, and in the process, deflects our attention from social outrage to personal violation.

In remembering and confessing the trauma worked on him at age eight—first to Pepper and then to the willing reader—he confirms that the waters of history, myth, narrative are now deadly, and nourish an evil world. The ritual of baptism, for example, is not a cleansing ceremony, but one of forced induction into a satanic world. Thus the Blue River is transmuted, first into a haven for poisonous snakes, then into a means of extending hell on earth, harbouring "fire, fire, fire flowing like a river, river, river" (84).

The textuality and intertextuality of *Handcarved Coffins* grows as the narrative accumulates. Capote implicitly yearns for the fixity and shelter of *In Cold Blood,* and more explicitly, seeks to undo the powers of death and evil by incorporating wholesale letters, telegrams, written telephone memoranda into the narrative. The waters are turbid, not unlike the muddy Alabama river into which he was dragged, and generic conflation soon appropriates the diary. The author includes twenty-three entries from 1975-1979, as if this disruption of the narrative, this insistence on displaying unmediated materials, can stop a mounting historical horror by violating the smooth surfaces of the text. If the desire for continuous narrative is to drink from a poisoned source, then perhaps health can be summoned by the sympathetic magic of conflation, deflection, indirection.

The river of narrative must somehow be turned aside, and this simultaneous movement of destruction and creation also takes place at the micro-level of prose style. From youth, Truman Capote was a master of literary style, writing with a true sense of the sound, rhythm, and texture of language, with a feel for trenchant detail and metaphor. But convinced that his prose had grown opaque and weighed him down, he soon turned to an absolutely reduced manner in *Music for Chameleons*, pruning and simplifying the rich descriptive language so powerfully turned loose in *In Cold Blood*. Diction, sound rhythm, syntax—all are attenuated here, for language itself is a poisoned spring.

This reduction of style is evident in every aspect of *Handcarved Coffins*, but especially in Capote's use of dialogue. Despite the gruesome deaths of the Roberts (by drugged rattlesnakes), the Baxters and their guests (fire), Clem Anderson (beheading), Dr. Parsons (poison) and Addie Mason (drowning), the pulse of the town remains quotidian. Their speech is slack, mildly slangy, colourless, bordering on direct recording. Seven "Conversational Portraits" (Part III) close *Music for Chameleons*, most of which continue the author's use of "commonplace conversation with everyday people" (xviii). Dialogue throughout is sunken in the text—quotation marks are not used—and the effect is that of a mechanism with a spent spring, one running on the lees of old energy.

Stylistic reduction is also evident in Capote's insistent parenthetical style. The frequent use of interrupting commas, ellipses, and dashes illustrates his diversionary technique: these all highlight disjointed thought rhythms undercutting plain language. Most explicitly, we see it in the regular stage directions for his cast—notations of their tones of voice, gestures, bodily movements—which are set off in parentheses. Parenthetical asides provide emphasis, nuance, elaboration or extension of (or from) a central notion, but in *Handcarved Coffins* the major action or mental state is held increasingly by parentheses, as if protected within lacunae of the marks themselves. On more than thirty occasions, the narrator isolates his perceptions or responses, as if to suggest that the tale of unavenged death by the Blue River is growing peripheral. The eye of the text moves to the psychic life of the narrator, and he hides these tender moments within convex walls, like pearls held in a bony shell.

Genre is conflated in *Handcarved Coffins,* and style reduced, but the role of the narrator expands considerably. Capote was no stranger to first-person narrative—almost all the early nonfiction collected in *The Dogs Bark* issues from an "I"—but he felt most comfortable and effective hidden, buried in the scapes of his narrative.

Capote's emblem is the chameleon, a creature surviving by assuming anonymity, save those rare, dangerous moments that it emerges from its backdrop, like the dozen "scarlet, green, lavender" chameleons seduced by Madame's piano, lured out on her terra cotta floor to create a living art, "a written arrangement of musical notes. A Mozartean mosaic" (12). They live in a deep lack of self-definition, an expression of the protean self. Similarly, the author finds ease in the protections of omniscient coloration.

He writes often with a keen nostalgia for a place on earth, a lost time of social and historical continuity. Many of his characters (human and beast) are driven to re-create that lost state of wholeness, and the efforts prove misguided, self-destructive. A pet raven in "Lola" is so tamed she forgets how to fly, "thought she was something else," and menaced by a cat, falls from a sixth floor balcony. A crippled boy in "Greek Paragraphs" falls in love with the Greek Isles through his reading of classical literature and convinces his doting mother to debark on an isolated speck. He wants "to see the temple by moonlight and sleep on the shores."[9] He is torn to pieces by starving rats; his mother flees into the sea, from which she watches all night. She survives in Nice, trapped mute in memory.

Even Detective Jake Pepper is an outsider, marked early as an alien—in part, the reason for his impotence—and lives six years in a motel while he stalks Bob Quinn. Pepper has no place here, can neither arrest Quinn nor save his own fiancée. Defeated, he retires to Oregon, deferring his role to the narrator.

But chameleons, confidence men, magicians, conjurers, artists survive and flourish in Capote's work. They live in their abilities to transform themselves, dwell in the illusions they create or embody.

As Jake Pepper fails, Capote succeeds him. "Just let me come there and look around," Capote implores him early on, and from that point on the narrative narrows down, the focus tightening from social threat and historical loss to the impact of each on the first-person narrator. Familiar with the point of view, Capote had usually limited it to the role of narrator-observer, almost never permitting it to swell to postmodern textual self-consciousness or self-reference.

Thus when he writes of a black mirror early in "Music for Chameleons" he signals a sudden, unexpected shift toward postmodern vision and technique: "I shall overly describe it—in the manner of those *'avant-garde'* French novelists who, having chosen to discard narrative, character, and structure, restrict themselves to page-length paragraphs dealing with the contours of a single object . . . a white wall with a fly meandering across it. So: the object in Madame's drawing room is a black mirror."[7]

The narrator of *Handcarved Coffins* is fully self-revealed, but merely a midpoint between the announced self-conscious and self-reflexive intentions in the passage above and the Siamese twin narrators of "Nocturnal Turnings," who talk themselves to sleep and close the collection. This is a postmodern *jeu d'esprit* comparable to that of John Barth in *Lost in the Funhouse.* Capote goes about as far as he can at this mid-point: his narrator intrudes to stage centre, and the narrative records his frustration and anger with the failure of history and myth—and with the agents (Pepper) who should continue these forces as modes of health. He projects himself further, asserting both his fear of what this drying up implies for him, as man and artist, and his resolve to take up Pepper's role as protagonist. Increasingly, he limns his inner life, puncturing the text frequently in a kind of self-flagellation caused by philosophic and literary frustration. Postmodern in impulse, yearning for what is lost and angry at failure, the narrative subsumes the fact of the death of history and older modes. Out of the failed quest grows a new power, though, and near the end of *Handcarved Coffins* he draws a strength from the flux of water run to fire.

Capote leaves Pepper behind at the Prairie Motel, and sets off to confront Bob Quinn, and, in doing so, his own trauma and fear. Quinn fishes waist-deep in the Blue River, and beckons the narrator to join him. He will not go. Capote now knows that Quinn will never be brought to trial. But his own sense of power grows, out of his knowledge that historical, literary, and literal rivers are all poisoned, and out of the decision not to be submerged. If water has turned to fire in nightmare, if history is a killing mother, and if the satanic has usurped the offices of divinity, Capote finds in embracing the irruption of the postmodern in his life and art a means of standing strong in narrative and character. It is enough, the end of his nonfiction novella suggests, to record the flux that runs without and within. As Quinn finally says, "'The way I look at it is: It was the hand of God.' He raised his own hand, and the river viewed between his spread fingers, seemed to weave between them like a dark ribbon. 'God's work. His will.'" (147).

NOTES

1. Truman Capote, *Handcarved Coffins*, in *Music for Chameleons* (New York: Random House, 1980). All subsequent references are to this edition and will appear in the text in parentheses.

2. Truman Capote, *Other Voices, Other Rooms* (New York: Random House, 1948); *A Tree of Night and Other Stories* (New York: Random House, 1949); *Local Color* (New York: Random House, 1950).

3. Truman Capote, *The Muses Are Heard* and "The Duke in His Domain," collected in *The Dogs Bark* (New York: Random House, 1973), 159-307; 308-353.

4. See Capote's comments to George Plimpton, "The Story Behind A Nonfiction Novel," in *Truman Capote: Conversations,* ed. M. Thomas Inge (Jackson: University Press of Mississippi, 1987), 47-68.

5. Truman Capote, *In Cold Blood* (New York: Random House, 1966), 316; 371; 375. All subsequent references are to this edition, and appear in the text in parentheses.

6. Capote, "Preface," *Music for Chameleons,* xiv.

7. Ibid., xvi-xvii.

8. Ibid., xviii.

9. Capote, "Lola" and "Greek Paragraphs," in *The Dogs Bark,* 129; 154.

IV

CAPOTE AND OTHERS

Gothic As Vortex: The Form of Horror in Capote, Faulkner, and Styron

J. DOUGLAS PERRY

An examination of Capote, Faulkner, and Styron reveals that modern American gothic is not only a matter of theme or image, as Irving Malin suggests,[1] but of narrative form as well, that certain basic modes of rendering are traditional to gothic, and that in structure, as in theme and image, writers like Capote, Faulkner, and Styron parallel Melville and Poe, and ultimately such gothicists as "Monk" Lewis and Mary Shelley.

A convenient rule of thumb for modern American gothic might be that its structures are analogous to its images and themes. If one considers gothic to be made up of the interaction of theme, image, and structure, Malin has covered two of the three areas. He identifies the three images of American gothic as the room, the voyage, and the mirror, and the three appropriate themes as confinement, flight—really two sides of the same coin—and narcissim.[2] It is with the remaining area, the three corresponding structural principles (which I have labeled *concentricity, predetermined sequence, and character repetition)* that this article will deal.

One more point should be made here. The most pervasive gothic theme, the most pervasive gothic image, points to the over-all gothic structure: the fear of being drawn in and the image of the whirlpool find their expression in a structural vortex, composed of a series of rings or levels which create a kind of hierarchy of horror, like Dante's inferno.

The three structural principles are simply ways in which a whirlpool is shifted from a visual representation to the printed page. The process down the side of the whirlpool becomes the sequential experiencing of levels, a series of events, funneling into the final one. The sequence is predetermined because the whirlpool cancels free will and random motion. To move through the whirlpool is to find oneself moving in smaller and faster circles; a novel conveys this

Modern Fiction Studies, 19 (Summer 1973): 153-59, 166-67.

sensation by repeating its initial event or situation in more and more strident ways, creating for us a sense of concentricity. Finally, there is the matter of character repetition, the recurrence of archetypal figures, or clusters of them, throughout the various subplots of the novel, in an obsessive and stereotypical fashion. This character repetition lets us see the workings of the gothic world, for as the main characters or their proxies reappear at successive levels, they become increasingly grotesque, distorted more and more by the whirlpool's pull.

In a sense, it is arbitrary and misleading to isolate these structures this way, because they are simply facets of the same process, even as the themes express each other: the room's boundaries both promote and define one's flight, and the mirror is not only what one flees, but what one flies to. Concentricity (which implies boundaries) and sequence (which is simply flight through the concentric events) have the same interlocking relationship. As readers, we experience the spatial arrangement of the novel (its chapters or levels) as a matter of duration, as though we ourselves flee downward through the circles of the vortex. The last structural element, character repetition (which expresses narcissism), is made possible through the interaction of the other two: it is observable because a series of human communities can exist simultaneously and be experienced concentrically in the novel.

All three of the structural principles are molded into a novel which, like the half-spent suction of the Pequod's whirlpool, sucks the reader in, only to throw him back out again, like Ishmael, or Poe's Maelstrom man. George Poulet's analysis of Poe, with slight modifications, can be applied to all American gothic:

> A sort of temporal circle surrounds Poe's characters. A whirlpool envelops them, which, like that of the maelstrom, disposes its funnel by degrees from the past in which one has been caught to the future in which one will be dead. Whether it moves in the limitless eternity of dreams or the limited temporality of awakening, the work of Poe thus always presents a time that is closed.[3]

The first principle, concentricity, is far easier for a spatial form, like painting, than for novels. Nevertheless, the novel can utilize what Hillis Miller calls "the Quaker Oats effect":

> A real Quaker Oats box is fictionalized when it becomes a picture of a Quaker Oats box which bears in turn another . . . and so on indefinitely, in an endless play of imagination and reality. The imaginary copy tends to affirm the reality of what it copies and at the same time to undermine its substantiality. To watch a play within a play is to be transformed from spectator into actor and to suspect that all the world may be a stage and the men and women merely players. To read a narration within a narration makes all the world a novel and turns the reader into a fictional character.[4]

Such an illusion becomes all the more desirable in the whirlpool world of gothic.

It is in just such a manner that Mary Shelley draws us into her tale. As we read *Frankenstein* we are, in effect, cutting across a series of interrupted and resumed narratives, drawing a straight line through the concentric circles made by her narrators. After Mary Shelley's own preface, voyager Robert Walton writes letters to his sister embodying the narrative of Dr. Frankenstein who in turn supplies the monologue of the monster. Each story teller is interrupted by the other and only allowed to finish when his interrupter has finished. One charts one's progress through the book by the level of hearsay.

A similar if more crudely manipulated concentricity occurs in *The Monk,* between Ambrosio's fall from innocence and his on-going corruption. In a hiatus of more than one hundred pages, a second plot is introduced, involving the narration of Don Raymond, who interrupts himself first for the autobiography of Marguerite and then for Agnes's capsule gothic tale. One is farthest from the surface and from a sense of reality here, for Agnes's story—the tale of the bleeding nun—is so fantastic that not even Agnes believes it until, in melodramatic fashion, Agnes and Don Raymond themselves succumb to the Bleeding Nun.

With so many tales being recounted successively, recurrence of character types is almost inevitable. It happens in *The Monk,* of course, but the classic example of this repetition occurs in the dark and fair heroes and heroines of *Wuthering Heights.* The confusion of names in *Wuthering Heights*—with so many overlapping Heathcliffes, Lintons, and Earnshaws for namesakes—becomes not merely a problem of multiple marriages and dense plotting, but the first source of disorientation in Lockwood's gothic encounter:

> In vapid listlessness I leant my head against the window, and continued spelling over Catherine Earnshaw—Heathcliffe—Linton, till my eyes closed, but they had not rested five minutes when a glare of white letters started from the dark, as vivid as spectres—the air swarmed with Catherines.[5]

Although there is no such confusion of names in *Frankenstein,* the character of the Promethean hero is central to each ring of the concentrically formed novel. His magnitude increases proportionately as one approaches the center of the book. The outermost ring is occupied by Mary Shelley herself who, despite her disclaimer that the novel was "commenced partly as a source of amusement, and partly as an expedient for exercising my untried resources of mind," provides the book with this envoi: "And now, once again, I bid my hideous progeny go forth and prosper. I have an affection for it, for it was the offspring of happy days, when death and grief were but words."[6]

At this point, the interaction of character repetition with concentricity and sequence becomes clear. The concentricity is apparent precisely because of the recurrence. At each new level, the reader finds the patterns obsessively reestablishing themselves. As a temporal experience, the growing horror is based partly on our recognition of the inevitable course of events, a sequence we have already faced in a milder form on the previous level.

Inversely, the concentricity and sequence strengthen the reader's impulse to make the analogies. For example, Robert Walton's uncompleted journey becomes much more sinister when one sees the horrible outcome of Dr. Frankenstein's idealistic quest.

I have started my discussion with these nineteenth-century examples both because the formal methods and patterns are clear, and because they are the prototypes, as Leslie Fiedler might say, in Capote, Faulkner, and Styron. In these American authors, the use of these techniques may be more elaborate, but the issues which are treated are of the same existential profundity and ambiguity as those of *Frankenstein. Other Voices, Other Rooms* concerns itself, as so many American novels do, with an adolescent's quest for identity. Joel Knox, like Robin Molienux before him, seeks out the fabled relatives that may give him identity and security. When he arrives at Skully's Landing, he finds only a madhouse inhabited by his long lost father (in a near catatonic state); his father's second wife in name only (Miss Amy), a Havisham-like relic of Southern womanhood; and his cousin Randolph, a homosexual and transvestite. These are Joel's role-models, the gothic family. It is cousin Randolph, Joel's ultimate alter-ego, who poses the gothic dilemma by linking the identity quest to the gothic whirlpool:

> What a subtle torture it would be to destroy all the mirrors in the world: where then could we look for reassurance of our identities? . . . Narcissus was no egotist . . . merely another of us who, in our unshatterable isolation, recognized, on seeing his reflection, the one beautiful comrade, the only inseparable love.[7]

This passage, which clearly demonstrates Malin's diagnosis of theme and image, mirror and narcissism, leads to the kind of motifs that Ishmael attaches to water in *Moby-Dick:*

> Still deeper the meaning of that story of Narcissus who because he could not grasp the tormenting mild image he saw in the fountain, plunged into it and was drowned. But that same image, we ourselves see in all rivers and oceans. It is the image of the ungraspable phantom of life; and this is the key to it all.[8]

Capote's horizon is narrower than Melville's partly because it is more exclusively gothic. The circle is vicious rather than transcendental. Joel enters the whirlpool and fails to resurface. As I have been suggesting earlier, this is a formal matter as much as a thematic one. Close to the end of the book, after Joel emerges from a series of progressively more sinister levels of gothic, he enters the final delirium, the delirium that renders him fit for Cousin Randolph's proclivities. The brief final section of the book opens with a description of the delirium as whirlpool, with Joel in his coffin at the center of a ring of grotesques—which includes every character in the novel but Joel:

> Miss Wisteria . . . leaned so far over she nearly fell into the chest: listen, she whispered . . . are the dead as lonesome as the living? Whereupon the room commenced to vibrate slightly, then more so, chairs overturned . . . a mirror cracked, . . . down went the house, down into the earth, . . . past the deepest root, into the furry arms of horned children whose bumblebee eyes withstand forests of flame. (C, p. 113)

The center of the final whirlpool is Randolph's window, where Joel, on his first day at Skully's Landing, saw "the queer lady" (C. p. 40). Joel's final submergence is accomplished by means of this specter, whom he now knows to be Randolph:

> Gradually the blinding sunset drained from the glass, . . . a face trembled like a white beautiful moth, smiled. She beckoned to him, shining and silver, and he knew he must go: unafraid, not hesitating, he paused only at the garden's edge where he stopped and looked back at the bloomless descending blue, at the boy he had left behind. (C, p. 127)

Unlike Poe's "Descent into the Maelstrom," there is no corresponding ascent; Joel makes his irrevocable choice.

To see the shape of the book, the gothic vortex, is to see only the symptom. The cause and ultimate meaning lie elsewhere. The reason why Joel must accept Randolph is that Randolph becomes the self-negating way out of an untenable and omnipresent situation: a perverted and sterile sexual triangle encountered, with different participants, not less than five times in the book. Joel finds either himself or Randolph at the apex, the variable element in each of these triangles, and each time Joel experiences or witnesses it, the triangle becomes more intense, more sinister. First Joel is a pawn in the sibling rivalry of the cruel Florabelle, totally feminine but totally self-centered, and the somewhat overbearing Idabelle, who has become a tomboy to escape the pressures of sexuality. All this can be accepted as part of the mildly confusing but normative world of adolescence. Not so healthy is the successive menage à trois of Ransom, Miss Amy, and the sexually ambivalent Randolph who, like Joel, drifts alone in the middle. Joel is then put between Zoo, feminine, warm, but somehow unattainable, and Randolph who is, at this point in the story, unacceptable.

Randolph's account of Ransom's incapacitating accident reveals a far more sinister triangle: Pepe, the stud prizefighter; Dolores, who, like Florabelle, lives only for self-worship; and Randolph, attracted differently by both, satisfied by neither. After hearing this story, Joel himself becomes the middle man in a similar but odder triangle with Miss Wisteria—a Florabelle transformed into a grotesque parody of the Southern Belle—and Idabelle, Miss Wisteria's inappropriate and hapless suitor. It does not help that Miss Wisteria in turn now covets the now terrified Joel.

The character repetition of this particular sequence makes Joel's end seem not only inevitable, but almost preferable. In effect, Capote has used the structures to turn the gothic inside out. The reader comes to understand that given the gothic nature of the outside world, which ravages Zoo, Ransom, and Randolph, the bond between Randolph and Joel—as perverse as it may be—is the most affirmative situation Joel can find.

Faulkner, in *Sanctuary,* also turns the gothic inside out. One finds in *Sanctuary,* as in *Other Voices, Other Rooms,* that while the center of the pool is the most dramatic, it is at the beguilingly calm margin that the real danger lurks. Not Popeye, but Narcissa is the real source of evil in *Sanctuary.* Faulkner uses the formal principles I have described to achieve this, but in a different way from Capote. For instance, instead of the slow but steady progress from the edge to the center, Faulkner flicks us back and forth between the two extremes. The novel begins with a confrontation, over a mirror-like pool, of Horace and Popeye who are, in some ways, the alpha and omega:

> The spring welled up . . . upon a bottom of whorled and waved sand
> . . . In the spring the drinking man leaned his face to the broken and
> myriad reflection of his own drinking. When he rose up he saw
> among them the shattered reflection of Popeye's straw hat.[9]

In one sense, this is a chance encounter between men from opposite poles: Horace, the respectable small town lawyer and family man; Popeye, the vicious and impotent bootlegger. Horace comes and goes at once, with no sense of participation in Popeye's world. Nevertheless, Horace first sees Popeye as an image mixed in with his own like the kaleidoscopic everyman shiftings of Joe Christmas's face when he dies. Horace is in flight from the sterile respectability of his marriage when Popeye, the social misfit, enters his life. In fact, as Olga Vickery points out, "there are certain startling similarities between these two morally antithetical figures":

> Popeye's rapt and unnatural absorption in watching Temple and Red
> perform an act in which he can never share is echoed by Horace's
> painful exclusion from the grape arbor where Little Belle casually

> experiments with sex. . . . Popeye's brutal act fuses with Horace's
> thoughts and culminates in the nightmare vision of the rape of a
> composite Temple-Little Belle.[10]

What Vickery notes about the men, and implies about Temple and Little
Belle, is even more applicable to the antipodal figures of Narcissa and Temple.
If Temple's father is a judge, the law runs rampant through the Benbow
family.[11] This familial tie with the law makes both women see law as a personal
convenience rather than an institution for human betterment. Both of them are
concerned with the appearance of respectability. "Honest women," Ruby sneers
at Temple. "Too good to have anything to do with common people. . . . Just let a
man so much as look at you and you faint away because your father the judge
and your four brothers might not like it" (F, p. 55). Miss Jenny has fainter but
similar scorn for Narcissa: "Do you think Narcissa'd want any of her folks could
know people who would do anything as natural as make love or rob or steal?"
(F, p. 115). In *Sanctuary,* the gothic world is synonymous with a loveless world,
and Temple and Narcissa match the impotence of Popeye and Horace with a
corresponding frigidity. Because they are not looking for adult relationships,
both Temple and Narcissa are drawn to Gowan, but only to a certain point, as
Horace's anecdote reveals:

> "He asked Narcissa to marry him. She told him that one child was
> enough for her. . . . So he got mad and said he would go to Oxford,
> where there was a woman he was reasonably confident he would not
> appear ridiculous to." (F, p. 161)

Imprisoned throughout the book, and standing as the sole exponents of the
nongothic world, are Lee Goodwin and Ruby, and it is their destruction, or
rather Lee's destruction and with it the meaning of Ruby's life, that finally
crushes Horace.

The feeling of character repetition is heightened by the structuring of the
narrative. Instead of moving from one situation to a more sinister one to a final
one, Faulkner shuttles back and forth between the respectable world of Jefferson
and the depraved worlds of Old Frenchman's Place and Memphis,
counterpointing his landscape and characters, holding to a strict chronological
sequence. A quick check of Cleanth Brook's chronology[12] reveals that only once
does Faulkner allow the two plots to slip out of synchrony; the result there is to
intensify the gothic.

In chapter XXII, Horace has learned from Clarence Snopes of Temple's
whereabouts, and in the next chapter, on June third, he interviews her. In
chapters XXIV and XXV, Faulkner jumps ahead to June seventeenth, describing
Popeye's murder of Red, Red's wake, and the departure of Popeye and Temple.
Yet when the reader returns to Horace in Jefferson (XXVI), it is still June
fourth: Horace is writing a letter to his wife in the aftermath of his horror over

Temple's recital; Narcissa is preparing for Horace's defeat at the hands of the district attorney; and Clarence Snopes is headed for Jackson. Thus, while Popeye and Temple move beyond his reach and arrangements are made with Judge Drake and a "Memphis Jew" lawyer, Horace continues to conduct his life at a snail's pace. At the beginning of chapter XXVII, it is still only June tenth for Horace, calling to make sure that his star witness is still safely in Memphis, a fact which may comfort Horace, but not the reader. Abruptly, Faulkner brings Horace to the eve of the trial. Temple has disappeared and only reappears to give the false testimony which convicts Lee.

Faulkner manipulates time to create a doubleness, to put Horace in molasses while evil moves by him on greased skids. The result is to make physically impossible what Miss Jenny knows to be societally impossible: "You won't ever catch up with injustice, Horace." (F, p. 115)

The final gothic twist, the final concentric pattern, is provided by Popeye's own trial. Here Popeye, that most impotent of the impotent men in *Sanctuary,* finds himself being defended by the ultimate parody of Horace's idealism: "His lawyer had an ugly, eager, earnest face. He rattled on with a kind of enthusiasm. . . . A fellow policeman, a cigar clerk, a telephone girl testified, while his own lawyer rebutted in a gaunt mixture of uncouth enthusiasm and earnest ill-judgment" (F, p. 303). Like the sideshow in *Other Voices, Other Rooms,* this courtroom comedy is the final degradation of and commentary on man's desire to act meaningfully. Both Horace's idealism and his actions are seen as if through the wrong end of a telescope, leaving a searing void like the fiery vortex which engulfs Goodwin in front of Horace's outraged eyes:

> Horace couldn't hear them. He couldn't hear the man who had got burned screaming. He couldn't hear the fire, though it swirled upward, unabated, as though it were living upon itself, and soundless: a voice of fury like in a dream, roaring silently out of a peaceful void. (F, p. 289)

In a slightly different manner from Capote, Faulkner has turned the gothic inside out. Evil seems initially a bizarre and isolatable element, confined to the aberrations of Popeye and Temple. Eventually, Horace's twin battles—with the natural world which threatens his sterile existence, and with the monstrous people who threaten his client—these merge. Nature itself, in all its forms, becomes the menace, menacing even the villains who become its victims, disrupting society, the law, and the community. When one recognizes that nature is gothic from Horace's point of view, one simultaneously realizes that Horace, all of us in fact, are unnatural, that good and evil are artificial, man-made concepts. In *Sanctuary,* Faulkner stops just short of what he later says in *As I Lay Dying* or *Light in August:* that it is man, not his universe, that is out of kilter, that the sensation of gothicness is man's projective response to the absurdity of his own existence in a totally consistent, self-sufficient, and alien universe.

If one characterizes Capote's subject matter as individual in its concerns, and Faulkner's as societal, one must call Styron's interpersonal. He is less concerned with Law and the coercions of the Community because he seems largely unconvinced that communal society can exist in America. The permanence of Jefferson, Mississippi, is negated by the transience of Port Warwick, VA:

> In America, our landmarks and our boundaries merge, shift, and change quicker than we can tell: one day we feel rooted. . . . Then . . . it is all yanked out from beneath us, and when we come down we alight on—what? The same old street, to be sure. But where it once had the solid resounding sound of Bankhead McGruder Avenue . . . now it is called Buena Vista Terrace ("It's the California influence," my father complained, "It's going to get us all in the end.")[13]

Even the name of the narrator, Peter Leverett, is invariably garbled and lost in introductions, becoming Levenson or Levitt, lending further evidence to a theory of instability: "There must be something basically unsound about the structure of my name," Peter observes (S, p. 141). For Styron, the same problem prevails that Capote and Faulkner documented: a sense of the void at the center of things, a conviction that chaos is about to rise up and swallow man's personal order. To Styron, this feeling manifests itself not among or within people, but between them, at that instant when one person tries to establish himself in terms of his relations to others. So, in *Set This House on Fire,* three major figures (and several minor ones) of distinct and somewhat antagonistic temperaments, establish a temporary equilibrium of their opposing tensions, only to lash out at each other in the end, all in the name of self-actualization. The two survivors— Cass Kinsolving and Peter Leverett, the murderer and the not-so-innocent bystander—are left with the task of rehearsing and reconstructing the significance of the triangle.

The theme of the void provides ample explanation for Styron's adaptation of gothic methods and form. In addition, because the problem is interpersonal in nature, a treatment of gothic as group dynamics, character repetition becomes a crucial and valuable structure in Styron's story. Instead of providing merely the grotesque commentary of Capote, or the suggestive analogies of *Sanctuary,* it boxes the compass of man's capacity for good and evil. Peter, Cass, and Mason, like the three somewhat similar brothers Karamazov, cover the spectrum of observing, doing, and embodying.

Yet it is not the variety of characters, but their sameness that finally emerges as important. Here again is where the gothic concentricity, the argument from character analogy plays the major part. Peter and Cass uncover their pasts by telling the history of their involvement with each other, to each other. In so doing, they also collaborate on Mason's history, piecing together motive and murderer, cause and effect, during the entire book. Gradually, the fact of their parallel pasts overshadows the sequence of events they are trying to reconstruct. All the men are nearly identical in age: Cass and Mason cross the watershed age of thirty just before the rape, murder, and apparent suicide which occur in Sambuco; Peter, a year younger, fails to confront the issues of Sambuco until after his return home, when a general kind of angst leads him to seek out Cass and the truth. Styron suggests something like Erik Eriksen's delayed identity crisis in these men. With the significant exception of Peter, accounts are given of each man's initial sexual encounter, invariably in the late teens: from Mason's *flagrante delicto* in boarding school to Saverio's rape-murder of Angelina. Thirteen years later, the mild anxiety of Peter is set over against Cass's almost classic nineteenth-century self-flagellation. Saverio murders mindlessly; Cass murders in an ecstasy of mistaken vengeance; and Mason, like Gatsby, attempts to realize himself in a grandiose self-conception, a pursuit of "the green light, the orgiastic future,"[14] only to find himself at an impotent dead end, pursued by Cass and the insatiable demands of his own unattainable fantasies.

In each man, one finds an inner compulsion, a need to establish his value by meeting the impossible standards he has set for himself. Like the overreachers in Mary Shelley's *Frankenstein,* each refuses to recognize his own human frailty, the underlying egotism of his idealism. Like Mary Shelley, Styron uses the concentricity to drive the point home. In an obsessive way, the form of the novel is a series of nightmarish self-confrontations, of gradually increasing intensity. The cosmic unfairness of it all is that, in each case, the characters confront their moment of truth at the time when they are physically and emotionally drained, and totally inadequate to the challenge.

As one might expect, the book begins with Peter who occupies the outermost circle of the vortex, who is least susceptible to the maelstrom, and whose encounter with the nightmare is the slightest. The novel is a series of descents, with the first unchronologically but appropriately Peter's descent to Carolina and Cass, by way of Port Warwick. The reader is next given, in flashback, not the main event he has come to expect, but Peter's tragi-comic arrival at Sambuco, gothic enough in Peter's near manslaughter, by car, of a half-wit Italian motorcyclist, but retrospectively mild in comparison to the novel's final outcome:

> DiLieto . . . lay face up on the road, blood trickling gently from nose and ears, and with a sort of lopsided, dreamy expression on his features, part agony, part a smile, as if in mindless repose. . . . One eye socket was pink and sunken (I thought this my doing), and with a grisly feeling I glanced around for the missing eye. . . . For what seemed like an endless time I kept trampling around the prostrate DiLieto, reeling with shock. (S. pp. 32-33)

Peter is given no time, at Sambuco, to regroup from the combination of the accident itself and the travel fatigue which precipitated it and, like Faulkner's Horace, never quite catches up. In fact, Peter attributes all his misfortunate to an initial sleepless night on the road: "Had I been able to sleep easily that night, I might very well have been spared my trouble of the next day. Without that misadventure, I most surely would have arrived in Sambuco fresh as a buttercup: not haggard, shattered, and cursed with a sort of skittish, haunted depletion of nerves from which I never quite recovered" (S, pp. 29-30). Peter observes that such second thoughts are no good, but both his and Cass's narratives are full of them. This is the first in a series of "if onlys" where the physiological state of the character predetermines the catastrophic outcome. Once more, sequence is all. From the moment Peter barges onto the movie set at Sambuco, until his groggy mid-afternoon awakening to the news of Mason's death, hallucination and illusion are his constant companions.

Cass repeats the pattern laid out for Peter. While in Paris where he has gone to study painting, Cass experiences a drunken hallucination, an Italian pastoral fantasy. He sets out for Rome and eventually Sambuco in quest of the sun-drenched South. When he arrives in Sambuco in a state of virtual collapse, he creates such a scene that he, like Peter, winds up confronting the local functionary. Cass's travel fatigue is heightened by his fall off the wagon. It is this alcoholic arrival, and relentless, ever-deepending alcoholism of his stay there that establishes the feeling of horrifying inevitability. His lack of money, his drunken desperation, his extra-marital involvement with Francesca, his acquiescence in Mason's sinister and ever growing domination over him, and his horror at Mason's rape of Francesca: all of these culminate in Cass's act of vengeance and self-liberation, the murder of Mason. Styron's vision becomes clearer at each level of the vortex. The nature of the universe is to demand more of man than he is equipped to deliver; the nature of our relations with our fellow man is to ask him to answer for our own inadequacies, to fulfill us; and the nature of our fellow man is such that he cannot do this. So each character projects his inadequacies and frustrations on the other: Peter lives vicariously through Mason's fleshed-out fantasies; Mason subjugates Peter and Cass for self-aggrandizement; Cass flees home, family, artistic responsibility, and self for an Italian Never-Never Land, an idyll with Francesca, and so unwittingly singles her out to be Mason's means of violating Cass through her. And if Francesca's hopes for herself and her family are projected on Cass, her fears are projected onto Saverio, bringing about a self-fulfilling prophecy:

> What Mason had done to her just that same evening clung to her flesh like some loathsome disease. . . . So it was that when she met Saverio in the shadows and he put out his fingers harmlessly . . . to stroke her, the intense male hand on her arm brought back, like horror made touchable, the touch and the feel and the actuality, and she found herself shrieking. (S, pp. 453-454)

She lashes out at him preemptively, and as he strikes back, she continues to scream, "unaware now that this was Saverio, or anyone, aware of nothing save that the whole earth's protuberant and insatiate masculinity had descended upon her in the space of one summer night" (S, p. 454). The half-wit kills her in self-defense, and so provides the most graphic example of the inevitably gothic dimension of all human relationships, the mutually destructive nature of people's needs for one another.

Nevertheless, the epilogue of *Set This House on Fire,* like the epilogue of *Moby-Dick,* is written by the survivors of the whirlpool, not its victims. In *Moby-Dick,* Ishmael, like Peter, is the one least involved with the cosmos of the story, and his survival is a demonstration of the difference in stature between him and Ahab. Cass is far closer to Ahab than Ishmael and suggests that Styron envisions another kind of survivor from one who returns merely to tell somewhat uncomprehendingly his tale. Cass has grown and learned, has learned that the gothic vision, with its Manichean values, its all or nothing philosophy, is out of kilter with human nature and self-actualization:

> But to be truthful, you see, I can only tell you this: that as for being and nothingness, the one thing I did know was that to choose between them was to choose being, not for the sake of being, much less the desire to be forever—but in the hope of being what I could be for a time. That would be an ecstasy. God Knows it would. (S. pp. 476-77)

The epilogue is two documents: one testifying to Cass's anticipated paternity, a reestablishment of creativity on several counts; the other Peter's reprieve in the miraculous recovery of DiLieto. Only Cass emerges as the clear victor, perhaps because we are dealing once again with a kind of double gothic. Perhaps the real gothic world is Peter's, a world of twilight perceptions, evanescent pleasures, vicariousness and lost opportunities, a world where the lack of a real dark night of the soul also means the impossibility of a real redemption.

Character repetition, sequence, and concentricity are the formal means of portraying the gothic sensation of existing in time and space. As such they apply to all of Faulkner, Styron, and Capote. The family resemblances of *Lie Down in Darkness* to *The Sound and the Fury* are only partly explained by influence, for in fundamental ways Faulkner and Styron differ at the start: Faulkner's concern with the Compsons turns on the family as microcosm of society; Styron sees the family as the most intense and glaring example of the failure of human relationships, the unendingly destructive demands of one on another. The similarities spring from Faulkner's and Styron's mutual fascination with time: with clocks and how to stop them, with existence, consciousness and its denial, with the sterile repetitiveness of family curses and familial neuroses, swirling on through time. Both writers stress subjective time, multiple narrations which substitute a series of fragmented and irreconcilable time-consciousnesses for a Greenwich stability. Capote's *In Cold Blood* is the archetypal horror machine of time, an inexorable pit and pendulum alternation, as Capote jerks the reader back and forth from Clutter farm to Kansas highway, in rigid chronological sequence and tightening geography, until the bright blue shotgun flash in the dark.

All three writers use the gothic form, with its denial of final absolute affirmation, tragic or otherwise, to capture the irony of our twentieth-century existence: the conviction that the search for self-awareness may not only be fatal, but fruitless, because it is equivalent to self-negation; that selfhood is an arbitrary but necessary construct of man's self-protective ignorance; that self-awareness and self-destruction are one and the same: "The intense concentration of self in the middle of such a heartless immensity, my God! Who can tell it?"[15]

NOTES

1. Irving Malin, *New American Gothic* (Carbondale, Ill.: University of Southern Illinois Press, 1962).

2. Malin, especially 79-80, 106-107, 126-128.

3. George Poulet, *Studies in Human Time* (Baltimore: Johns Hopkins Press, 1956), 333-334.

4. J. Hillis Miller, *The Form of Victorian Fiction* (Notre Dame, Ind.: University of Notre Dame, 1968), 35.

5. Emily Bronte, *Wuthering Heights* (New York: Dodd, Mead & Co., 1942), 37.

6. Mary W. Shelley, *Frankenstein* (New York: Dell, 1970), 8, 14.

7. Truman Capote, *Other Voices, Other Rooms* (New York: Signet, 1958), 78. In subsequent references to this book, page numbers will appear after the citation, in parentheses, with the author's initial: (C, p. 78).

8. Herman Melville, *Moby-Dick* (New York: Bobbs-Merrill, 1952), 26.

9. William Faulkner, *Sanctuary* (New York: Vintage, 1958), 3. See note 7.

10. Olga Vickery, "Crime and Punishment: *Sanctuary*," reprinted in *Faulkner: A Collection of Critical Essays* (Englewood Cliffs, N.J.: Prentice-Hall, 1966), 132.

11. Robert Kirk thinks Narcissa's father may be Judge Benbow of *Absalom, Absalom!: Faulkner's People* (Berkeley: University of California Press, 1963), 323. William Volpe makes the same assumption in his Sartoris family tree: *A Reader's Guide to William Faulkner* (New York: Noonday, 1964), 66.

12. Cleanth Brooks, *The Yoknapatawpha Country* (New Haven: Yale University Press, 1963), 287-289.

13. William Styron, *Set This House on Fire* (New York: Signet, 1961), 14-15. See note 7.

14. F. Scott Fitzgerald, *The Great Gatsby* (New York: Scribners, 1953), 182.

15. Melville, 529.

Glimpses of "A Good Man" in Capote's In Cold Blood

JON TUTTLE

Truman Capote's *In Cold Blood*[1] was praised in early reviews for its "factual reporting"[2] and "admirable honesty,"[3] even to the extent of being "stuck in the mire of factuality."[4] Capote himself tells of the "tremendous amount of research," the "endless interviews" and the 6000 pages of notes that he accumulated in the process of writing the book.[5]

What he does not mention in his apparent indebtedness to a literary work published twelve years earlier, Flannery O'Connor's short story "A Good Man is Hard To Find" (1953).[6] The principal similarity, the massacre of a family, would be of no consequence except that at two points in his "nonfiction novel" Capote seems to have sacrificed authenticity for thematic texture and "borrowed" from O'Connor.

This implies nothing new as far as Capote is concerned. His first novel, *Other Voices, Other Rooms,* was described as "reflecting" such southern writers as Faulkner and Welty, or as being "a minor imitation" of Carson McCullers,[7] especially *The Heart Is a Lonely Hunter* and "A Tree. A Rock. A Cloud." Gore Vidal was more explicit, claiming that Capote "plundered Carson McCullers for *Other Voices, Other Rooms,* [and] abducted Isherwood's Sally Bowles for *Breakfast at Tiffany's*: in short, was ruthless and unoriginal."[8] The plunderings in question here would have been made by Capote to provide what *In Cold Blood* has been criticized as lacking: psychological dimension.

That both Bonnie Clutter in *In Cold Blood* and the Grandmother in "A Good Man" are hypochondriacs and martyrs is arguably coincidental. What may not be coincidental is the similarity between the speeches both deliver when they realize they are about to be murdered. Perry recounts Bonnie Clutter's last moments: "Mrs. Clutter was still crying, at the same time she was asking me about Dick. She didn't trust him, but said she felt I was a decent young man. I'm

ANQ: A Quarterly Journal of Short Articles, Notes and Reviews 1 (October 1988): 144-46.

sure you are, she says, and made me promise I wouldn't let Dick hurt anybody" (p. 242). The Grandmother, making a futile appeal to the Misfit's sense of decency, offers a similar plea: "I know you're a good man. You don't look a bit like you have common blood. I know you must come from nice people! . . . [Y]ou shouldn't call yourself The Misfit because I know you're a good man at heart. I can just look at you and tell" (p. 22, p. 23).

While the speeches are not identical, the similarities in situation are significant. In both cases, the women are fearing for their lives and the lives of their families; they are treated by their murderers with ironic courtesy; and the families are murdered in roughly the same order—Bonnie Clutter and the Grandmother being the last to die. The character of Bonnie Clutter is never so interesting as she is just before her death; whether or not that is O'Connor's influence is the question.

Perry and Dick never provide a motive for the murders they commit. The only insight *In Cold Blood* offers about their provocation is supplied by James Latham, another murderer sentenced to die: "It's a rotten world. . . . There's no answer to it but meanness. That's all anybody understands—meanness. Burn down the man's barn—he'll understand that. Poison his dog. Kill him." To this Latham's accomplice adds, "Anyway, anybody you kill, you're doing them a favor" (p. 323). The problem in Capote is that such an explanation, arriving as it does at the end of a book-length inquiry into criminality, is unsatisfying, as it fits no particular context, answers no questions, and, finally, means almost nothing. On the other hand, the "favor" the Misfit feels he does by killing is explained by his unique crime-and-punishment polemic, which he words in a similar way: "Jesus was the only One that ever raised the dead . . . and He shouldn't have done it. He thrown everything off balance. If He did what He said, then it's nothing for you to do but throw away everything and follow Him, and if He didn't, then it's nothing for you to do but enjoy the few minutes you got left the best way you can—*by killing somebody or burning down his house or doing some other meanness to him. No pleasure but meanness*" (p. 28, my italics). A generous reader with one eye on O'Connor might make sense of Latham's justification, if he can allow that Perry and Dick's "resurrection" from prison matched that of the Misfit's and bred the same hostility and philosophy, or if he can apply the web of religious symbolism and inference in "A Good Man" (e.g. the lost Eden motif of the plantation) to Perry and Dick's return to and destruction of the Edenic world of the Clutter farm. But such an application might be a quantum leap for most readers, as Capote offers few guideposts other than Latham's single rhetorical flourish.

Regarding the energy spent in assembling the material for his book, Capote noted that "there's only so much you can give to art."[9] In short, in acknowledging that artistic effort frequently falls short of its author's ideal, Capote demonstrates the necessity of also drawing on worthy predecessors, in this case Flannery O'Connor, to enrich his own creative efforts.

NOTES

1. Truman Capote, *In Cold Blood: A True Account of a Multiple Murder and Its Consequences* (New York: Modern Library, 1968). References to this edition are noted in the text.

2. Michael Novak, "The Nameless Evil in Strangers," *Critic*, 24 (1966): 65.

3. Clifton Fadiman, rev. of *In Cold Blood*, by Truman Capote, *Book of the Month Club News,* (Jan. 1966): 5.

4. Robert Kuehn, "The Novel Now: Some Anxieties and Prescription," *Wisconsin Studies in Literature,* 7 (1966): 127.

5. Haskel Frankel, "The Author," *Saturday Review* (22 Jan. 1966): 37.

6. Flannery O'Connor, *A Good Man Is Hard to Find and Other Stories* (New York: Harcourt, Brace, 1955). References to this edition are noted in the text.

7. Elizabeth Hardwick, "Much Outcry; Little Outcome," *Partisan Review*, 15 (1948): 376.

8. Gore Vidal, "*Playboy* Interview: Gore Vidal," *Playboy* (June 1969): 96.

9. Frankel, 37.

Variations on a Dream:
Katherine Anne Porter and Truman Capote

WILLIAM L. NANCE

One of the best-documented facts about the American mind is that it is possessed by a dream. The dream takes many forms, finding perhaps its most comprehensive embodiment in that American Adam whom R. W. B. Lewis described as "a figure of heroic innocence and vast potentialities, poised at the start of a new history." It has been one of the principal functions of the writer in America to examine this dream, revealing the repressed guilt that underlies such innocence reminding the nation that potentialities may be evil as well as good.[1] The writer does not do this by somehow abjuring American experience and rising above it to a superior viewpoint from which foibles stand out more clearly. While we may in some sense attribute this strategy to the European novelist of manners, the American writer's approach is better described in this observation by James Baldwin: "That the tensions of American life, as well as the possibilities, are tremendous is certainly not even a question. But these are dealt with in contemporary literature mainly compulsively; that is, the book is more likely to be a symptom of our tension than an examination of it."[2] Like the rest of us, the writer lives within the dream; he is, in fact, the dreamer *par excellence,* speaking characteristically through symbols, taking as his field of vision his own subconscious mind and that of the nation and, at his best, finding them identical.

It is not too surprising, if somewhat paradoxical, that, in what Evelyn Waugh has called "a nation of waifs and strays," the writers we find most essentially American should usually prove to be in some sense outsiders. Very little of our significant literature has come from what we might call the "dead center" of American society (presided over, let us say, by Benjamin Franklin). On the other hand, a remarkable number of our writers have come from alienated classes, or have in some other way been made unusually aware of the limitations

Southern Humanities Review, 3 (Fall 1969): 338-45.

of life. There are, for example, the Jews, the Negroes, the homosexuals; there are those who have experienced war or in some other way come close to death. And, finally, there are the Southerners. In attempting to explain the Southern literary renaissance, C. Vann Woodward makes the point that the South's experience of defeat, humiliation, and poverty has given it a kind of knowledge not shared by the rest of the United States.[3] Hence the South is at least a partial exception to this observation of Northerner James Baldwin's: "Europe has what we do not have yet, a sense of the mysterious and inexorable limits of life, a sense, in a word, of tragedy."[4]

I have, in accord with common practice, been using the word "dream" quite broadly, to designate the American mind's insistent and more or less confident drive toward some ideal condition. I wish now to narrow my use of it to a more nearly literal meaning and speak of the dream as a vision of the ideal existence, precisely formulated and projected into an admittedly unattainable realm beyond time and place. In this form—as neoplatonic paradisal vision—the American dream has been primarily a Southern phenomenon, a reaction to the Southerner's intense awareness of the heavy, downward pull of life and related, certainly, to his old habit of looking back, with ever-diminishing hope, to an idealized past. In the fiction of Katherine Anne Porter and Truman Capote this dream takes especially interesting and somewhat contrasting forms.

Katherine Anne Porter is a frontier Southerner who spent her childhood, at the end of the nineteenth century, on a farm in the plains country of central Texas. She was raised by her widowed grandmother, a stern, self-reliant woman whose name she adopted as a writer and whom she made one of her favorite fictional characters. Her harsh, matriarchal background may account for the fact that Miss Porter's work, in the mid-twentieth century, reflects a thematic pattern which Leslie Fiedler associates with the second half of the nineteenth, in which "women eternally suffer not from sexual assault but from the general failure of males—not, that is to say, from men's potency but from their weakness: their cowardice, lack of moral firmness, insufficient intelligence, proneness to get drunk or ill, or to die when most needed."[5] A sense of deprivation, of missed possibilities dominates Miss Porter's fiction, but in seeking its cause she has gone beyond the anti-male stereotype to the fact of death itself. Her fine short story, "The Jilting of Granny Weatherall," is a blending of the two themes in the last, delirious thoughts of a dying woman. But it is her short novel "Pale Horse, Pale Rider" that contains her most direct confrontation with death, and this work, by Miss Porter's own testimony, is an attempt to record an actual experience.[6]

In 1918, ten years before she began publishing her important fiction, Katherine Anne Porter came close to dying of influenza and had what she has described as a vision of "heaven." This experience, set against the background of a love affair frustrated by war, sickness and death, is the central episode of the story. The title of another Porter story, "The Downward Path to Wisdom," well describes the movement of "Pale Horse, Pale Rider." As the story begins, Miranda notices the first signs of illness encroaching upon her hectic routine of newspaper work and occasional dates with Adam, her new boyfriend, soon to leave for the front. The narrative of her waking life is interrupted by impressionistic, stream-of-consciousness dreams, then yields completely to the long series of delirious visions that represents her illness of several weeks. The sequence of Miranda's dreams and visions combines several meanings. Symbolically a record of her physical descent to a point very near death, it is also a characteristically American study of the nature of thought and language. Miranda's mind—like Melville's, always in pursuit of the final truth about life, however frightening it may be—refuses to rest in the possession of any traditional formula, any generally accepted category imposed on the flux of experience. Profoundly skeptical throughout her life (as we see it recorded in several other stories), she has refused compromise of any sort—intellectual, political, marital—and has consequently been an isolated wanderer, increasingly oppressed by a sense of loss which is most explicitly treated in the short story "Theft." As the heroine of that story acknowledges, there has been a profound ambivalence in her pursuit of the ideal of complete knowledge, complete happiness. In its thoroughgoing rejection of life as experienced in the present, it resembles a pursuit of death. In "Pale Horse, Pale Rider," we see that ambivalence dramatized with perfect clarity, though veiled from the protagonist's full awareness by the circumstance of physical illness.

Miranda's visions bring her progressively closer to the real nature of death. She sees it first as the pale horseman of Biblical and romantic Southern tradition, then as a jungle full of savagery and decay, next as invisible flying arrows killing those she loves. There is a gradual simplifying of imagery and an increasing realization that death consists of privation. In the climactic vision she first returns to her "childhood dream of danger," seeing herself as lying on a narrow granite ledge overlooking a bottomless pit. She thinks, "There it is, there it is at last, it is very simple; and soft carefully shaped words like oblivion and eternity are curtains hung before nothing at all."[7] The concept is then refined even further, with the reflection that "granite walls, whirlpools, stars are things. None of them is death, nor the image of it. Death is death, and for the dead it has no attributes." With this recognition the seeking mind comes to rest, and she feels herself sink "through deeps under deeps of darkness until she lay like a stone at the farthest bottom of life," enduring there only as "a minute fiercely burning particle of being that knew itself alone, that relied upon nothing beyond itself for its strength; not susceptible to any appeal or inducement, being itself composed entirely of one single motive, the stubborn will to live." It is at this lowest point of life that she has her vision of paradise, which begins with an alteration in the particle of light that represents herself:

At once it grew, flattened, thinned to a fine radiance, spread like a great fan and curved out into a rainbow through which Miranda, enchanted, altogether believing, looked upon a deep clear landscape of sea and sand, of soft meadow and sky, freshly washed and glistening with transparencies of blue. Why, of course, of course, said Miranda, without surprise but with serene rapture as if some promise made to her had been kept long after she had ceased to hope for it. She rose from her narrow ledge and ran lightly through the tall portals of the great bow that arched in its splendor over the burning blue of the sea and the cool green of the meadow on either hand.

The small waves rolled in and over unhurriedly, lapped upon the sand in silence and retreated; the grasses flurried before a breeze that made no sound. Moving towards her leisurely as clouds through the shimmering air came a great company of human beings, and Miranda saw in an amazement of joy that they were all the living she had known. Their faces were transfigured, each in its own beauty, beyond what she remembered of them, their eyes clear and untroubled as good weather, and they cast no shadows. They were pure identities and she knew them every one without calling their names or remembering what relation she bore to them. They surrounded her smoothly on silent feet, then turned their entranced faces again towards the sea, and she moved among them easily as a wave among waves. The drifting circle widened, separated, and each figure was alone but not solitary; Miranda, alone too, questioning nothing, desiring nothing, in the quietude of her ecstasy, stayed where she was, eyes fixed on the overwhelming deep sky where it was always morning.[8]

The vision is doomed to fade almost instantly. Suddenly she notices a flaw in the scene and thinks, "Where are the dead?" Then, "as if a curtain had fallen, the bright landscape faded, she was alone in a strange stony place of bitter cold, picking her way along a steep path of slippery snow, calling out, Oh, I must go back! But in what direction?" Miranda lives on, but only reluctantly, alone, and without hope.

The story, certainly a sort of ultimate in American literature, presents the dream as engulfed in a nightmare chilling in its finality. And there has been something fixed and final in all of Katherine Anne Porter's work, as though that early encounter with death had somehow short-circuited her sense of life's possibilities. She has stuck by her austere vision, and her works, on the whole, read as if she had judged each experience by the standard of this impossible paradise and, inevitably, found it wanting.

The career of Truman Capote has been as marked by deliberate change as Katherine Anne Porter's has been by a sort of deliberate fixity. While her dramatization of the paradisal vision seems only to confirm a feeling of captivity, Capote's use of a similar kind of dream seems to have been for him a means of liberation.

Capote's early stories are dream-like in technique, conveying, with various degrees of surrealistic distortion and symbolic complexity, the sensation of submersion in an alienated, fear-ridden mind. They are nightmares, each dominated by a threatening figure analogous to the Wizard Man who embodies the terrors of childhood. His first novel, *Other Voices, Other Rooms,* is set in a similarly nightmarish atmosphere, and completes, with amazing symbolic intricacy, the pattern of the early stories. The familiar threatening figure is shown to be, on different levels, the father, the unknown part of the self (the id), and finally death. By coming to terms with this multiple presence, the young hero escapes from fear and achieves a sense of his own identity. The principal means by which he does this is a loving acceptance of his fate, and in particular of Randolph, a sort of anti-father who is a homosexual but represents primarily the need of others for love and of the darker self for acceptance. The same fundamental pattern is duplicated in the less gothic portion of the book which deals with Idabel Thompkins, initiating a new pattern which Capote has retained up to the present, even in his "nonfiction novel," *In Cold Blood.* Idabel is a tomboyish girl of Joel's own age who becomes, in a precarious way, his friend. In a tentative sexual encounter he learns that conventional love is not possible for them, and while he comes to love her just as he does Randolph, he finally relinquishes her sadly to what Capote suggests will be a life of wandering, suffering, and dreaming. (Idabel wears colored glasses in a particularly futile search for the ideal.) Virtually every one of Capote's later stories and novels has been built around such a dreamer-victim, usually female, and in each case based on a real person Capote has known. In the frankly autobiographical "A Christmas Memory," he returns to the prototype, an elderly cousin who acted as a mother to him during much of his childhood. In a sense, his early life with her, as idealized in this story, is Capote's "dream," nostalgically surrendered to time. The same is true of the brief sojourn in the tree house in *The Grass Harp,* which ends with the old lady's death and the young hero's entrance into maturity, this time on a much less symbolic level than in *Other Voices, Other Rooms.*

In other cases, however, the dream is formulated in a manner comparable to that of "Pale Horse, Pale Rider." Miss Bobbit of "Children on Their Birthdays" says, "Not that I live here, not exactly. I think always about somewhere else, somewhere else where everything is dancing, like people dancing in the streets, and everything is pretty, like children on their birthdays." The worldlier Holly Golightly, in another story whose title designates the dream, would like to wake up some morning and have breakfast at Tiffany's. Meanwhile, she goes to Tiffany's for a sense of security when she is especially oppressed by the "mean reds," that is, the fear of death.

Each of these dreamers is, of course, a projection of elements in Capote himself. It is his childhood with its wildness, its aspirations and fears, that he has embodied in them and relinquished "as a bittersweet memory." The phrase is Leslie Fiedler's, applied to another writer entirely. Fiedler continues, "It is the final tribute of the white Romantic to the world of untamed nature and the id, which he can bring himself neither to live by nor disown. . . . The bourgeois world could not afford to let so apt a symbol of its divided heart die out of the literature while that division lived on; and in America in particular it throve especially, both in the form Scott gave it [*Rob Roy*] and in the adaptation of James Fenimore Cooper."[9] With a considerable shift in time and mores, it still thrives in Truman Capote. His strategy of blended acceptance and relinquishment is supported, in the stories, by a philosophy of love which is distinctly Platonic in nature and which is shared, as critics have noted,[10] by Carson McCullers and to some extent by several other Southern writers. In this view the beloved, who may be of either sex and any conceivable human form, is an ideal completion of the self, serving merely as the stimulus for a love which remains essentially solitary (and which, if analyzed, turns out to mean perfect bliss). While in Carson McCullers this philosophy seems to reflect a despair comparable to Katherine Anne Porter's, in Capote it has proved much more flexible.

Capote's discovery of new possibilities at the time of *Other Voices, Other Rooms* was followed by an important change in technique. He began to tell his stories from the point of view of a dramatized semi-autobiographical narrator, thus moving himself away from the center of interest, which was now occupied by the dreamer-heroine. Thereafter, each work was both an evocation of the dream and a further state in the campaign to exorcise it. Capote has explained, "I did at one time feel an artistic need to escape my self-created world. I wanted to exchange it, creatively speaking, for the everyday objective world we all inhabit."[11] The final product of this desire was, of course, *In Cold Blood,* in which Capote tried to remove himself completely from the story, meanwhile contemplating its real-life characters with perfect objectivity and universal sympathy. He did not, of course, attain these inherently impossible goals, but he came remarkably close to doing so. Even more remarkable, he managed to continue the pattern he had established in his fiction, for, while moving himself almost completely out of the book, he managed to find in Perry Smith, the killer (by "psychological accident") of the Clutter family, another wandering dreamer pursued by death—another surrogate Truman Capote.

The dream, then, can serve varying purposes. Born as a response to the apprehension of death, and existing only somewhere beyond it, it may be tirelessly pursued, with all the life-death ambivalence of that pursuit, or left as a haunting reminder as one goes about the business of accommodating to this imperfect world. Our literature has achieved its greatest triumphs following the former route, but the latter is no less typically a part of us. Both Katherine Anne Porter and Truman Capote have shone a bright, and Southern, light on American possibilities.

NOTES

1. See Leslie Fiedler, *Love and Death in the American Novel.* London: Jonathan Cape, 1967.

2. James Baldwin, *Nobody Knows My Name.* New York: Dell Publishing Company, 1961, 22.

3. *The Burden of Southern History.* New York: Vintage Books, 1961.

4. Baldwin, 23.

5. Fiedler, 219.

6. See my discussion in William L. Nance, *Katherine Anne Porter and the Art of Rejection.* Chapel Hill: University of North Caroline Press, 1964, 131-155.

7. Katherine Anne Porter, *Pale Horse, Pale Rider: Three Short Novels.* New York: Random House, 251.

8. Nance, 151-152.

9. Fiedler, 178-179.

10. See Frank Baldanza, "Plato in Dixie," *The Georgia Review,* 12 (1958), 151-167.

11. *New York Times Book Review* (January 16, 1966): 2.

An American Tragedy and In Cold Blood: Turning Case History into Art

JOHN J. McALEER

When Truman Capote's *In Cold Blood* was published in 1965 the *London Sunday Express* hailed it as "one of the stupendous books of the decade." The *New York Review of Books* agreed. Capote's book was "the best documentary of an American crime ever written." And in *Harper's* Rebecca West wrote: "Nothing but blessings can flow from Mr. Capote's grave and reverend book." Yet the editor of the *Atlantic Monthly,* Edward Weeks, who might be supposed to know something about fact-based novels since Nordhoff and Hall wrote the Bounty trilogy at his behest, demurred: "In *In Cold Blood,*" he wrote, "Truman Capote is providing the readers with a high-minded, aesthetic excuse for reading about a mean, sordid crime." In the pages of the *New Republic* Stanley Kauffman supported him: "It is ridiculous in judgment and debasing of us all to call this book literature. Are we so bankrupt, so avid for novelty that, merely because a famous writer produces an amplified crime feature, the result is automatically elevated to serious literature?"

While contending critics framed their avowals with matching ardor and indignation, only one, Granville Hicks, thought to praise *In Cold Blood* at the expense of another crime novel—Theodore Dreiser's *An American Tragedy*—which on its appearance forty years earlier likewise met a divided critical response. Applauding Capote's restraint in limiting "himself to ascertainable facts," Hicks told readers of the *Saturday Review:* "If Dreiser had done the same sort of thing with the Gillette-Brown Case . . . *An American Tragedy* might have been a better book."

Although Dreiser, unlike Capote, unabashedly had fictionalized his source, critics berating *An American Tragedy* picked grounds similar to those Capote's detractors would occupy when they denounced *In Cold Blood.* Russell Blankenship, for example, had dismissed it as "simply a mammoth example of

Thought, 47 (Winter 1972): 569-86.

the reporter's art." No one suggested, however, that Dreiser had exploited a lurid situation for mere sensationalism. Unlike Capote, Dreiser had a thesis that went deeper than a demonstration of form. Critics could and did dispute Dreiser's thesis yet there could be no pretending that he lacked one.

To Joyce Cary *An American Tragedy* was "a great book," to H. G. Wells it was "one of the great novels of this century," to Joseph Wood Krutch, "the greatest American novel of our generation." Anderson, Lewis, Bennett, Fitzgerald, Agee, Dos Passos, Wright, Warren, Bellow, Mailer—to seek for commentary only among Dreiser's fellow novelists—also have lauded Dreiser's achievement. Just lately C. P. Snow has written: *"An American Tragedy* has its place among the 'great' novels in a sense, and to an extent, that no other American novel has, and, I might add, in a sense not possessed by any English novel since *Little Dorrit."* If, then, *In Cold Blood* is a better book than *An American Tragedy,* Capote's success has been notable. To determine if it has been, let us see his book in overlay to Dreiser's.

Basing a literary work on an actual murder is not a twentieth-century innovation. The sixteenth-century play, *Arden of Feversham,* once attributed to Shakespeare, was based on a real-life murder. So were Poe's "Mystery of Marie Roget," Dostoevsky's *Crime and Punishment,* and Browning's *Ring and the Book.* Yet in literature, to draw from life, even a life that deals in death, is no sure guarantee of merit. What is crucial is the writer's success in transcending the meanness of his materials to give them universal significance. As Goethe expressed it: "The artist has a twofold relation to Nature. . . . He is her slave, inasmuch as he must work with earthly things, in order to be understood; but he is her master, inasmuch as he subjects these earthly means to his higher intentions, and renders them subservient."

Capote's own account of why he wrote *In Cold Blood* centers on one fact—he wanted to give the nonfiction novel status as an art form. He had, he admits, "no natural attraction to the subject matter," choosing it on the theory that "Murder is a theme not likely to yellow with time." Even then he was ready to abandon this topic if he found another that suited his purpose better. Since Capote makes no declaration of intention in writing *In Cold Blood* beyond stating his desire to illustrate the feasibility of his form, we must wonder if his announced resolve really took him beyond the goal of achieving a dramatic ordering of facts, in felicitous prose, to serious consideration of how the potentials of his materials might be utilized to express a true, universalizing experience. Capote seems to have mistaken craft for art.

Dreiser did not write *An American Tragedy* to establish a literary method, nor was murder incidental to his purpose. Like Capote he did have trouble choosing his starting point, like Capote, it took him five years to complete his book once it was under way. But he had no doubts about the area in which he intended to work. He believed that murders such as the one Chester Gillette had committed were indigenous to America and his book was to be about the typicality of such a murder—murder carried out under the auspices of the American Dream. He researched "ten or fifteen" such murders and weighed their narrative potential before he chose the Gillette-Brown case [1906]. He was not interested in the crime as a crime but in the social pressures which fostered it. He tells us:

> I had long brooded upon the story, for it seemed . . . so common to every boy reared in the smaller towns of America . . . so truly a story of what life does to the individual—and how impotent the individual is against such forces. My purpose was . . . to give, if possible, a background and a psychology of reality which would somehow explain, if not condone, how such murders happen. . . .

An American Tragedy, then, has a social direction. Its author wishes to identify and condemn a social evil which, under the pretext of opening the way to self-realization, lures men to ruin. This therapeutic aim does not mean that *An American Tragedy* is a tract; that is hardly better than calling it an expanded exercise in journalism. Art is not always vanquished by preachment, and in his ultimate handling of his subject Dreiser detaches himself from society and its failings to write with insight and power of problems of the human condition which transcend time and place—and to chronicle the history of a cosmic hunger found in every human heart, though beyond man's reckoning in common hours. *"An American Tragedy,"* says Robert Penn Warren, "is conceived as a drama involving both the individual and the universe."

Regardless of the reason each author gave to explain his choice of subject, any record of the parallels between *An American Tragedy* and *In Cold Blood* must begin with awareness of how each author quarried from his own past, episodes which let him identify with his protagonist and, through such identification, draw upon an inner store of psychic perceptions. Neither author was new to the practice. *The 'Genius'* (1915), with its near American Tragedy ending (its protagonist, Eugene Witla, actually wishes his wife, Angela, dead, so that he might marry a young girl with whom he is infatuated), fictionalized Dreiser's own unhappy life up till the age of forty. Capote admits that *Other Voices, Other Rooms* (1948) is "all about" himself.

Both Dreiser and Capote have insisted that, in childhood, they never were wanted enough. In his own early poverty and aspirations Dreiser found a pattern that paralleled the history of Chester Gillette, whom he fictionalized as Clyde Griffiths. Warren says of Dreiser's autobiographical volumes: "In *Dawn* and in the first twenty-two chapters of *A Book About Myself*, Not only the basic personality and life pattern of Dreiser himself have been presented and analyzed, but the basic characters, situations, and issues of *An American Tragedy* have been projected." Warren concludes that "in the strange metabolism of creation" Dreiser's source materials, both personal and derived, "are absorbed and transmuted into fictional idea, fictional analogy, fictional illusion." Thus: "This book is 'created,' and therefore generates its own power, multiplying the power implicit in the materials."

Dreiser then refashioned his own experiences to give verisimilitude to portions of Clyde's history. Although fealty to facts would not allow Capote to interpolate such data into his novel, it could not keep him from seeing himself in one of his protagonists—Perry Smith. Novelist Harper Lee, who was at Capote's side during those months when he made a final assessment of the materials he had gathered for *In Cold Blood,* relates: "I think every time Truman looked at Perry he saw his own childhood." The early years of both Smith and Capote were nomadic. Both hungered to escape from poverty and obscurity. Both were estranged from their fathers, neglected by their mothers. Both had talents which went unrecognized and therefore unencouraged. Although these are riches that go unclaimed, there is fully as much of Truman Capote in Perry Smith as there is in the autobiographical child-protagonist of *Other Voices, Other Rooms*—Joel Knox.

As a boy in Vincennes, Indiana, Dreiser had shared the same living quarters with a youth, Jimmie Dooney, executed later for murder (1901 or 1902) by the State of New York. Without success Dreiser had petitioned the governor for commutation of sentence. It required no great force of imagination for Dreiser to see himself in Dooney's place. Neither Dreiser nor Capote propose that the Dooneys, Gillettes, and Smiths of this world could have been Dreisers and Capotes had they made of their talents and opportunities a wiser use. On the contrary, their anguish and compassion seem rooted in their conviction that what they are recording might have been, save for the caprices of fortune, their own destiny.

To turn from the authors to their protagonists, Clyde, Perry, and Perry's companion in crime, Dick Hickock, both Dreiser and Capote incorporate the reader into their lives at a level of compassion and sympathy which deplores not only the treatment which society dispenses but what Dreiser identifies as "the substance of the demands of life itself"—those circumstances which are the soil in which tragedy ripens toward its season of reaping. All three have experienced poverty, inequality, lack of success in satisfying basic needs, insecurity, frustration, and futility of quest. Clyde and Dick had godfearing parents. Perry's father, as well as his institutional keepers, tried to instill moral lessons. Yet both books insist that powerful moral influences are actual incentives to rebellious behavior when blind authority and emotionalism would try to enforce them.

Now consider how society deals with these protagonists as transgressors. Although in both books the crowds—society made visible—are amazed that such well-appearing boys could have committed the crimes they are charged with, no one thinks to investigate this paradox. We become aware, instead, of the morbid curiosity of a public which, despite its alleged Christian adherence, is titillated by the unfolding drama. A carnival atmosphere takes over as Roberta's letters are hawked in the street at Clyde's trial, along with peanuts, hotdogs, and popcorn. A local church sponsors a gala auction of the effects of the Clutter family. Hotdogs and soda pop are sold to the crowd gathered to see Dick and Perry arraigned. Though the defendants want a change of venue, their lawyers dissuade them on the theory that the community is religious-minded and will deal leniently with them. Yet, in each instance, the prosecution calls down Old Testamental wrath on their heads. Defense attorneys, in both books, ultimately ask the court if a fair trial is possible in a community so emotionally aroused. The limited mentality of the jurors is stressed. Farm people are the victims and farm people sit in judgment on the accused. In *In Cold Blood,* when the verdict is reached the judge himself has to be fetched from his farm. The governor, who refuses clemency, is, like the murdered man, a rich farmer. Both books disclose that forthcoming elections influence the conduct of the trials. For Orville Mason, in *An American Tragedy,* and Al Dewey, in *In Cold Blood,* stalwarts of the law, a verdict of guilty becomes an epic obsession. And in Kansas, as in New York, the aristocracy of the community holds aloof from the trial.

The post-trial phase of legal justice, in the reversal of public interest which occurs, becomes society's subtlest barbarism. Legal postponements in the death house are excruciating. Dreiser deplores the "unauthorized cruelty and stupidity and destructive torture" which these delays constitute. Capote finds that the state exacts a thousand other deaths besides the one which the sentence calls for. In *An American Tragedy* Dreiser relates that the dimming of the prison lights as a man is electrocuted, is a psychological ordeal for other occupants of the death house.[1] In *In Cold Blood* Capote says that the sound of the floor dropping on the gallows constitutes mental torture for others, confined within earshot, who await hanging. In both books the point is made that money keeps people from execution. One recalls that on June 25, 1906, two weeks before Chester Gillette killed Grace Brown, Harry Thaw, in the same State of New York, with impunity shot Stanford White.

Concerning the underlying causes of the crimes—what Dreiser speaks of as "the substance of the demands of life itself"—both books convey an "only in America" emphasis—a strong sense of America as the logical environment sponsoring these murders. As Margaret Mead has noted, the title itself records Dreiser's intent "to make it [*An American Tragedy*] universal, at least for the American scene." The Dream of Success is paramount. Hence Alfred Kazin's remark: "Roberta's rival is not just a rich girl; it is, literally, the American Dream." And Leslie Fiedler's conclusion: "Clarissa is seduced here not by Lovelace but by Horatio Alger." Dreiser and Capote, indeed, each strikes a blow at the "bootstrap myth." In *An American Tragedy* a boy comes out of the West, into the East, seeking material fulfillment, only to find that conditions responsive to his expectations no longer exist. The Clutter murders truly appall because the crime occurs within the premises of paradise. Clutter himself says: "an inch more of rain and this country would be paradise—Eden on earth." The mythic Garden of the World is violated. In this context, observe that a condition of happiness, an archetypal situation as ancient as Eden, is imposed. Clyde is told that he must, under no circumstances, fraternize with girls working in the Griffiths' factory. Perry and Dick are forbidden to fraternize with former convicts. In each case the tragedy becomes possible when this injunction is flouted. That Dreiser appreciates this fact is affirmed by Clyde's Adamic lamentation, after his condemnation, that his failure to heed the mandate had cost him paradise. For Capote, it is simply another fact, stored among an array of facts, and left unevaluated. It is, as we shall see, this misguided reluctance on Capote's part to make functional use of his facts, save at the most literal level, that causes the two books to cleave apart. This point can be illustrated in another way. Corollary to the loss-of-Eden theme in both books, estrangement from Nature is basic to the misfortunes of the protagonists. Dreiser illustrates it in that memorable episode in which Clyde drops on all fours to run through a barren field, again in Roberta's death scene, the spot enclosed by dead trees with the weir-weir bird hovering and, finally, in causing Clyde to be taken by the posse at the margin of a woodland which beckons as a refuge—a classic ameliorative retreat to the wilderness situation. Capote, for his part, is satisfied to allude vaguely to Perry's lost Cherokee heritage and abortive Alaskan frontier adventure. A further parallel use of Nature offers additional illustration. In *An American Tragedy* water lilies equate with purity and death. Roberta's courtship begins and ends with them. A latter-day Persephone, Roberta, in Milton's parlance, gathering flowers is herself gathered. In *In Cold Blood,* Mrs. Clutter looks at her flower garden and sighs for bygone innocency. Dreiser functionally assimilates details from the Gillette-Brown case, making himself responsive to their mythic potential. Confronted with comparable riches, Capote ventures a grace note.

Although Capote, unlike Dreiser, makes an elaborate use of flashbacks to cover the early histories of Perry and Dick, thereby precipitating the reader at once into a gory drench, he pays a steep price for the dramatic appeal gained. Emphasis falls on effect rather than cause, a predictable consequence for an operational plan which gives to method precedence over matter. That Capote recognized an obligation to do something more may be inferred from the several efforts he made to provide a context for the crime. Among his notations, a principal instigating cause for the murder of the Clutters leaps to prominence. But Capote himself does not see it. He tries to mask his bewilderment by offering a succession of probable causes, creating for the reader a veritable solve-it-yourself packet. And that, of course, gives head to chaos.

When the film version of *In Cold Blood* was made, the moviemakers proffered one of Capote's implied secondary causes—Perry's Oedipal frustrations—as chief cause of the murders. When Perry cut Mr. Clutter's throat, Hollywood suggested, he thought he was butchering his father. When he climbed the gallows he saw his father as hangman. These Freudian revelations do not appear in Capote's book. When, however, the evidence is evaluated as Capote ought to have evaluated it, but failed to do, the cause of the murders of the Clutters proves to be identical with the cause of Roberta Alden's death, that is, blind pursuit of the American Dream. That is the theme Capote gropes for throughout *In Cold Blood* and which, despite his floundering, he most nearly proved valid. Ironically, someone in Hollywood sensed this. As Dick and Perry drive to Holcomb to commit the murders, they pass a theater the beckoning marquee of which announces its feature attraction—"A Place in the Sun," a movie version of *An American Tragedy.*

Capote says that when he saw the completed film of *In Cold Blood* he was "increasingly gripped by a sense of loss," as he viewed it. Since he himself did not know what it was that he had tried to say through his book, Capote's complaint was without focus. It did not occur to him that Hollywood, possibly because it did not want to march to Dreiser's music, had eschewed the one theme that held together his narrative. Nor were matters improved by the effort Hollywood made to bolster the fragile theme it had built the film around by tagging on to it the adjunctive notion that the book mounts an assault on capital punishment. Even Capote would not go along with that. After the film was released he told an interviewer that he believes in capital punishment and wishes only that it could be evenly enforced and used more generally.

In truth, in his preoccupation with form, Capote did not give enough thought to what conclusions his materials would lead to. Perhaps he believed that if he kept serving up facts they would supply their own logic—make their own gravy—with no assistance from him. As fiction writer Dreiser was free to deal with the uncut gem in his possession in whatever way best served his aims so long as he took into full account its natural planes of cleavage. As documentary-novelist, Capote was shackled by commitments which permitted him neither to release fully the potentials of his materials nor to concentrate their power for maximum effectiveness.

Capote's topic of prime focus is, like Dreiser's, the destructive encroachments of the American Dream. Although preoccupation with his experiment in form caused him to look on this theme and other lesser themes as intrusive, it surfaces too often not to be recognized. We have his word for it. He assures us: "The arbitrary act of violence springs from the poverty of Perry's life. . . ." Perry's resentment of those making good is illustrated in his attitude toward his sister, Bobo: "One fine day he'd pay her back . . . spell out in detail the things he was capable of doing to people like her, respectable people, safe and snug people, exactly like Bobo." In striking down the Clutters, Perry is striking at the embodiment of the American Dream—not, however, because he disapproves of it, but because he cannot get in on it. In a revealing statement, Perry confesses: "They [the Clutters] never hurt me, maybe it's just that the Clutters were the ones who had to pay for it." Capote says that the key to Perry's personality is "self-pity."

Dick's thinking parallels Perry's. At the trial a psychiatrist explains: "He secretly feels inferior to others . . . and dissatisfaction with only the normal slow advancement he could expect from his job. . . . These feelings seem to be overcompensated for by dreams of being rich and powerful . . . spending sprees when he has money." The Christmas following the killings, Dick and Perry are in Miami. "'Didn't I promise you we'd spend Christmas in Miami, just like millionaires?'" Dick asks Perry. But they are not millionaires and Dick soon shows the same kind of resentment that caused Perry to kill the Clutters. They see a shapely blonde masseuse hovering over a wealth racketeer, at poolside at the Fountainebleau. We are told that Dick mused: "Big-shot bastards like that had better be careful or he might open them up and let a little of their luck spill on the floor." Capote seeks the key to Dick's personality as "envy." Self-pity and envy—defects of character which Clyde Griffiths shares and which impel him in pursuit of the American Dream.

Consider the trip to Mexico, the dreams of sunken treasure, a hill of diamonds, of Cozumel, the island paradise. Contrast with these things the ignominy which Perry feels wriggling on his belly beneath Nancy Clutter's bed, in pursuit of a keepsake silver dollar. The disparity between his hopes and his gains, produces a rage and shame which leads directly to the killings. In prison, awaiting execution, Perry whimpers: "'I was better than any of *them.*'" Why should the "haves" have while he has not? This thought makes a murderer of him.

Perry's last thoughts, at the foot of the gallows, are of his father and his father's "hopeless dreams." Here is the point about Perry's father which Capote must have wanted to implant in the reader's consciousness. The failure of the elder Smith to attain the American Dream, yet his relentless quest for that Dream, contributed much to Perry's discontent. Perry could and probably did hate his father for the false hopes he had engendered. Yet he could not rid himself of the habit of hoping which his father had implanted in him. He did not reject his father's goals, only his idealistic methods of pursuing them. When he killed Herbert Clutter he was not cutting his father's throat, he was splitting open a money bag.

When the Clutters were murdered their neighbors sensed at once that they had been killed because they emblemized the American Dream. One such neighbor laments: "'Feeling wouldn't run half so high if this had happened to anyone except the Clutters. Anyone less admired. Prosperous, secure. But that family represented everything people hereabouts really value and respect, and that such a thing could happen to them—well, it's like being told there is no God. It makes life seem pointless.'" Capote himself has described the Clutters to an interviewer as "a perfect embodiment of the good, solid, landed American gentry." Their neighbors wonder, indeed, if a wealthier family, living near the Clutters, had not been the intended victims, since they were even more representative. Perry's and Dick's dreams of riches are, after all, the dreams of the community that judges them. That really is why it had admired the Clutters. Accordingly the community is outraged not so much by the murders as by the assault on the American Dream which the murders signify. The community hates the persons who have sullied that Dream and, by implication, challenged its validity. An ironic feature of the tragedy is that the Clutters were not that much to be envied. Imagine winning, as a prize, a weekend with the Clutter family! Clutter himself, perched in his chair, as on the night of the murders, reading *The Rover Boys,* trying to escape back into the untroubled days of his boyhood. The Clutter children, Nancy and Kenyon, restively testing their father's fundamentalist authoritarianism. Daft Mrs. Clutter shut away in her room, as she has been for years, her neuroticism a likely by-product of her husband's obsessive concern with piling up riches. To pursue the American Dream he had neglected her emotional needs. Even on the eve of his death plans for newer and greater business ventures jostled for place in his head with new plans for her rehabilitation. Here, indeed, is a household the occupants of which are leading "lives of quiet desperation." Thus, both Perry and Clutter are double victims of the American Dream. Pursuing the Dream and persuading his son to pursue it, Perry's father had destroyed his home life. In pursuit of the Dream, Clutter, too, had destroyed his family life, and was slain, at last, by someone pursuing the Dream who envied him his apparent attainment of it. This game had no winners.

At the close of *In Cold Blood* a reporter opines that the only good that came of the Clutter case was that a lot of newspapers had been sold. The final irony: the Clutter murders had been good for business, good for someone's pursuit of the American Dream. Inevitably, critics would say that Truman Capote's dream had come true, also, when *In Cold Blood* brought him a fortune amounting to millions. Dreiser had known the same opprobrium, if not the same rewards.

A further dilemma faced Truman Capote as author of a nonfiction novel based on the Clutter case. He had dual protagonists. Now Chester Gillette had been the protége of not one but two uncles. He had courted not one but three society girls. Not committed, as Capote was, to presenting facts without variance, Dreiser was able to merge the uncles into one, and to alloy the three belles. As co-protagonist, alleged instigator of the Clutter killings but not the actual killer, Dick Hickock is an encumbrance to Capote as storyteller. He "doesn't fit," as Capote himself has owned. Capote's narrative would have gone better if he could have dispensed with him entirely. His rapport was with Perry. It was Perry who wrote him a ten thousand word farewell letter and kissed him goodby before ascending the gallows. Capote lavished every attention on him. That is not surprising if, as Harper Lee surmises, Capote saw himself in Perry, just as Dreiser saw himself in Clyde. Dick's role, on the other hand, seems like something thrown in to strike the bargain. Since Dreiser sifted through at least ten American tragedies before he settled on Chester Gillette as the representative victim of the American Dream, it might be supposed that other victims of the same illusion, insofar as they approach typicalness, would resemble Clyde Giffiths. Dick does not. Perry does, in numerous particulars.

Dick's get-it-easy attitude and good looks remind us of Clyde. Otherwise he is nonrepresentative—an unwanted excrescence. Had Dreiser found such a personage bulking on the landscape of the Gillette-Brown case, he would have excised him without a pang, or telescoped his salvageable parts into a single characterization, just as he did with the dual uncles and triad of society girls. A good artist must have the surgical touch and apply it as needed. Capote's attempts to handle Hickock peripherally show that he realizes this. But he had to retain him because the scheme he had bound himself to demanded it. Hickock further illustrates, then, the quagmire the writer steps into who supposes that a work of art can be shaped from uninterpreted facts.

The parallels between Perry and Clyde, unlike those between Dick and Clyde, are both intimate and sustained:

Neither has a father with whom he can identify.

Both seek mother surrogates.

Both are unable to establish lasting and meaningful relationships.

Both despise religious rigorism.

Both are rootless, nomadic, and in flight from failure.

Both envy prosperous relatives.

Both are quick to excuse the conduct of sisters who have shared in their hardships.

Both are described as following a "mirage."[2]

Both dream of coming into possession of fabled riches—Aladdin's treasures; a hill of diamonds.

Both have in their natures a strain of tenderness, vivid but ephemeral—a by-product of their own hardships and disappointments.

Both are sentimentalists and betrayed by their sentimentalism.

Both morbidly hoard memorabilia touching on their emotional ties with others.

Both antagonize those whom they might look to for help: Gilbert won't help Clyde or let his father help him; Bobo won't help Perry or let her husband help him.

Both are wary prior to the crimes, reluctant to proceed, eager to call them off.

Each must assume a new personality to be capable of killing: Clyde joins forces with the afrit; Perry fuses his personality with Dick's.

Both think they have been shrewd but leave damaging clues behind.

Both attract comforters to them in prison.

Both see someone in the courtroom who reminds them of their victims and are haunted by that fact: Clyde, a girl who looks like Roberta; Perry, a brother of Clutter's who resembles Clutter.

Both are superstitious: For both a bird is harbinger of death; both regard Kansas City as "a place of bad luck."

Both are specifically charged in court with having murdered "in cold blood."

Both are perplexed by the role they have played: Clyde, legally innocent, feels morally guilty; Perry, legally guilty, feels morally innocent.

Both go to their deaths believing they have not received justice.

Granting the reality of coincidence, we must none the less concede that many of these parallels go beyond chance. Certainly if an anthropologist turned up so many matching bones we would not hesitate to concede that they probably came from creatures of the same species. Yet even if we did not know that Capote was working from facts alone, it would be unwise to conclude that he had plundered *An American Tragedy* for confirming touches for his narrative. On the other hand, if Dreiser's fictionalization had postdated Capote's nonfiction novel, how many critics would have been ready to bring in an indictment against him, charging plagiarism! Actually, when two authors are mining the same vein such duplications are inevitable. What is unforgettable is the realization that much of what Capote dug from the bedrock in his role as documentarian, Dreiser, through a remarkable use of the creative faculty, was able to provide out of his own intuition. Dreiser's sense of the American Tragedy type of individual was so unerring, he was able to identify with such a personage so totally, that he summoned up, out of his own innate sense of what was probable about such a man, a wealth of details which find actual substantiation in Capote's true-life record of Perry Smith.

Dreiser met none of the principals involved in the Gillette-Brown murder case, but he rowed to Moon Cove on Big Moose Lake where the murder occurred and lingered there for two hours; he sat in a cell on Death Row with a man awaiting execution, he went to a shirt factory and studied the process of shirt manufacturing, all in preparation for writing *An American Tragedy* And he went beyond these physical preparations, beyond a scrutiny of the trial record and newspaper accounts, to take on an actual sense of the identify of Chester Gillette. In doing that he created as honestly as Michelangelo did when he summoned David from his marmoreal cerements. Only a wraith of the Clyde Griffiths whom Dreiser created exists in the Chester Gillette of the trial record, yet in the truth of the characterization we are given an archetypal grasp of the American Tragedy type of protagonist, and of his dilemma, such as no dossier ever has been ample enough to hold. And all future portrayals of him, to the extent that they correspond to the facts, must resemble that archetype.

In 1838 William Ellery Channing wrote:

> You must have taken note of two classes of men, the one always employed on details, on particular facts, and the other using these facts as foundations of higher, wider truths. . . . One man reads a

history and can tell you all its events, and there stops. Another combines these events, brings them under one view, and learns the great causes which are at work. . . . So one man talks continually about the particular actions of this or another neighbor; whilst another looks beyond the acts to the inward principle from which they spring, and gathers from them larger views of human nature . . . strives to discover the harmony, connection, unity of all. . . . To build up that strength of mind, which apprehends and cleaves to great universal truths, is the highest intellectual self-culture.

By fictionalizing his material Dreiser gained vastly more in truth of nature than Capote did when he deployed his material without creative intervention. Capote's nonfiction novel format kept him from sorting out his major theme from secondary ones. It shackled him to petty data, kept him from soaring, from taking creative possession of his material. Lacking a viable artistic alternative, he let a debilitating morbidity, sponsored by his closeness both to the events and personages involved, and perhaps by his own narcissistic needs, inundate the resultant vacuum. The result is a work which avoids what Warren calls "the dreary factuality of an old newspaper account" solely by its dependency on an exalted style and on an emotionalism which combines Gothicism and sentiment in equal measure.

Dreiser's liberating method lets us enter into a bona fide relationship with Clyde. Chester Gillette admitted murdering Grace Brown. By qualifying Clyde's guilt in Roberta's death, Dreiser lays stress on society's role in the failure of his protagonist. By making Clyde a situational criminal impelled by circumstances, rather than an habitual criminal whose conduct is complicated by a twisted psyche, as is true of Dick and Perry, Dreiser is better able to convince us of the compelling force of the American Dream. After *An American Tragedy* was published Dreiser received letters from many readers who told him—"Clyde Griffiths might have been me." Readers could, in fact, identify with Clyde. Rare is the reader who will see himself as Dick or Perry. By the time he has read of Perry's Oedipal anxieties, his paranoia, his pathological drives, his craving for notoriety, of Dick's check-bouncing mentality and feelings of sexual inadequacy, he must be able to relate to them about as well as he could to *Australopithecus robustus.*

As a shaper of materials who does not have to answer to any person or pattern of events, Dreiser can place his emphasis where it will best support his thesis. Clyde reaches his decision to kill Roberta because of his wish to safeguard his American Dream prospects. Perry kills out of frustration at not attaining them. It is easier to relate to Clyde in his efforts to preserve his hopes than to Perry in his exasperation at not attaining his. Clyde's actions are consistent with his aspirations, Perry's a gesture of spite which negates the whole thrust of his ambitions—an acknowledgment of defeat. Dreiser thus is able to keep a positive emphasis, consistent with pursuit of the Dream, but Capote is compelled to deal with an act which repudiates it, with a protagonist who, at the start of his quest, has forsaken his goal. What is to be said of the Horatio Alger hero who loses faith when he experiences a setback in his progress toward success?

Not committed to rote delivery of hard facts, Dreiser is able to make the pace of his narrative less deliberate than Capote, to convey better a sense of Clyde's stumbling progress through life, with things falling out for him, as they do, by caprice rather than calculation. Against this pattern the pathos of his own petty scheming is better grasped and the reader prepared both for the ineptitude which characterizes his plan of murder, and the irony which lets chance make of it a foolproof vehicle for his destruction.

Dreiser is able to speak openly, too, of the inadequacies of the law. Capote, dealing with actual people, many of whom will be searching his narrative for grounds for libel, has to report on their shortcomings inferentially. Recognizing, also, that the appeal of his book is blunted by the absence of a love plot, Capote patches on an extraneous account of Nancy Clutter's lost love. Indeed, because Capote does not know how to tie together his facts, the whole final portion of *In Cold Blood* is fragmentary. He might have assured harmony, as Dreiser did with the use of a relay character, like the Reverend Duncan McMillan who could carry on the protagonists' quest and help them to order their thoughts on their ordeal. Dreiser was free to invent McMillan to serve this end and to invent little Russell whose role, at the close of the book, is to affirm that the action of the novel is about to unwind itself again, and will continue to do so, *ad infinitum*, until society itself alters. Wanting such characters, Capote loses his final chance to force an assessment of the true meaning of the Clutter murders.

Lilies, seasons, sports, the dance, cars, birds, boats, trees, colors all intrigue at the level of the symbol to give *An American Tragedy* expanding dimensions of subtlety and strength. Some are supplied out of Dreiser's creative imagination, others germinated by some actual circumstance of the Gillette-Brown case which Dreiser's imagination could restructure without reproach. By such measures was Dreiser able to enlarge the scope of his thesis and produce what Sergei Eiesenstein would salute as an "epic of cosmic veracity." Moreover, while Capote must grind under foot anything that looks like an undocumented assumption, Dreiser is free to give to his material a mythic sweep by invoking in Roberta the image of Persephone, and in Clyde, the transgressing Adam.

We have remarked that in *An American Tragedy*, Dreiser, without being on the scene as Capote was, or privy to confessional disclosures, again and again accurately intuited what was classic in such instances. The documentation which Capote provides on an American Dream sponsored murder in *In Cold Blood* confirms Dreiser's extraordinary instinct for the relevant in crimes of this specific kind. *In Cold Blood*'s chief value then—the real blessing which flows from it—may well be its affirmation, as an accurate but uninventoried stockpile of American Tragedy details, of the soundness of Dreiser's intuitions and methods. It is striking proof of the timeless integrity of *An American Tragedy*.

What Dreiser saw as true in 1925, is shown by Capote's documentation forty years after to be true still. Capote has reported on an event. Transcending time (and, indeed, as Mason Gross has observed, there is by design little in *An American Tragedy* to confine it to an era), Dreiser has reported on the truth of human nature. After all, materialism is, as E. M. Forster long ago noted, "the old, old trouble which eats the heart out of every civilization."

Dreiser's achievement confirms the essential role of the creative faculty and its generosity in supplying authenticating detail when the author acts from an understanding of the human condition founded on genuine responsiveness to the universe. By its very amplitude, it affirms the pity of a creative faculty stifled by limiting forms, of which the nonfiction novel, at least in Capote's understanding of it, is a repelling example. Capote's facts adorn him like leg irons. He is, in turn, jailer to imprisoned archetypes, myths, and symbols, inherent in his material, but denied liberty. They stare out at us like bugs in amber. Through Dreiser's method they could gorgeously soar. Even when style approaches the luminosity of Holy Writ, and Capote's sometime does, that is not enough if the facts strain for release, without avail, against the membrane of words enclosing them.

"Fact," says Norman Mailer, "is nothing without nuance." These words hint at a larger truth which Dreiser saw. In his edition of *The Living Thoughts of Thoreau,* Dreiser expresses admiration for this statement of Thoreau's:

> When facts are seen superficially, they are seen as they lie in relation to certain institutions, perchance. But I would have them expressed as more deeply seen, with deeper references; so that the reader or hearer cannot recognize them or apprehend their significance from the platform of common life, but it will be necessary that he be in a sense translated in order to understand them. . . . A fact truly and absolutely stated is taken out of the region of common sense and acquires a mythologic or universal significance.

As author of *An American Tragedy,* Dreiser can cite this passage with the authority of someone who has confronted truth and been caught up in its vastness. In the failing light of the void we live in, Capote, footloose amid the lovely lawns of his lyricism, is merely the most fragrant of the ineffectual angels who woo us. To see facts wholly, to be enveloped in verities that are eternal, we still must go to Dreiser.

NOTES

1.   The notoriety Dreiser's book gave to this circumstance eventually brought the desired reform. Electric chairs now are powered by a dynamo separate from those which supply prisons electricity for normal use.

2.   *Mirage* was Dreiser's original choice of a title for *An American Tragedy.* Clyde's
      aspirations are twice spoken of as a mirage.

V

BIBLIOGRAPHY

Major Works and Themes

PETER G. CHRISTENSEN

Writing a bibliographical essay on post-1978 critical literature on Truman Capote represents a challenge on several counts. First, his achievement declines precipitously after the 1966 publication of *In Cold Blood*, his best novel. The many problems of his personal life from the November 28, 1966 "Party of the Decade" to his sorry death in 1984 parallel his decline in literary productivity and fall from critical favor.

Second, critical commentary has been stranded in various ruts. We have Capote as the author of dark stories and light stories who abandons both to take up a form of journalism in the 1960s. The lack of connection between these three literary styles becomes almost emblematic of a personality that is ultimately seen as torn apart from within. Yet the attempt to read Capote's work as a coherent whole runs the opposite risk of preserving his reputation as a person who more obsessionally than artistically explored the same themes again and again.

Third, the huge amount of publicity attendant on *In Cold Blood*, Capote's often ill-advised reaction to it, and his misleading statements have led to an overemphasis on the theoretical issue of the nonfiction novel at the expense of penetrating thematic analyses of the work. Even the bulk of the theoretical literature on the nonfiction novel ultimately did not come out in Capote's favor, despite such well-written defenses of Capote by Jean Mouton and Mas'ud Zavarzadeh.

Fourth, Capote pretended to be above questions of literary influence, and in this sense he made up elements of his career just as he made up elements of his

---

Editor's Note: This essay has been formatted to be in the same style as the Introduction. We have accommodated occasional overlaps in coverage among the essay, the Introduction, and Robert J. Stanton's bibliography whenever they are mutually complimentary. As in the case of the Introduction, all items covered in the essay are included in the general bibliography.

biography. Capote was influenced by Welty, McCullers, and Flannery O'Connor, but did not wish to be typecast as a Southern writer. He bristled when it was suggested that he borrowed from these and other writers, and always insisted on the image of himself as a small child who hid in his bedroom to write. His talent began, he would argue, *ab ovo*, uninfluenced by any other sources.

Ten dissertations at least in part on Capote, particularly on *In Cold Blood*, have been completed since 1981, yet not one of them has been published, probably an indication that Capote's work is not in the front line of today's critical battles. Although Régis Durand in 1980 could write of Capote as an author who had gone very far to reduce the writer to his "skeletal minimum" ("On Conversing," 1980), most critics avoided such poststructural exuberance and grew embarrassed at Capote's publicity stunts and public appearances while intoxicated or on drugs. Capote's apparent indifference to gay liberation has also lost him potentially sympathetic critics in the highly visible field of gay and queer studies. My essay on gay themes and gay/queer reading of Capote which appears earlier in this anthology ("Truman Capote: A Career Retrospective") contains my comments on the memoir and biographical literature on Capote as well as a helpful bibliography on the topic.

Aside from memoirs, the only published full-length literary study of Capote since his death is Helen S. Garson's *Truman Capote: A Study of His Short Fiction* (1992), an item in the Twayne's Study in Short Fiction series, which fits into the restricted format of a career overview supplemented by reprints of articles and parts of essays by earlier critics. Kenneth T. Reed's 1981 *Truman Capote*, also published by Twayne, had been the last literary monograph on him, succeeding the earlier survey by William L. Nance (*The Worlds of Truman Capote*, 1970).

Prof. Garson, herself the author of the third book-length overview in English of Capote's work, a volume in the Ungar series (1980), has written a well-informed and researched study but does little to open up new ground. She tries to make the best of *Handcarved Coffins*, "Dazzle" and "Mojave" in *Music for Chameleons*, but, not surprisingly, can find little good to say for the three stories republished from *Esquire* as *Answered Prayers*. Most interesting is her comparison of the way misogynistic comments are filtered through character dialogue in "Mojave" but presented at face value in "Unspoiled Monsters" from the incomplete novel. Garson also notes a significant strain of cold self-absorption that extends from Walter Ranney, the protagonist of "Shut a Final Door" to B. P. Jones, the unpleasant narrator of *Answered Prayers,* whom she considers Capote's alter ego.

Garson provides a quick, though judicious, overview of the earlier literature on Capote, which I will not recapitulate here. Although she resists extremely critical views of Capote as person and author, she concedes that Capote fell apart like such other early American successes as Hemingway and Fitzgerald.

All were death-driven, and as in the case of Hemingway, Capote's later works amount to parodies of the earlier ones. Since Garson's book is a study of Capote's short fiction, it necessarily leaves out his most sustained achievements, *Other Voices, Other Rooms,* and *In Cold Blood.*

What is needed at this point in Capote criticism are skillful contextualizations which will neither overvalue nor undervalue the merit of his best work, while putting dated works such as *The Muses Are Heard* and *The Dogs Bark* to the side and burying *Answered Prayers.* One example of such an approach comes from Stefano Tani, who, in "L'Esperimento del Professor Hawkline: Case Stregate e sogno americano da Brown a Brautigan" (1984) places *Other Voices, Other Rooms* in a tradition of American Gothic from Ichabod Crane, Roderick Usher, the heroes of James's ghost stories, and Richard Brautigan's *Hawkline Monster* (1974).

Only a few reviews of Capote's career appeared in the period after his death, and the ones that did appear were more tribute than analysis. James Dickey was asked by the American Academy and Institute of Letters to compose a tribute to Capote after his death, and although he barely knew Capote, he offered an essay for the Academy's Proceedings (*Paris Review,* 1985) in which he praised Capote as a stylist, particularly in *Other Voices, Other Rooms.* For him Capote's gift is lyrical and poetic with a flair for the "scene stunning with rightness and strangeness, the compressed phrase, the exact yet imaginative word." In another tribute to Capote after his death, William Styron indicated that as an apprentice writer he was so taken with Capote's first publications that he felt an envy for him that paralleled Salieri's for Mozart.

In a positive overall career evaluation Chris Anderson speaks of Capote as a master of the "rhetoric of silence" ("The Art of Truman Capote," 1987). Capote was correct in his view of himself as a master of a prose style of understatement and conciseness. He is a paradigmatic writer of American prose because like Joan Didion and Tom Wolfe he uses very spare connecting explanation for his scenes and dialogues, and dramatized moments." More critical is Bruce Bawer, who in his overview, "Capote's Children," (1985) maintained that in his later years Capote was "neglecting his obligation as a literary artist to create, to order, and thereby to serve not merely personal and superficial truths but universal ones."

The bulk of the most significant reviews of *In Cold Blood* are conveniently available in the Casebook on the novel by Irving Malin (1968). Many excerpts from these and other reviews and articles up to 1987 also appear in the fifty pages of *Contemporary Literary Criticism* Vol. 58 (1990): 84-136, devoted to *In Cold Blood,* including an important interview with Capote as well as a reprint of the controversy in *The Observer* between Kenneth Tynan and Capote. All of the exchanges in this controversy can be found reprinted in Tynan's *Tynan Right and Left* (1967) as well as in *Contemporary Literary Criticism* 58.

Malin's Casebook appeared before 1978 and is covered in the Introduction to this volume. But two publications also appeared before 1978 which the editors and I feel should be included in this essay because they serve as convenient transitions into a discussion of post-1978 criticism of *In Cold Blood*, and because they merit more extensive treatment than they would get in the Introduction.

Jean Mouton's *Littérature et sang-froid: un récit véridique de Truman Capote pose des questions au roman* (1967), remains the one full-length study of the novel, although as it is in French, it is not often cited in the critical literature. Mouton begins by asserting that *In Cold Blood* caused just as much controversy in Europe as in the United States, but that the debate was more concerned with issues that had already been addressed concerning both prison literature and the French "nouveau roman." On the one hand, Alberto Moravia hated the book; on the other hand, J. M. G. Le Clézio admired it greatly.

Mouton suggests reading *In Cold Blood* in the light of André Gide's autobiographical *Souvenirs de la Cour d'assizes,* in which Gide tries to figure out what happened in the life of a condemned man before he committed his crime and what happened after his condemnation in court. Of comparable interest is Marcel Jouhandeau's *Trois Crimes rituels*, an exploration of the bloody murders which the noted author learned of through the court system, the crimes of the so-called "amants de Vendôme."

Mouton's second chapter compares Paul Claudel's journalistic account of the Japanese earthquake of 1923 with Capote's reportage in terms of their objective distance from the event and also with respect to the event's innate public interest. Mouton finds Capote not guilty of exploiting a shocking event for cheap purposes, and points out that most crime stories do not succeed in really illuminating the most horrible deeds. Capote, like Euripides in *Medea,* at least provides some illumination about the murder of innocent people who serve as surrogates for others who are seen as the source of injustice but who cannot be touched.

Mouton feels that Capote has written in a way that tries to avoid the trap that Sartre finds most novel writers falling into when creating their characters. The novelist risks placing before us an actor who is playing a role rather than a living being caught up in the change of circumstances and the mobility of time. However, Capote fails to go in the direction of the "nouveau roman" because the new novel requires not only a great deal of specialized concentration from the reader but also the reader's willingness in letting him/herself be taught a new literary discipline and approach to experience.

Perhaps most provocative in Mouton's analysis is his comparison of the motivations of Camus' Meursault in *The Stranger* with those of Perry in *In Cold Blood.* He comments that Meursault likes night but only to the extent that it is the time when people are finally silent. The self-reflective interrogation caused by the night is insupportable to him. In contrast Perry accepts his own entry into the night, even into the great night which is his own death. Reading Mouton's book, one feels that existential themes of *In Cold Blood* have not been totally tapped.

More theoretical and less wide ranging in his comparisons is Mas'ud Zavarzadeh whose section on Capote in his *The Mythopoeic Reality: The Postwar American Nonfiction Novel* (1976) is perhaps the most famous defense of Capote's *In Cold Blood.* For Zavarzadeh the writer of a nonfiction novel is not the creator of a fictional universe but rather the midwife of experiential reality. The view of reality recreated in the nonfiction novel is local and epistemologically different from the "global Weltanschauung of the totalizing novel." Zavarzadeh concedes that the ending of *In Cold Blood* is weak and open to severe criticism for being sentimental, but the fault is less with Capote's writing than with the ontology of the nonfictional novel. Indeed, "Any ending in such narratives will be to a certain degree 'false,' since an ending is an arbitrary and artificial but required imposition of a medium on the uninterruptible flow of life, whose movements the nonfiction novel follows." The ending is a concession that stands in the way of the open-endedness of life itself.

Zavarzadeh defends Capote's use of what seems to be the traditional omniscient narrator of Dickens and George Eliot, but Capote's omniscience is of an "empirical" type based on strong research rather than imaginative authority. Zavarzadeh continues:

> While the fictive novelist's authority for shaping and presenting his reality through his control of the point of view is his totalization of the experimental *donnée*, the authority of the nonfiction novelist is obtained through exegesis of his *données*. In using "empirical omniscience" in *In Cold Blood,* the all-knowing author substantiates his authority by weaving the narrative web from interviews, official documents, autobiographical sketches, and even the article in the learned journal.

Surprisingly, what is more jolting about *In Cold Blood* is less the author's omniscience than such bizarre facts that Mr. Clutter had bought a double indemnity insurance policy on the very day of his murder. The irony developed is less from "situational suspense" based on unknown events and new permutations in the plot line but on the "inscriptional suspense" of the bizarre items. Finally, for Zavarzadeh, *In Cold Blood* captures an event that is so strange that it escapes from the standards of fact and fiction. We are left with wonder and puzzlement because the confessions fail to give the events enough meaning.

Alan Collett wishes to claim that *In Cold Blood* is even more radical than Zavarzadeh finds it. His "Literature, Criticism, and Factual Reporting" (1989) defends *In Cold Blood* as a "successful result of an intention to create a literary work whose literariness is inseparable from the truth or falsity of its report sentences." By resisting the time-honored distinction between literary and factual works, it makes a virtue of its "lack of coherence and plausibility." Although the novel has much resonance, one should not consider that Capote resorts to overworked symbolism for, in effect, he has "succeeded in conveying an instance of life imitating art." For Collett, "If we insisted in reading *In Cold Blood* as a fictional account of real-life events we would condemn as crude precisely those examples of creativity which we praise as 'ironic' or 'significant' when we read the novel as Capote says we should. Collet hopes that this rethinking of the truth claims of *In Cold Blood* can expose as false the "popular view that the novel is a 'moral allegory of an innocent family struck down by killers who are themselves victims of fate' and that Mrs. Clutter was the scapegoat for the collected wrongs of Smith's life." Collett's reading, although provocative, seems to arrive at the point that any apparent weakness in a novel can become a virtue if looked at in a new way.

Collett directly critiques John Hollowell's "Truman Capote's 'Nonfiction Novel,'" a chapter in his *Fact & Fiction* (1977). Hollowell feels that *In Cold Blood* becomes "universal in a way that most reportage is not." One of Capote's big successes is his sympathetic portrait of Perry. Hollowell works under the belief that Capote has been scrupulous in his observance of factual events, a view that does not hold up, and goes on to say that the novel "suggests the impossibility of any 'objective' history. Ultimately the novel ends with a type of "mythic significance." In this reading, "The destiny of an archetypal American family crosses paths with warped killers whose vengeance is portrayed more as the result of fate than human motivation." The Clutters are representatives of the American dream cut down by the murderers they never met who are "agents of fate more than culpable human beings."

Other essays see limitations in Capote's approach to his raw materials but do not express wholesale disapproval. Ronald Weber, in *The Literature of Fact* (1980), considers *In Cold Blood* a success in Capote's terms, but unfortunately the documentary materials which make the book seem authentic reduce the emotional effects that the account can offer. Weber ultimately believes that Capote's earlier fiction is richer, as now he cannot "invent 'facts' in order to penetrate his characters all the more or enrich the implications of the account."

Less sympathetic evaluations of the novel come from critics who stress matters of factual accuracy. Robert Agustin Smart in *The Nonfiction Novel* (1985) presents various examples of Capote's distortion of the facts; the point in the chain of events when Perry confesses the four murders, the auctioning of the Clutter equipment, Smith's relationship with Mrs. Meier, and Smith's purported apology before his death, among other matters. Smart believes that Capote's own formula for fiction was that of the "conventional realistic novel," not the nonfiction novel. The use of setting, centers of consciousness, and neutral omniscience are all part of this tradition of the realistic novel. Capote believed that timelessness of theme, unfamiliarity of setting, and large cast of characters would contribute to the nonfiction novel, yet the end result is conventionality rather than genre adventurousness or an inquiry of the truth value of fiction.

Jack De Bellis in "Visions and Revisions" (1979) pointed out that, among the five thousand revisions of *In Cold Blood* made in the preparation of it for book publication from its original magazine appearance in *The New Yorker*, nineteen are in direct quotations. Here we have another bit of evidence which has eroded the average reader's belief in the truth value of Capote's "nonfiction novel." The similarity of Perry to Capote's early heroes may also lead one to believe that Capote has tampered with the characters.

Eric Heyne ("Toward a Theory of Literary Nonfiction," 1987) is also critical of Capote, in this case, for violating his own rules. However we feel about the possible ways of distinguishing or not distinguishing between fiction and nonfiction, for Heyne the fact remains that Capote did not play by his own principles. He should not have employed an omniscient perspective, "telling his story from the perspectives of a variety of characters but never entering the narrative as a character or making explicit value judgments as a narrator." Either Capote made up key scenes or else transferred his own experiences to other characters. Consequently the achievement of the book is substantially weakened.

Phyliss Frus McCord ("The Ideology of Form," 1986) also argues that Capote is naïve: he never deals with the question of the ownership of the defendants' story. He simply takes the $4 million that follows along from his claim that he has the true story. Capote's mistake is to believe that the true story "exists apart from its creation by a 'subjective' journalist conditioned to compose using certain patterns of words and images and in a language constructed by a complex culture." In this view, Capote is, reprehensibly, a "positivist."

Although, as the critical literature shows, most scholars have concluded that *In Cold Blood* is more novel than nonfiction novel, it has not generated the number of readings one would expect once the issue of the novel's truth value is bracketed out of consideration. One such attempt to read the novel as novel comes from Brian Conniff in "'Psychological Accidents': *In Cold Blood* and Ritual Sacrifice," (1995) which draws on elements of René Girard's *Violence and the Sacred*. Conniff feels that the court's refusal to consider psychological evidence that may have made jurors more sympathetic to Perry and Hickock was evidence of the attempt of a community to reassure itself that justice was being done while setting up sacrificial victims for itself. Nevertheless, instead of giving Capote credit for writing a novel with this message, he assumes that Capote is part of the blinded community itself. He writes, "Capote does not really want to consider the disturbing truth that this center of the American psyche, this vision of justice as a vengeful God who must be propitiated so that the 'natural and social order can be restored, is only reached by luck—or to put it in his own terms, by a 'psychological accident.'" The completely fictional final scene with its appeal to normalcy is Conniff's main backing for Capote's failure to realize that what he has been doing in the novel is defending American complacency.

Not surprisingly, *Music for Chameleons* has garnered much less critical attention than *In Cold Blood*. Again, as with the greater book, reactions are mixed. Robert Siegle in "Capote's *Handcarved Coffins* and the Nonfiction Novel," (1984) while appreciating the artistry of this "nonfiction" novel cannot agree with Capote's idea of discovering the "truly true" because for him it falsely implies that "truth is the indwelling meaning of events or entities themselves." Siegle does not want to concur that the "nonfictional discourse to which [Capote] resorts will give him privileged access." For him the "hermeneutical crisis" over the relation of fictional to nonfictional narrative cannot be handled adequately by logical deduction, including the logical deductions implicit in a mystery story. "Thus, in short, Capote's 'invention' of the nonfiction novel is both hoax and ingenious gathering of the full cultural resources of the act of narration, even if those resources have always been in fiction."

In contrast to these postmodern perspectives on *Handcarved Coffins* is David Lodge's review of it under the title of "Getting at the Truth" (1981). Lodge finds it very hard to believe that *Handcarved Coffins* could have been based on a true story. Not only is it nebulous in terms of date and place, but it follows through with the Sherlock Holmes mystery story paradigm too much not to suggest Conan Doyle as a model. Believing that the story is without any literary merit, Lodge suspects that Capote has labeled it nonfiction in order to increase its stature among critics. Lodge claims, "Truth is so much stranger than fiction these days, that the reading public will apparently give credence to the most hackneyed and sentimental stereotypes of fiction masquerading as fact."

John Hersey in "The Legend on the License" (1986) is even more hostile to *Handcarved Coffins*. He maintains that there is a sacred rule of journalism that nothing must be made up. For him a great threat to journalism is posed by the "distortion that comes from adding invented detail." *Handcarved Coffins* strains credulity beyond belief, and not because of any stripped-down quality but because it has a "much-too-muchness about it." The bizarreness of the murder details is simply 'over the top.' The story resembles a game of blindman's bluff with the reader blindfolded, for the story "takes place in an invisible place." Although the characters are "**there**, they are unseeable as real people," for their names have been changed. Such distortions have contributed in Capote, as in Norman Mailer and Tom Wolfe, to reprehensible "befogging of the public vision, to subtle failures of discrimination, and to the collapse of an important sense of trust."

John Fowles could not care less if *Handcarved Coffins* is fact or fiction. For him, it is a "fascinating tale about a bizarre chain of murders in the Midwest, and as grippingly readable as a Raymond Chandler—or *In Cold Blood*" ("Capote as Maupassant," 1980). Fowles admires all of *Music for Chameleons* and believes that Capote was the subject of much hostile criticism because of his willingness to expose for ridicule the lives of the rich. Fowles's Capote is the Polonius of his age, and the heir of Flaubert, Maupassant, and Proust as well. Although this favorable view of *Music for Chameleons* is atypical, it points to the possibility of future sympathetic reevaluation of the volume, and it reminds us of Capote's favor in the eyes of other novelists, such as Dickey and Styron.

If we ask how many of the articles about Capote mentioned in this essay are truly remarkable, we are forced to admit that although most provide useful information and some new insights, the overall quality is not outstanding. Zavarzadeh and Hersey offer contrasting points of view for entry into the issue of the nonfiction novel. Conniff and Hollowell deal most explicitly with the theme of murder and sacrifice in *In Cold Blood* taken as a novel. Surprisingly little criticism has developed from the fact that some readers see the novel as showing Capote's sympathy with the world of the Clutters, whereas others find him to be using the murderers to attack what the Clutters represent. Much of the richness of the novel lies in this ambiguity created by the withdrawn narrative consciousness.

In Cold Blood is for some critics an extension of Capote's gothic fiction extending back to his work of the 1940s. *Other Voices, Other Rooms* has been well discussed in terms of gothic fiction, but except for Tani's recent article, this vein of criticism appears to have run dry, to be replaced by the usually brief examples of gay criticism of the novel discussed in my earlier article. Nevertheless, the gay subtext of *In Cold Blood* has neither been examined in any detail nor connected to its gothic qualities.

With the renewed popular interest in Capote—two versions of "A Christmas Memory" have appeared on television, as has "The Thanksgiving Visitor"; the film of *In Cold Blood* appeared on television in Dec. 1997, along with a televised biography of Capote; and the one-man play starring Robert Morse as Capote was a Tony winning success—it is probable that there will be a renewed critical interest in the man and his work. Some directions which it might take include not only the gay subtext of his work but detailed analyses of his dramatic writing, especially the screenplays of *The Innocents, Beat the Devil,* and *Laura,* and a careful examination of his relationship with and debt to French, German, and Italian literature.

SELECTED BIBLIOGRAPHY

Adams, Steven. *The Homosexual as Hero in Contemporary Fiction.* New York. 1980.

Aldridge, John W. "America's Young Novelists: Uneasy Inheritors of a Revolution." *Saturday Review* 32:6-8, 36-37, 42 (12 Feb., 1949).

_____. "The Metaphorical World of Truman Capote." *Western Review* 15:247-60 (Summer, 1951).

Algeo, Ann M. "The Courtroom as Forum: Homicide Trials by Dreiser, Wright, Capote, and Mailer." Ph.D. dissertation, Lehigh University, 1992.

Allen, Walter. "London Letter." *New York Times Book Review,* 12, 14, 16 (10 April, 1966).

_____. "New Novels." *New Statesman* 36:445-46 (20 Nov., 1948).

_____. *Tradition and Dream.* London; Phoenix House, 1964.

Allen, William. "New Short Stories." *New Statesman* 56:888-90 (20 Dec., 1957).

Almendinger, Blake. "The Room Was Locked with the Key on the Inside." *Studies in Short Fiction* 24:279-88 (Fall, 1987).

Anderson, Chris. "Fiction, Nonfiction, and the Rhetoric of Silence." *Midwest Quarterly* 28:340-53 (Spring, 1987).

Anon. "Gershwin in Russia." *Times Literary Supplement,* 408 (5 July, 1957).

Anon. "'In Cold Blood' An American Tragedy." *Newsweek* 67:59-63 (24 Jan., 1966).

Anon. "Is That A Fact?" *Times Literary Supplement,* 1061-62 (25 Nov., 1965).

Anon. "Story or Documentary?" *Economist* 218:1140 (19 Mar., 1966).

Anon. "Stranger Than Fiction." *Times Literary Supplement,* 215 (17 Mar., 1966).

Anon. "The Country Below the Surface." *Time* 87:83 (21 Jan., 1966).

Anon. Review of *Other Voices, Other Rooms. Virginia Kirkus' Bookshop Service* 15:629 (15 Nov., 1947).

Anon. Review of *In Cold Blood. Virginia Kirkus' Bookshop Service* 33:1139 (1 Nov., 1965).

Arvin, Newton. "The New American Writers. *Harper's Bazaar* 81:196-97, 292, 294, 296, 298-99 (March, 1947).

Atkinson, Brooks. "Truman Capote's First Drama." *New York Times* (28 March, 1952).

Austen, Roger. *Playing the Game: The Homosexual Novel in America.* New York. 1977.

Baker, Carlos. "Deep South Guignol." *New York Times Book Review,* 5 (18 Jan., 1948).

_____. "Nursery Tales from Jitter Manor." *New York Times Book Review,* 7, 33 (27 Feb., 1949).

Balakian, Nona. "The Prophetic Vogue of the Anti-Heroine." *Southwest Review* 47:134-41 (Spring, 1962).

Baldanza, Frank. "Plato in Dixie." *Georgia Review* 12:151-67 (Summer, 1958).

Barzun, Jacques. "Delicate and Doomed." *Harper's* 196:386, 388 (April, 1948).

Baro, Gene. "Truman Capote Matures and Mellows." *Herald Tribune,* 4 (30 Sept., 1951).

Barry, Iris. "Short Stories of Truman Capote." *Herald Tribune,* 2 (27 Feb., 1949).

Bawer, Bruce. "Capote's Children." *New Criterion* 10:39-44 (June, 1985).

Baxandall, Lee. "The New Capote and the Old Soviet Advice." *Studies on the Left* 6:92-100 (March/April, 1966).

Bentley, Eric. "On Capote's Grass Harp." *The New Republic* 126 (14 April 1952): pp. 22-23.

Boles, Paul Darcy. "Legend of Holiday the Lost." *Saturday Review* 41:20 (1 Nov., 1958).

Brannerman, James. "Capote's Unanswered Questions." *Maclean's* 79:42 (5 Mar., 1966).

Brown, Cecil M. "Plate du Jour: Soul Food: Truman Capote on Black Culture." *Quilt* 136-42 (1981).

Bryer, Jackson. "Check List" in *A Critical Handbook,* ed. by Irving Malin. Belmont [CA]; Wadsworth Publishing Co., 1968, pp. 239, 69.

Cardinal, Esther. "Journalistic Fiction: A Development from Early American Realism." Ph.D. dissertation, Kent State, 1981.

Chapman, John. "'House of Flowers.'" *New York Daily News* (1 Jan., 1955).

Chiu, Hanping. "Nonfiction Novel, Historical Novel, and the Crisis of the Novel." Ph.D. dissertation, University of Minnesota, 1991.

Christensen, Peter. "Capote As Gay American Author." In *Contemporary Gay American Novelists.* Westport [CT]; Greenwood Press, 1993.

Christensen, Peter. "Truman Capote: Major Works and Themes." An original essay in this anthology.

Clarke, Gerald. *Capote.* New York; Ballantine Books, 1988.

Clurman, Harold. "Theater." *The Nation* 176:421-22 (16 May, 1953).

_____. "Theater." *The Nation* 180:106-07 (29 Jan., 1955).

Coindreau, Maurice E. "Preface to *Other Voices, Other Rooms,*" in *The Time of William Faulkner.* Columbia [SC]; Univ of South Carolina Press, 1971, pp. 123-31.

Collett, Alan. "Literature, Criticism, and Factual Reporting." *Philosophy and Literature* 13:282-96 (Oct., 1989).

Connell, Evan S. Jr. "A Dissenting Voice." *This World Magazine,* 32, 34 (16 Jan., 1966).

Connelly, Cyril. "Introduction." *Horizon* 16:1-11 (October, 1947).

Conniff, Brian. "Psychological Accidents." *Midwest Quarterly* 35:77-95 (Autumn, 1995).

DeBellis, Jack. "Visions and Revisions." *Journal of Modern Literature* 7:519-36. (1979).

Dickey, James. "Proceedings: Truman Capote." *Paris Review* 97:184-89 (Autumn, 1985).

Dupee, F. W. "Truman Capote's Score." *New York Times Review of Books* 6:3-5 (3 Feb., 1966).

Durand, Regis. "On Conversing." *Sub-stance* 27:47-51 (1980).

Eisinger, Chester. *Fiction of the Forties.* Chicago; University of Chicago Press, 1963, pp. 237-43.

Farrelly, John. "Fiction Parade." *New Republic* 118:31-32 (26 Jan., 1948).

Fiedler, Leslie. "Capote's Tale." *The Nation* 168:395-96 (2 April, 1949).

Fineman, Morton. "Heir to Terror and Love." *Philadelphia Inquirer,* 5 (18 Jan., 1948).

Follows, Arthur J. "A Strange First Novel." *Milwaukee Journal,* 5 (25 Jan., 1948).

Fowles, John. "Capote as Maupassant." *Saturday Review* 7:52-53 (July, 1980).

Friedman, Melvin J. "Towards an Aesthetic: Truman Capote's Other Voices," in *A Critical Handbook,* ed. by Irving Malin. Belmont [CA]; Wadsworth Publishing Co., 1968, pp. 163-76.

Galloway, David. "Real Toads in Real Gardens," in *Gattungsprobleme in der Anglo-Amerikanischen Literatur,* ed. by Raimund Borgmeier. Tübingen: Niemeyer, 1986.

_____. "Why the Chickens Come Home to Roost in Holcomb, Kansas," in *A Critical Handbook,* ed. by Irving Malin. Belmont [CA]; Wadsworth Publishing Co., 1968, pp. 154-63.

Garrett, George. "Crime and Punishment in Kansas." *The Hollins Critic* 3:1-12 (Feb., 1966).

Garson, Helen. *Truman Capote.* New York; Frederick Ungar Publishing, 1980.

_____. *Truman Capote. A Study of the Short Fiction.* New York; Twayne, 1992.

Gehman, Richard B. "Where Are the Postwar Novels?" *Esquire* 31:74, 91 (March, 1949).

Glicksberg, Charles I. "The Lost Self in Modern Literature." *Personalist* 43:527-38 (Autumn, 1962).

Goad, Craig M. "The Literary Career of Truman Capote." Ph.D. dissertation, University of Missouri, 1993.

Good, Craig M. "Daylight and Darkness, Dream and Delusion. . . ." *Emporia State Research Studies* 16:5-57. (Sept. 1967).

Gossett, Louise Y. *Violence in Recent Southern Fiction.* Durham [NC]; Duke University Press, 1965.

Goyen, William. "That Old Valentine Maker." *New York Times Book Review,* 5, 38 (2 Nov., 1958).

Guilfoil, Kelsey. "Exotic Tale of Youth in Odd Setting." *Chicago Sunday Tribune,* 5 (18 Jan., 1948).

Haack, Dietmar. "Faction. . . ." in *American Literature in the 20ᵗʰ Century*, ed. by Dietman Haack and Alfred Weber, Göttingen; Vandenhoeck & Ruprecht, 1971, pp. 127-46.

Habas, Ralph. "First Novel." *Chicago Sun Times*, 7 (1 Feb., 1948).

Hardwick, Elizabeth. "Much Outcry; Little Outcome." *Partisan Review* 15:374-77 (March, 1948).

Hardy, John E. "Truman Capote's Diamond Guitar." *Commentaries on Five American Short Stories*. Germany; Diesterweg, 1962, pp. 3-6.

Harriss, W. E. Review of *Other Voices, Other Rooms. Commonweal* 47:500 (27 Feb., 1948).

Hassan, Ihab. "Birth of a Heroine." *Prairie Schooner* 34:78-83 (Spring, 1960).

_____. "The Daydream and Nightmare of Narcissus." *Wisconsin Studies in Contemporary Literature*, 1:5-21 (Spring-Summer, 1960).

Hayes, Richard. Review of *The Grass Harp. Commonweal* 55:73-74 (26 Oct., 1951).

_____. "The Stage." *Commonweal* 61:454-55 (28 Jan., 1955).

Hellmann, John. "Death and Design in *In Cold Blood." Ball State University Forum* 21:65-78 (Spring, 1980).

Hersey, John. "The Legend on the License," *Yale Review* 75:289-314 (Winter, 1986).

Heyne, Eric. "Toward a Theory of Literary Nonfiction." *Modern Fiction Studies* 33:479-90 (Autumn, 1987).

Hicks, Granville. "A World of Innocence." *New York Times Book Review*, 4 (30 Sept., 1951).

Hicks, Jack "Fire, Fire, Fire Flowing Like a River, River, River," in *History and Post-War Writing,* ed. by Theo D'haen and Hans Bertens. Amsterdam; Rodopi, 1990, pp. 171-84.

Hill, Pati. "The Art of Fiction XVII: Truman Capote." *Paris Review* 16:34-51 (Spring-Summer, 1957).

Hoffmann, Frederick. *The Art of Southern Fiction*. Carbondale [IL]; Southern Illinois University Press, 1967.

Hollowell, John. *Fact and Fiction: The New Journalism and the Nonfiction Novel.* Chapel Hill [NC]; University of North Carolina Press, 1977.

Howe, Irving. "Realities and Fictions." *Partison Review* 26:130-36 (Winter, 1959).

Hutchens, John K. "Book Review." *Herald Tribune,* 17 (4 Nov., 1958).

Inge, M. Thomas. *Truman Capote: Conversations.* Jackson [Miss]; University of Mississippi Press, 1987.

Jackson, Katherine Gauss. "Books in Brief: *The Grass Harp." Harper's* 203:121-22 (November, 1951).

Jacobs, J. U. "The Non-Fiction Novel." *Unisa English Studies Pretoria* 9:17-22 (Sept., 1971).

Kael, Pauline. "'The Innocents,' and What Passes for Experience." *Film Quarterly* 15:21-36 (Summer, 1962).

Kanfer, Stanley. Music for Chameleons." *New Republic* 176:30-32 (6, 13 Sept., 1980).

Kauffmann, Stanley. "Capote in Kansas." *New Republic* 154:19-21 (22 Jan., 1966).

Kazin, Alfred. *The Open Form.* New York; Harcourt Brace, 1961.

_____. "The World As a Novel." *New York Review of Books* 16: 26-30 (8 April, 1971).

_____. "Truman Capote and the Army of Wrongness." *Reporter* 19:40-41 (November, 1958).

Kerr, Walter. "New Play with Beauty, Style, and Little Drama." *Herald Tribune* (6 April, 1952).

_____. "The Grass Harp" Revived at Circle in the Square." *Herald Tribune* 28 April, 1953).

Kirby, John Pendy. "Fashions in Sinning." *Virginia Quarterly Review* 28:126-30 (Winter, 1952).

Klein, Alexander. "Nothing Ordinary." *New Republic* 121:17-18 (July, 1949).

Klein, Marcus. *After Alienation.* Cleveland; World Publishing Co., 1964.

Kramer, Hilton. "Real Gardens with Real Toads." *New Leader* 49:18-19 (31 Jan., 1966).

LaFarge, Oliver. "Sunlit Gothic." *Saturday Review* 34:19-20 (20 Oct., 1951).

Langbaum, Robert. "Capote's Nonfiction Novel." *American Scholar* 35: 570, 572-80 (Summer, 1966).

Lazarus, H. P. "A Blizzard of Butterflies." *The Nation* 173:482 (1 Dec., 1951).

LeMaire, Marcel. "Fiction in the U.S.A.: From the South." *Revue de Langues Vivant* 27:244-53 (1961).

Levine, Paul. "Review." *Georgia Review* 12:350-52 (Fall, 1959).

_____. "The Intemperate Zone. . . ." *Massachusetts Review* 8:505-23 (Summer, 1967).

_____. "The Revelation of the Broken Image." *Virginia Quarterly Review* 34:600-17 (Autumn, 1958).

Lodge, David. "Getting at the Truth." *Times Literary Supplement* 4064:185-86 (20 Feb., 1981).

Ludwig, Jack. *Recent American Novelists.* Minneapolis [MN]; University of Minnesota Pamphlets on American Writers, No. 22, 1962.

MacDonald, Dwight. "Cosa Nostra." *Esquire* 65:44, 46, 48, 58, 60 (April, 1966).

Mailer, Norman. *Advertisements for Myself.* New York; G. P. Putnam, 1959.

_____. *The Naked and the Dead.* New York; Rinehart & Co., 1948.

Malin, Irving. *A Critical Handbook.* Belmont [CA]; Wadsworth Publishing Co., 1968.

_____. "From Gothic to Camp." *Ramparts*:60-61. (1964).

_____. *New American Gothic.* Carbondale [IL]; Southern Illinois University Press, 1962.

McAleer, John J. "*An American Tragedy* and *In Cold Blood*: Turning Case History into Art." *Thought* 47:569-86 (Winter, 1972).

McCord, Phyllis. "The Ideology of Form." *Genre* 19:59-79 (Spring, 1986).

McCormick, John. *Catastrophe and Imagination.* London; Longmans, Green and Co., 1957.

McGrory, Mary. "Truman Capote . . . Takes a Flight into Non-Fiction." *Washington Star,* 6-3 (17 Sept., 1950).

Mengeling, Marvin E. "*Other Voices, Other Rooms*: Oedipus Between the Covers." *American Imago* 19:361-74 (Winter, 1962).

Merrick, Gordon. "How to Write Lying Down." *New Republic* 139:23-24 (8 Dec., 1958).

Michener, James. "Foreword" to Lawrence Grobel. *Conversations with Capote.* New York. 1985.

Moravia, Alberto. "Two American Writers." *Sewanee Review* 68:473-81 (Summer, 1960).

Morris, Lloyd. "A Vivid, Inner, Secret World." *Herald Tribune,* 2 (18 Jan., 1948).

Morris, Robert K. "Capote's Imagery," in *A Critical Handbook,* ed. by Irving Malin. Belmont [CA]; Wadsworth Publishing Co., 1968, pp. 269, 299, 312.

Morris, Willy. "Capote's Muse Is Heard." *New Republic* 169:21-22 (3 Nov., 1973).

Mouton, Jean. *Litterateur et sang-froid.* Paris; Desclee De Brouwer, 1967.

Nance, William L. *The Worlds of Truman Capote.* New York; Stein and Day, 1970.

————. "Variations on a Dream: Katherine Anne Porter and Truman Capote." *Southern Humanities Review* 3:338-45 (Fall, 1969).

Nathan, George Jean. "The Grass Menagerie." *Theatre Arts* 36:17-19 (June, 1952).

O'Gorman, F. E. *Best Sellers* 18:296 (1 Nov., 1958).

Ozick, Cynthia. "Reconsideration: Truman Capote." *New Republic* 168:31-34 (27 Jan., 1973).

Parone, Edward. "Truman in Wonderland." *Hartford Courant,* 14 (10 Dec., 1950).

Pavlov, Grigor. "Truman Capote." *Publications of the University of Sofia* 63:149-70 (1969).

Perry, J. Douglas. "Gothic As Vortex: The Form of Horror in Capote, Faulkner, and Styron." *Modern Fiction Studies* 19:153-59, 166-67 (Summer, 1973).

Phillips, Robert. "William Goyen: The Art of Fiction LXIII." *Paris Review* 17:58-100 (Winter, 1976).

Phillips, William, "But Is It Good Literature?" *Commentary* 41:77-80 (May, 1966).

Pizer, Donald. "Documentary Narrative As Art." *Journal of Modern Literature* 2:105-18 (Sept., 1971).

Plimpton, George. "The Story Behind a Nonfiction Novel." *New York Times Book Review,* 2-3, 38-43 (16 Jan., 1966).

Plimpton, George. *Truman Capote.* New York; Doubleday and Co., 1997.

Prescott, Orville. "Books of the Times." *New York Times,* 23 (21 Jan., 1948).

————. "Books of the Times." *New York Times,* 25 (2 Oct., 1951).

Rafferty, Terrence. "A Final Door." *The New Yorker,* 113-19 (21 Sept. 1987).

Reagan, Betty Ann Adams. "The Rhetoric of Criminal Defense: Ethos, Logos, and Pathos in Selected American Works." Ph.D. dissertation, Texas Woman's University, 1982.

Reed, Kenneth T. *Truman Capote.* Boston; Twayne Publishers, 1981.

Riedell, Karyn Lea. "The Struggle Toward Androgyny: A Study of Selected American Writers." Ph.D. dissertation, Arizona State, 1984.

Rosenfeld, Isaac. "Twenty-Seven Stories." *Partisan Review* 16:753-55 (July, 1949).

Rubin, Louis. "The Curious Death of the Novel. . . ." *Kenyon Review* 28:305-25. (June, 1966).

Ruoff, Gene W. "Truman Capote: The Novelist As Commodity," in *The Forties*, ed. by Warren French. Deland [FL]; Everett/Edwards, 1969, pp. 261-69.

Siegle, Robert. "Capote's *Handcarved Coffins* and the Nonfiction Novel." *Contemporary Literature* 25:437-51 (Winter, 1984).

Smart, Robert A. *The Nonfiction Novel.* New York; University Press of America, 1985.

Smith, Harrison. "Sizing Up the Comers." *Saturday Review* 32:9-11 (12 Feb., 1949).

Stanton, Robert J. *A Primary and Secondary Bibliography.* Boston; G. K. Hall, 1980.

Styron, William. "Adios a Truman Capote." *Quimera* 44:43-45 (1985).

Sullivan, Walter. "The Continuing Renaissance: Southern Fiction in the Fifties." *South: Modern Southern Literature in Its Cultural Setting.* Ed. by Louis B. Rubin Jr. New York; Doubleday and Co., 1961, pp. 376-91.

Tanner, Tony. *City of Words.* New York; Harper & Row, 1971.

————. "Death in Kansas." *Spectator* 216:331-32 (18 Mar., 1966).

Tanrisal, Meldan. "New Journalism and the Nonfiction Novel: Creating Art Through Facts." Ph.D. dissertation, Hacettepe University (Turkey), 1989.

Tompkins, Phillip. "In Cold Fact." *Esquire* 65:125, 127, 166-68, 170-71 (June, 1966).

Trilling, Diana. "Capote's Crime and Punishment." *Partisan Review* 33:252-59 (Spring, 1966).

————. "Fiction in Review." *The Nation* 166:133-34 (Jan., 1949).

Trimmier, Dianne B. "The Critical Reception of Capote's *Other Voices, Other Rooms.* West Virginia University Philological Papers* 17:94-101 (June, 1970).

Trousdale, Marion. "Reality and Illusion in the Theatre." *Critical Quarterly* 11:347-59 (Winter, 1969).

Turner, Dixie Mae. "Structural Patterns and Principles of Design . . . Literature in Secondary Schools." Ph.D. dissertation, University of Illinois, 1988.

Tuttle, Jon. "Glimpses of 'A Good Man' in Capote's *In Cold Blood" ANQ* 1:144-46 (October, 1988).

Tynan, Kenneth. "The Kansas Farm Murders." *The London Observer,* 21 (13 March, 1966).

Vidal, Gore. *Williwaw.* New York; E. P. Dutton, 1946.

Waldmeir, John C. "Religion and Style in *The Dogs Bark* and *Music for Chameleons."* An original essay in this anthology.

Waldmeir, Joseph J. "Introduction" to this anthology.

Weber, Ronald. *The Literature of Fact: Literary Nonfiction in American Writing.* Athens [OH]; Ohio University Press, 1980.

West, Paul. *The Modern Novel.* London; Hutchinson University Library, 1963.

West, Ray B. *The Short Story in America.* New York; Books for Libraries Press, 1968.

West, Rebecca. "A Grave and Reverend Book." *Harper's* 232:108, 110, 112-14 (February, 1966).

Wiegand, William. "The 'Non-Fiction' Novel." *New Mexico Quarterly* 37:243-57 (Autumn, 1967).

Wilson, John S. "Building a House of Flowers." *Theatre Arts* 39:30-31, 91 (January, 1955).

Young, Marguerite. "Tiger Lilies." *Kenyon Review* 10:516-18 (Summer, 1948).

Yurick, Sol. "Sob-Sister Gothic." *The Nation* 202:158-60 (7 Feb., 1966).

Zavarzadeh, Mas'ud. *The Mythopoeic Reality: The Postwar American Nonfiction Novel.* Urbana [IL]; University of Illinois Press, 1976.

Zolotow, Maurice. "The Season on and off Broadway." *Theatre Arts* 39:90-91 (March, 1955).

Zunbrunnen, Wanita Ann. "A Literary Search to Identify Factors Necessary for an Individual Sense of Justice." Ph.D. dissertation, University of Iowa, 1987.

VI

INDEX

INDEX

Agee, James, 22, 121, 122, 206
Aldridge, John W., 5, 6, 7, 9, 10, 13,
    15, 37-47, 52, 55, 63, 81, 84, 88, 89,
    99, 100, 105
Allen, Walter, 8, 14, 19, 20
Almendinger, Blake, 28, 29
American Dream, 23, 24, 30, 145, 152,
    198, 207, 209, 211, 212, 213, 216,
    217
Anderson, Chris, 9, 10, 206, 223
Arlen, Harold, 11, 77
Arvin, Newton, 11, 12
Atkinson, Brooks, 10
Austen, Roger, 17, 62

Baker, Carlos, 12, 14
Balakian, Nona, 7, 63
Baldanza, Frank, 29, 63, 203
Baldwin, James, 5, 33, 197, 198, 203
Bannerman, James, 21
Barnes, Djuna, 8
Baro, Gene, 17
Barry, Iris, 12
Barth, John, 28, 167, 168, 176
Barzun, Jacques, 14
Bayandall, Lee, 21
Bellow, Saul, 5, 19, 32, 33, 109, 206
Bentley, Eric, 10, 69-72
Bowles, Paul, 7, 8, 48, 84
Bowles, Sally, 19, 29, 113, 193
Brickell, Herschel, 1, 11
Brooks, Peter, 11

Brown, Cecil M., 5, 31-36
Bryer, Jackson R., 22, 30

Capote, Truman (Works cited):
    Answered Prayers, 4, 6, 19, 20, 26,
        27, 61, 66, 115, 116, 118, 119,
        120, 153, 155, 165, 171, 222, 223
    "Beat the Devil," 3, 49, 229
    Breakfast at Tiffany's, 1, 3, 6, 11,
        17, 18, 20, 29, 50, 51, 61, 96, 97,
        109, 110, 112, 113, 117, 135, 144,
        193
    "Children on Their Birthdays," 12,
        39, 51, 79, 80, 83, 85, 88, 110,
        201
    In Cold Blood, 1, 3, 4, 6, 8, 9, 10,
        13, 17, 20, 21, 22, 23, 24, 25, 26,
        28, 29, 30, 61, 63, 64, 65, 66, 67,
        119, 121, 122, 123, 130, 131, 132,
        135, 137, 143, 144, 146, 147, 148,
        149, 152, 153, 154, 160, 168, 170,
        171, 172, 173, 174, 191, 194, 195,
        201, 202, 205, 206, 207, 208, 209,
        210, 211, 213, 215, 217, 221, 222,
        223, 224, 225, 226, 227, 228, 229
    "A Diamond Guitar," 7, 61, 63, 65,
        66, 113
    The Dogs Bark, 3, 25, 26, 27, 155,
        156, 159, 160, 161, 162, 165, 166,
        174, 175, 176, 177, 223
    The Grass Harp, 1, 3, 6, 7, 8, 10, 11,
        16, 17, 18, 19, 23, 29, 50, 51, 52,

56, 58, 59, 66, 67, 69, 70, 71, 73,
88, 91, 92, 107, 110, 113, 117,
201
Handcarved Coffins, 4, 10, 26, 28,
61, 153, 161, 163, 164, 165, 166,
167, 169, 170, 171, 172, 173, 174,
175, 176, 222, 228
House of Flowers, 3, 11, 50, 77, 114
"The Innocents," 11, 229
"La Côte Basque," 20, 116, 117, 118
"A Lamp in the Window," 27, 157
Local Color, 3, 25, 26, 49, 155, 160,
169, 176
"Miriam," 1, 39, 50, 79, 80, 85, 89,
109
"Mojave," 19, 115, 116, 222
The Muses Are Heard, 3, 25, 26, 27,
49, 96, 119, 145, 159, 169, 176,
223
Music for Chameleons, 4, 19, 25, 26,
27, 28, 61, 116, 119, 153, 155,
156, 157, 158, 161, 166, 170, 171,
174, 175, 222, 228, 229
Other Voices, Other Rooms, 1, 3, 6,
13, 16, 28, 29, 38, 39, 46, 47, 50,
52, 53, 54, 56, 61, 62, 64, 66, 67,
79, 80, 81, 84, 88, 89, 90, 96, 99,
100, 104, 109, 115, 117, 143, 155,
159, 160, 169, 169, 176, 182, 184,
186, 191, 193, 201, 202, 207, 208,
223, 229
"Shut a Final Door," 13, 50, 80, 88,
95, 109, 117, 118, 222
"My Side of the Matter," 29, 51, 80,
83, 110
"The Thanksgiving Visitor," 3, 155,
229
A Tree of Night, 3, 6, 8, 9, 11, 12,
16, 23, 38, 50, 52, 61, 79, 80, 81,
87, 88, 95, 96, 109, 155, 169, 176
"A Voice from a Cloud," 27, 155
"The Walls Are Cold," 1, 81
"Why I Live at the Post Office," 28
Chapman, John, 11
childlike, 8, 20, 90, 102, 117
Christensen, Peter G., 6, 7, 30, 61-68,
221-30
Clurman, Harold, 10
Clarke, Gerald, 5, 65
Coindreau, Maurice Edgar, 16

Commonweal, 10, 11, 15, 17
Connell, Evan, 21
Connelly, Cyril, 12

daylight, metaphor, 6, 13, 19, 40, 49,
50, 51, 56, 59, 82, 83, 84, 85, 88, 89,
91, 93, 95, 105, 109, 110
De Bellis, Jack, 25, 65, 227
Documentary, 2, 21, 22, 25, 29, 30,
131, 135, 146, 147, 148, 149, 205,
211, 226
Dreiser, Theodore, 30, 146, 205, 206,
207, 208, 209, 210, 211, 213, 214,
215, 216, 217, 218

Economist, 21
Eisinger, Chester, 8
Esquire, 4, 19, 21, 61, 115, 116, 151,
222
exotic, Capote's fascination with, 8, 18,
26, 77, 88, 95, 113, 169

fantasy, 8, 15, 16, 17, 26, 48, 62, 70,
73, 74, 80, 82, 126, 147, 189
Farrelly, John, 14
Faulkner, William, 2, 14, 23, 28, 49,
136, 169, 179, 182, 184, 185, 186,
187, 189, 190, 191, 193
Fiedler, Leslie, 12, 30, 79-80, 182, 198,
201, 203, 209
Fineman, Morton, 14
Firbank, Ronald, 26
Follows, Arthur J., 14
Friedman, Melvin J., 23

Galloway, David, 23, 25, 28, 143-54
Garrett, George, 21
Garson, Helen, 5, 63, 222
Gehman, Richard, 15
Glicksberg, Charles I., 17
Goad, Craig, 9, 63
Gossett, Louise Y., 8, 9, 10
Gothic, 7, 8, 15, 17, 20, 27, 28, 49, 51,
62, 66, 79, 88, 95, 96, 97, 99, 137,
153, 155, 160, 161, 169, 179, 180,
181, 182, 183, 184, 185, 186, 187,
188, 190, 191, 201, 216, 223, 229
Goyen, William, 18
Grobel, Lawrence, 5
grotesque, 2, 6, 7, 9, 12, 14, 23, 39, 48,

54, 62, 82, 83, 86, 87, 89, 91, 93,
    102, 172, 180, 183, 184, 187
Guilfoil, Kelsey, 14

Haack, Dietmar, 24
Habas, Ralph, 14
Hardwick, Elizabeth, 14, 195
Hardy, John E., 7, 8
Harriss, W.E., 14
Hassan, Ihab, 6, 8, 13, 15, 19, 49-60,
    63, 99, 100, 104, 105, 106, 109-114
Hayes, Richard, 10, 11, 17, 77-78
Hellman, John, 24, 25
Herald Tribune, 10, 12, 18
Hersey, John, 24, 137, 146, 147, 148,
    154, 228, 229
Hickock, Dick, 2, 3, 63, 65, 67, 123,
    124, 125, 126, 127, 129, 130, 138,
    170, 171, 172, 208, 213, 214, 227
Hicks, Granville, 17, 205
Hicks, Jack, 28, 158, 165, 166, 167-78
Hill, Pati, 5
Hoffmann, Frederick, 15, 17
Hollins Critic, 21
homosexuality, 6, 7, 17, 40, 61, 62, 64,
    66, 106
Horizon, 12
horror, 3, 6, 15, 18, 22, 28, 39, 47, 51,
    79, 110, 117, 122, 150, 158, 173,
    174, 179, 182, 185, 189, 191
Howe, Irving, 18
Hutchens, John K., 18

Inge, M. Thomas, 5, 63, 176

Jackson, Katherine Gauss, 17, 22
Jacobs, J. U., 24

Kael, Pauline, 11
Kanfer, Stanley, 27
Kauffmann, Stanley, 21
Kazin, Alfred, 18, 24, 26, 96, 146, 154,
    209
Kenyon Review, 15
Kerr, Walter, 10
Kirby, John Pendy, 16
Klein, Alexander, 12, 15
Klein, Marcus, 8
Kosinski, Jerzy, 28, 167, 168

La Farge, Oliver, 17
Lemoire, Marcel, 7
Levine, Paul, 9, 12, 13, 19, 63, 81-94
Ludwig, Jack, 7

MacDonald, Dwight, 21, 138
Mademoiselle, 3
Mailer, Norman, 1, 5, 18, 24, 25, 28,
    33, 143, 144, 148, 149, 150, 151,
    153, 154, 168, 169, 206, 218, 228
Malin, Irving, 8, 13, 15, 22, 27, 64, 65,
    95-98, 154, 179, 182, 191, 223
Manchester, William, 29
McAleer, John J., 30, 205-19
McCormick, John, 26
McCullers, Carson, 2, 8, 12, 14, 17, 26,
    28, 29, 49, 50, 58, 62, 66, 81, 83, 87,
    88, 90, 92, 108, 114, 193, 202, 221
McGrory, Mary, 26
Mengeling, Marvin E., 15, 99-106
Merrick, Gordon, 18
Michener, James, 5
Moravia, Alberto, 8, 15, 224
Morris, Lloyd, 15
Morris, Robert K., 23
Morris, Willy, 27, 159
Mouton, Jean, 22, 221, 224

Nance, William L., 5, 24, 29, 63, 154,
    197-204, 222
narcissism, ist, 6, 7, 8, 9, 15, 16, 52,
    89, 149, 179, 180, 182, 216
Nathan, George Jean, 10, 73-76
Nathan, Robert, 17
Nation, 10, 11, 14
New Republic, 12, 14, 21, 27, 166, 205
New Statesman, 14, 19
The New Yorker, 3, 19, 20, 25, 65, 81,
    97, 121, 130, 131, 143, 170, 227
New York Review of Books, 21, 154,
    205
New York Times, 10, 17, 20, 132, 154,
    203
Newsweek, 20
nocturnal, metaphor, 6, 13, 19, 50, 51,
    56, 59, 82, 84, 85, 87, 88, 91, 99,
    109, 110
"Nonfiction Novel," 24, 25, 144, 226,
    228

Oberman, Harold, 11
Observer, 22, 129, 144, 223
O'Connor, Flannery, 2, 7, 8, 23, 28,
    29, 193, 194, 195, 221
O'Gorman, F. E., 18
Ozick, Cynthia, 16, 28, 67

Parone, Edward, 26
Partisan Review, 12, 14, 22, 195
Pavlov, Grigor, 23
Perry, J. Douglas, 28, 179-92
Pizer, Donald, 29
Plimpton, George, 5, 20, 63, 132, 133,
    154, 176
Podhoretz, Norman, 5, 33
Poe, Edgar Allan, 7, 8, 15, 28, 50, 51,
    56, 143, 146, 153, 179, 180, 183,
    206
Prescott, Orville, 14, 17
Pynchon, Thomas, 28, 167, 168

Rafferty, Terrence, 19, 115-20
Reed, Kenneth T., 5, 13, 63, 222
Rosenfeld, Isaac, 12, 15
Rubin, Louis, 17, 66
Russia, 3, 26, 96, 119, 145

Saroyan, William, 10, 17, 73, 74
Saturday Review, 12, 18, 195, 205
Selected Writings, 11
Sewanee Review, 15
Shaw, Irwin, 5, 33
Smith, Harrison, 12
Sontag, Susan, 15

Spectator, 20
Stanton, Robert J., 30, 221
Starosciak, Kenneth, 30
Sullivan, Walter, 7

Tanner, Tony, 20, 24
Theatre Arts, 11, 73
Times Literary Supplement, 26
Tompkins, Phillip K., 21, 65
Trilling, Diana, 14, 21, 22, 25, 64, 121-
    28
Trimmier, Dianne B., 16, 63
Truesdale, Marion, 23
Tuttle, Jon, 29, 193-96
Tynan, Kenneth, 21, 22, 25, 65, 129-
    34, 139, 144, 223
Vidal, Gore, 1, 29, 61, 143, 193, 195
violence, 6, 9, 15, 21, 23, 48, 50, 53,
    54, 59, 64, 109, 126, 137, 139, 211

Waldmeir, John, 27, 28, 30, 155-66
Waldmeir, Joseph, 1-29
West, Paul, 8
Wiegand, William, 22, 135-42
Williams, Tennessee, 5, 6, 10, 17, 31,
    50, 61, 65, 66, 73, 74
Wilson, John S., 11
Wolfe, Tom, 25, 28, 143, 148, 151,
    152, 153, 154, 168, 223, 228
Wright, Richard, 5, 33, 206

Young, Marguerite, 15

Zolotow, Maurice, 11

About the Editors

JOSEPH J. WALDMEIR is Emeritus Professor of English at Michigan State University. He is the author or editor of several books, and his articles have appeared in such journals as *Modern Fiction Studies, Southern Folklore Quarterly, Studies in Short Fiction, Journal of American Culture, The Hemingway Review*, and *Journal of Modern Literature*.

JOHN C. WALDMEIR is Associate Academic Dean and Assistant Professor of English at Loras College. He is the author of *The American Trilogy 1990–1937: Norris, Dreiser, Dos Passos and the History of Mammon* (1995) and has published in such journals as *English Language Notes* and *Journal of American Culture*.